LEISURE EDUCATION

MORE ACTIVITIES AND RESOURCES

SECOND EDITION

Leisure Education II
More Activities and Resources

Second Edition

compiled and edited by
Norma J. Stumbo, PhD, CTRS

Venture Publishing, Inc. • State College, Pennsylvania

LEISURE EDUCATION II:

MORE ACTIVITIES AND RESOURCES

SECOND EDITION

NORMA J. STUMBO

VENTURE PUBLISHING, INC.

STATE COLLEGE, PA

Copyright © 2002

Venture Publishing, Inc.
1999 Cato Avenue
State College, PA 16801
Phone: (814) 234-4561
Fax: (814) 234-1651

Production Manager: Richard Yocum
Manuscript Editing: Valerie Paukovits, Richard Yocum

Library of Congress Catalogue Card Number 2001098994
ISBN 1-892132-28-1

TABLE OF CONTENTS

SOCIAL INTERACTION SKILLS ACTIVITIES

Musical Compliments (Witt Nilson)
Asking for Help (Stumbo)
You Said What?!?" (Pringnitz Guerrier)
Pick Me Up Bouquet (Rodgers, Tense & Lundin)
Leisure Uno (Church)
Wheel of Leisure Charades (Harrs)
Group Yahtzee (Sauer)
What Shall I Wear? (Nesheim Larson & Witt Nilson)
Social Situations
Leisure Observation (Folkerth)
I Give. . .
Discovering Your Leisure Partners
Are You Listening?
What I See in You
Communication Blocks
Negotiating Conflicts
Play It Again, Sam
Holiday Recollections (O'Neil)
Sports Card Collecting (Magafas)
Recipe for Friendship
Friendship Poem

LEISURE RESOURCES ACTIVITIES

The Place Where I Play
Leisure Resource Scavenger Hunt (Noble)
Where's That Leisure (Jones & Folkerth)
What a Site! (Potter, Holian, Bramlet, Watson, Jester, Miller & Folkerth)
An Evening Out (Folkerth)
Resource Tic-Tac-Toe (Folkerth)
Towel Volleyball (Potter, Holian, Watson, Jester, Miller, Bramlet & Folkerth)
Scrambled Resources (Clawson & Folkerth)
Unit Scavenger Hunt (Gordon)
Where Do You Go?
Resource Values and Priorities
Your Town: Finding the Way (Hoover & Williams)
Nature Awareness: Recycling (Smith & McCord)

INTRODUCTION

The term leisure education has been in our professional vocabulary for over 30 years. It has been defined in a variety of ways but generally means helping the participant to gain knowledge and/or skills so that he or she is empowered to make choices and participate in leisure activities of his or her choosing. The end result is that the participant has adequate resources to participate as independently as possible in a variety of personally satisfying leisure pursuits.

For most individuals this happens naturally throughout the course of life, but for participants within therapeutic recreation services this is not the case. These individuals often have barriers, both real and perceived, to meaningful leisure involvement.

LEISURE BARRIERS

A variety of barriers continue to exclude individuals with disabilities or illnesses from full participation in recreation and leisure opportunities, including societal attitudes, architectural and transportation barriers, and the effects of segregated services. Many individuals have not had adequate opportunities to acquire normalized, appropriate leisure and social skills. They have not had the same participatory opportunities as their nondisabled counterparts and therefore do not have the knowledge, skills, and experiences that enable full participation in leisure and community life. This in turn often affects their own attitudes and self-concept in relation to their own competence and ability to make decisions. Some of the more typical leisure barriers experienced include:

- Not valuing leisure as an important aspect of one's total lifestyle
- Inability to participate in leisure without chemical or substance use
- Inability to identify or use personal resources for leisure involvement
- Inadequate planning and decision-making skills for leisure participation
- Inability to transfer previous skills for leisure involvement after an accident/illness

- Not having diverse activity skills for a variety of experiences
- Lack of accessible and usable leisure facilities in the community
- Inability to identify other people (leisure partners) with whom to participate in leisure experiences
- Inability to identify psychologically and physically healthy behaviors for leisure involvement
- Lack of knowledge of available community resources for leisure participation
- Inability to take responsibility for leisure involvement
- Inadequate social skills for participation in dual or group activities

The purpose of leisure education is to assist participants in eliminating or reducing barriers to enjoyable participation. It is provided to prepare or enable individuals to enhance the quality of their lives through individually selected patterns of recreation and leisure involvement. Healthy leisure values and attitudes, adequate social interaction skills, knowledge of leisure resources and their utilization, and a sufficient base of leisure activity skills are all important prerequisites to a balanced and healthy leisure lifestyle.

This manual intends to aid therapeutic recreation specialists in identifying and using appropriate leisure education activities to assist participants in overcoming leisure barriers and participating fully in leisure. To meet this aim, the manual includes a variety of resources and information.

THE CONTENTS OF THIS MANUAL

This manual serves as a comprehensive resource guide designed to facilitate the implementation and improvement of leisure education services. It is meant to be a starting point from which to create new and different creative leisure education programs and activities. Users are encouraged to not be bound by the activities provided, but to create, develop, and adapt activities to suit their purposes. It is divided into six sections:

- Chapter 1: Importance of Outcomes for Therapeutic Recreation Practice
- Chapter 2: Writing Goals for Leisure Education
- Chapter 3: Designing Games and Activities for Leisure Education
- Leisure Awareness Activities
- Social Interaction Skills Activities
- Leisure Resources Activities

TARGET PARTICIPANT POPULATION

This manual intends to be generic in nature and to serve a wide variety of clientele through its use. Most activities are appropriate for a diversity of populations and settings; only a few activities are designed with a specific population in mind. Users are encouraged to modify and adapt activities in the manual as they see fit to meet the needs of the participants and the intent of the program.

CHANGES FROM THE FIRST EDITION

The activities have been modified in this second edition, focusing on improving goals and adding debriefing questions so that participant outcomes will be more obvious. It is hoped that these additions and changes will make the second edition even more usable and valuable in practice. The three activity sections contain over 100 activities, including 13 newly developed activities. It should also be noted that throughout the second edition the term "participant" is used instead of or interchangeably with "patient" or "client." It was felt that this term was more inclusive to involve those individuals served within community facilities and services.

DIVERSITY OF CONTRIBUTORS

Several practicing professionals and educators across the nation contributed activities used in their own facilities. These professionals practice in a wide variety of clinical and community settings, including long-term care facilities, pediatric units, mental health centers, recreation departments, substance abuse centers, physical medicine and rehabilitation centers, and youth facilities. Many thanks to the individuals below who shared their talents and activities.

LIST OF CONTRIBUTORS

Gail Alexander	Mary Miller
Denise Berry	Sue Myers
Peggy Bramlet	Gretchen Nachazel
Cynny Carruthers	Kathy Nesheim Larson
Jennifer Church	Lisa Noble
D. Clawson	Pat O'Dea-Evans
Maureen Cullerton	Kelly O'Neil
Michelle DelGuidice	John Paule
Dena Filisha	Cheryl Potter
Jean Folkerth	Tami Pringnitz Guerrier
Cheryl Gordon	Michelle Roach
Jerri L. Harding	Julie Robbins
Marian Harrs	Cynthia Rodgers
Carol Holian	Ruth Roeder
Carol Hoover	Barb Sauer
Dan Hotchkin	Susan D. Schmunk
Sharon Jester	Tracy Smith
Ray Jones	Lisa Stretch-Dodson
Gary Koenig	Steve Swanson
Barbara Kolb	Marilyn Tense
J. Kriemer	Diane Wagner
Bobbie Jean Leonard	Kim Watson
Penelope J. Levenberry	E. M. Williams
Anita Magafas	Lois Witt Nilson
Patricia Malik	Robert Wolfe
Patrick McCord	

CHAPTER 1
IMPORTANCE OF OUTCOMES FOR THERAPEUTIC RECREATION PRACTICE*

The future of the therapeutic recreation profession depends on therapeutic recreation specialists' competence to define, measure, and document important client outcomes. The interest in outcomes is everywhere these days, from education to industry to business to healthcare. In most of these arenas, the underlying focus is measuring the productivity of the total endeavor—for example, determining whether workers are accountable for their actions or whether the process used is the straightest line to producing the desired outcome. Attention to measuring outcomes ensures that both the *inputs* (the right clients in the right programs) and *outputs* (the right outcomes for the right clients) of these accountability systems are appropriate and the best they can be.

It is less clear, however, how to define outcomes and how exactly to measure them, especially in healthcare. Although a significant amount of attention has been paid to client outcomes in the last decade, more serious effort on the part of the profession is needed to ensure that outcomes are consistent and meaningful. "While there is general agreement among therapeutic recreation professionals that patient outcome measurement needs to be developed, there exists little consensus as to what actually constitutes valid outcome measures or how we should monitor them" (Riley, 1991b, p. 53). This chapter introduces the basic concepts of defining and producing outcomes in therapeutic recreation services. After an introduction of outcomes background and terminology, several issues and concerns for producing outcomes in therapeutic recreation will be discussed.

*Adapted from: Stumbo and Hess, 2001; Stumbo, 2000; and Peterson and Stumbo, 2000

THE DEFINITION OF CLINICAL ENDPOINTS OR OUTCOMES

According to Stumbo and Hess (2001) three forces have converged to shape the dominance of client outcomes in the healthcare arena:

1. External accreditation agencies such as the Joint Commission on Accreditation of Healthcare Organizations (aka the Joint Cormission or JCAHO) and the Rehabilitation Accreditation Commission (aka the Commission on Accreditation of Rehabilitation Facilities or CARF)
2. Third-party payers such as insurance companies
3. Healthcare consumer groups

These three entities have synergized the significant shift to outcomes in the healthcare industry. The newest focus is on defining quality, identifying clinical endpoints (outcomes), using clinical performance measures, and increasing accountability at all points of service. Quality is measured by and equated with outcomes (Aral & Peterman, 1998; Horn, 1997; Margison et al., 2000; Powe, 1996; Scalenghe, 1991; Stumbo, 2000; Stumbo & Hess, 2001). Outcomes assist in defining the quality of services, defending the value of services in the competitive healthcare environment, and in applying for third-party reimbursement (Kloseck, Crilly, Ellis & Lammers, 1996).

Clinical outcomes have been defined by the Joint Commission as "the results of performance (or nonperformance) of a function(s) or process(es)" (JCAHO, 1995, p. 717). Shank and Kinney (1991) expanded on this definition:

> Outcomes are the observed changes in a client's status as a result of our interventions and interactions, whether intended or not. Outcomes are the complications, adverse events, or short-term or long-term changes experienced by our clients, and represent the end results of our care. Outcomes can be attributed to the process of providing care, and this should enable us to determine if we are doing for our clients that which we purport to do. (p. 76)

Riley (1991b) clarified client outcomes as "the direct effects of service upon the well-being of both the individual and specified populations; the end result of medical care; what happened to the patient in terms of palliation, control of illness, cure, or rehabilitation" (p. 58). Others have explained outcomes simply as "clinical results" (Scalenghe, 1991, p. 30).

Gorski (1995, p. 33) identified four major healthcare outcome categories:

1. Change in clinical status (effect of treatment on patient's symptoms)

2. Change in functionality (effect of treatment on patient's lifestyle)

3. Change in utilization of medical resources (effect of treatment on using additional healthcare services)

4. Recidivism (examining patterns of relapse or reentry into the medical system)

Given these broad outcome dimensions, each healthcare professional must determine the appropriateness of their targeted and most valued outcomes. It seems reasonable to assume that therapeutic recreation will concentrate primarily on changes in functionality, healthcare utilization, and recidivism.

WHY THE FOCUS ON CLIENT OUTCOMES?

Eight factors that have contributed to the current demand for health outcomes information were identified by the United Kingdom Clearing House on Health Outcomes (1997, p. 1):

1. Eliminate poor/unnecessary practice and promote good practice

2. Aid negotiations between purchasers [of healthcare] and providers

3. Increase the accountability of services following separation of purchasers and providers

4. Develop means to evaluate services for the chronically ill

5. Empower consumers and involve them in service evaluation and planning

6. Evaluate new services

7. Inform priority setting and resource allocation

8. Help to set, monitor, and improve standards of care

These factors clearly support the growing urgency for outcome development that stems from a concern for cost containment as well as for quality improvement in the delivery of healthcare services. The push behind these purposes has risen primarily from external accreditation bodies, third-party payers or insurance companies, and healthcare consumer groups (Stumbo & Hess, 2001). Each of these three forces will be reviewed briefly to show their impact on the mandate for healthcare outcomes.

EXTERNAL ACCREDITATION AGENCIES

The Joint Commission on Accreditation of Healthcare Organizations is the largest and most influential accrediting organization (Loeffler & Henley, 1997). The Joint Commission "is a non-governmental, nonprofit national organization whose mission is to improve the quality of care provided to the public through accreditation and related services" (Schyve, 1996, p. 54). Accreditation indicates a status of recognition and is awarded to organizations that demonstrate overall compliance with applicable standards of care provision. The Joint Commission currently has standards manuals for hospitals, ambulatory care, behavioral health, long-term care, home care, and health networks. For complete and up-to-date information, see http://www.jcaho.org.

Previously it was sufficient for healthcare providers to illustrate the quality of their services by answering JCAHO's question of "Can this organization/department provide quality healthcare?" (Scalenghe, 1991, pp. 30–31). Underlying the intent of this question were standards of structure and process. *Structure standards* focused on things such as the availability of resources (such as staff and equipment) for client participation while *process standards* were concerned with the actions or events taking place between the therapist and the client (JCAHO, 1995).

More recently, in response to the emphasis on cost containment and quality improvement, the Joint Commission has restructured its standards. It has become "no longer sufficient to demonstrate that structures and processes are in place, but, in addition, to demonstrate that the patient has changed as a result of such care" (Scalenghe, 1991, p. 31). Therefore, "the Commission has implemented an evaluation process that assesses *actual performance*, rather than only *capacity*" [emphasis added] (Schyve, 1996, p. 54). Joint Commission standards now equate quality with the ability of a service to produce client outcomes or functional gains in health status.

CARF (2000) accredits five types of services for individuals with disabilities:

1. Adult day services
2. Assisted living
3. Medical rehabilitation
4. Behavioral health
5. Employment and community services

CARF recently has reengineered some of their standards that focus on outcome achievement. For complete and up-to-date information, see http://www.carf.org.

CARF adheres to a client self-determination and customer-centered service model and advocates for outcomes important to the consumer rather than the service provider. "The movement to which CARF has subscribed says that we as service providers should help determine what is important to people, then hold ourselves accountable for it, make our performance visible, and establish efforts to get better. This is a radical departure from the definitions of quality and assessment procedures that have subjugated the lives of the individuals served to bureaucratic needs" (CARF, 2000, p. ix). According CARF:

> Quite simply, the quality that matters is the quality of life of the individual served, and services of high quality are ones that make substantial positive contributions to the quality of life of the individuals served. In the past quality assessment efforts have focused on standards related to physical facilities, staffing, or programs that would seldom be included in any individual's definition of important aspects of quality of life. But in the future the quality of human services will be increasingly viewed not as a status to be assessed and certified, but as a process in which the persons served, the service providers, family members, friends, and other will articulate life goals, establish plans

for reaching those goals, and work effectively toward those goals. Quality of services will be seen as manifested in the achievement of desired outcomes by the people served. (2000, p. viii)

This shift from "capability" or *potential* for quality healthcare delivery to "clinical and organizational performance" or *demonstrating* quality healthcare has been adopted by both JCAHO and CARF, and therefore affects virtually every healthcare provider in the nation (Scalenghe, 1991, p. 31). For healthcare delivery services currently in place, their continued existence depends on their ability to define, measure, and monitor exactly what they deliver, as external accrediting agencies now base accreditation exclusively on the ability to deliver and define outcomes (Campbell, 1997). Researchers claim that "outcomes will mainly be used to preserve the integrity of the [accreditation] process and help JCAHO target problem areas in healthcare systems" (Campbell, 1997, p. 13). Both organizations want to ensure that data-based, integrated, and standardized monitoring systems determine the acceptability of treatment processes and results.

THIRD-PARTY PAYERS

Healthcare financing has changed dramatically in the last century, and the changes have accelerated in the last two decades. "In the early 1900s, financing health services was relatively simple. People went to their physicians, were treated, and paid out of their own pockets for the services they received" (Reitter, 1989, p. 239). This payment system was replaced by a retrospective, cost-based reimbursement system. Retrospective cost-based reimbursement was meant to minimize the escalating costs of healthcare services individuals were required to pay out of their own pockets by relinquishing a portion of healthcare charges to third parties (insurance companies). Under defined regulations established by third-party payers, hospitals were permitted to be reimbursed by insurance companies after-the-fact for "reasonable costs" of providing services to patients (Reitter, 1989, p. 240). Retrospective cost-based reimbursement had a tremendous impact on healthcare. National expenditures for healthcare tripled and continued to rise unchecked (Reitter, 1989). "The virtually limitless financial resources permitted by retrospective reimbursement stimulated growth of the healthcare industry" (Reitter, 1989, p. 240).

Retrospective cost-based reimbursement was replaced by the Medicare prospective payment system in 1983, with many private insurance carriers following the government's lead (Reitter, 1989; Olsson, 1986; Scott, 1984). This shift from retrospective cost-based reimbursement to the prospective payment system (price determined prior to payment) brought dramatic changes to healthcare. As the earlier system promoted increased quantity of services, this latter system decreased the quantity of services while maintaining quality (Reitter, 1989).

Other factors in the reduction of healthcare costs include diagnostic related groups (DRGs), preferred provider organizations (PPOs), capitation, and managed care (see O'Morrow & Carter, 1997; Petryshen & Petryshen, 1993/94; Thompson, 2001; Touchstone, 1997). Although these efforts have not stymied healthcare costs as they once were purported to do, they have brought other significant changes to healthcare.

> [Capitation] requires the provider to carefully plan their service and deliver it efficiently or cost effectively. There is no question that therapeutic recreation is much cheaper and a more productive service...If the therapeutic recreation professional can provide a quality experience and improvement in functional and behavioral change, then they become very valuable to us in the [healthcare] industry. (Touchstone, 1997, p. 147)

The relationship between accreditation and financing is significant. Through earning accreditation, hospitals/healthcare providers demonstrate eligibility for government-sponsored Medicare and Medicaid reimbursement (Loeffler & Henley, 1997). Private insurance companies have followed suit in embracing cost-containment strategies.

HEALTHCARE CONSUMER GROUPS

There was once undeniable public trust in the healthcare system (O'Morrow & Carter, 1997; Vorderer, 1997). Healthcare decisions and outcomes were determined by physicians and other healthcare providers. However, this began to change as individuals began to assume more responsibility for their own health and become better consumers of their own healthcare. With heightened awareness "that there is wide variability in utilization rates, practice patterns, and clinical results, the public (through government, business, insurers, consumers, and other interest groups) [began] seeking information concerning how much of this variation reflects actual quality difference" (Scalenghe, 1991, p. 30).

Even greater awareness and advocacy by consumers is on the immediate horizon. "Americans will have to become real partners with their chosen providers in the diagnostic and therapeutic clinical process. Providers are getting accustomed to the trend of patient-oriented questions, challenges, second opinions, cost and track record/competence inquiries and the like. Patients must become equally comfortable with this relationship" (Vorderer, 1997, p. 131).

Consumer groups have been successful in changing how healthcare does business, and how it defines quality outcomes. "Many patients today are filled with the sense of 'I want to know about my role in my treatment'" (Gerber, 1994/95, p. 4). This is evidenced by a greater number of consumer health information outlets, such as the Internet, magazines, and newsletters.

These three threads of accreditation, reimbursement, and consumerism have resulted in massive changes in the healthcare industry. Performance measures, clinical outcomes, accountability, and quality are now common language among healthcare professionals and consumers.

TERMINOLOGY OF CLIENT OUTCOME ACHIEVEMENT

Common language contributes to a shared understanding among professionals. Like many other emerging knowledge bases, the field of outcomes measurement has constructed a common sets of definitions. Some of the most prominent terms and definitions used today are outlined here.

Effectiveness characterizes how an intervention works under everyday circumstances in routine clinical practice (Aral & Peterman, 1998; Powe, 1996).

The effectiveness of an intervention is the impact an intervention achieves in the real world, under resource constraints, in entire populations, or in specified subgroups of a population. It is the improvement in a health outcome achieved in a typical community setting. (Aral & Peterman, 1998, p. 3)

Efficacy characterizes how an intervention performs under ideal or more controlled circumstances (Aral & Peterman, 1998; Powe, 1996). "Efficacy is the improvement in health outcome achieved in a research setting, in expert hands, under ideal circumstances" (Aral & Peterman, 1998, p. 3). In comparing *effectiveness* and *efficacy*, Aral and Peterman (1998) explained:

Effectiveness of an intervention is the product of its efficacy, the penetration or reach of the intervention into the population, and the compliance of the population with the intervention. In general, effectiveness is lower than efficacy, though theoretically, it could be higher. (p. 4)

Effectiveness research compares different healthcare practices or interventions (e.g., medical technologies such as drugs, devices, or procedures) covering the following areas: mortality, morbidity, symptoms, satisfaction, quality of life, preferences, and costs (Powe, 1996).

Outcomes-based management research incorporates similar methods to compare performance under different providers (e.g., physicians, hospitals, clinics, facilities), often for purposes of quality assessment and utilization review (Powe, 1996).

In additional to more traditional methods *patient outcomes research* uses new markers of health status and quality of life, symptoms (particularly those that are bothersome), patient preferences, patient satisfaction, costs, and cost-effectiveness (Powe, 1996).

Near-patient testing (Delaney et al., 1999) or *point-of-care methods* (Dufault & Sullivan, 2000; Hudson, Christenson, Newby, Kaplan & Ohman, 1999) research is performed in locations where treatment decisions are made and care is delivered based on the results of these tests (e.g., research conducted in an outpatient clinic or an emergency room).

Evidence-based medicine means that the practice of medicine should be based on the best available scientific knowledge or evidence of its efficacy (Linde, 1999; Margison et al., 2000; Waise, 1999). *Practice-based evidence* is the complementary activity in which research reflects routine clinical practice or evidence of its effectiveness (Margison et al., 2000)

Clinical practice improvement examines the steps of a care process to determine how to achieve the best medical outcomes at the least necessary cost over the continuum of a patient's care (Horn, 1997).

Clinical importance may be contrary to reported statistical significance in the findings of a particular research study, but results still would lead to the conclusion of an important difference in patient outcome and in patient health status (Hatala, Holbrook & Goldsmith, 1999). These authors advocate using clinical judgment to determine clinical significance or importance versus statistical significance.

MANDATES FOR MEASURING OUTCOMES

As Stumbo and Hess (2001) noted, targeted outcomes must be based on solid evidence of empirically-based, integrative, and standardized treatment that produces predictable, measurable changes in the client's health status. This takes a combination of research that improves practice (evidence-based practice) and practice that lends itself to replicable research (practice-based evidence). These complementary activities must occur within therapeutic recreation, as well as all healthcare disciplines, if outcomes are to be defined, measured, and have meaning.

Outcome development within therapeutic recreation does not need to be thought of as an impossible mission or even unreasonably difficult. Although "it may be challenging for practitioners to specify and measure client outcomes related to involvement in their programs" (Dunn, Sneegas & Carruthers, 1991, p. 109), outcomes are essential to accountability. Challenge can no longer be an excuse, it is time to rise up and "demonstrate accountability for those services that we all have always 'known' and 'felt' in our hearts to be an essential component of quality care" (Scalenghe, 1991, p. 41). A number of authors have encouraged therapeutic recreation professionals to respond to this call for a variety of reasons, including:

- To verify appropriate and quality services (i.e., treatment effectiveness) rather than just "knowing" and "feeling" in our hearts that valuable services are provided (Kloseck, Crilly, Ellis & Lammers, 1996; Scalenghe, 1991; Shank & Kinney, 1991)

- To measure the relationship between various program/treatment protocols for specific illness/diagnostic category and the associated outcomes of those treatments (i.e., treatment efficiency) (Kloseck, Crilly, Ellis & Lammers, 1996; Riley, 1991b)

- To lay a legitimate claim to a portion of the competitive healthcare dollar and to prove that therapeutic recreation services may lower overall healthcare costs (Kloseck, Crilly, Ellis & Lammers, 1996; Shank & Kinney, 1991)

- To spur continued acceptance and enhanced growth and support of the profession (Riley, 1991b; Shank & Kinney, 1991)

- To provide valuable information for the future improvement of programs (Dunn et al., 1991, p. 107)

All of these reasons rest on the premise that the therapeutic recreation profession can provide solid evidence of *empirically-based*, *integrative*, and *standardized* treatment that produces predictable, measurable changes in the client's health status. According to Scalenghe (1991), now is the time for therapeutic recreation as a profession to become even more proactive and take a major role in defining appropriate and quality services—primarily by conducting the necessary research, making the appropriate clinical decisions, and forming coalitions across the country to standardized treatment protocols.

CRITERIA FOR DEFINING AND MEASURING OUTCOMES IN THERAPEUTIC RECREATION

What are the criteria for outcomes associated with evidence-based practice and practice-based evidence? These criteria require that outcomes and their measurement focus on *relevance*, *importance*, and *attainment* (Peterson & Stumbo, 2000; Riley, 1991b). When planning outcome measurement, keep in mind that outcomes must be:

Identified. Identification of outcomes must be done before undertaking other measurement tasks (Peterson & Stumbo, 2000, p. 64; Stumbo & Hess, 2001). What outcomes from therapeutic recreation services are important to clients seen at this facility? What target outcomes fit within the scope of therapeutic recreation practice that will benefit these clients? Do they fall within the intent of this facility and its other healthcare disciplines?

Measurable. While most healthcare providers believe their services contribute to the overall, global health and well-being of their clients, these measures often are deemed too broad and lack meaning in today's healthcare. There is greater interest in defining outcomes more specifically and in smaller terms. For some professions, this might amount to VO_2 max performance levels, changes in blood gases, or other biomedical indicators. Many professions, such as therapeutic recreation, do not have such biomedical markers, and rely on other less exact but not less important indicators. What important outcomes of therapeutic recreation services are measurable? How and when will they be measured? Will these measurements be sensitive to change within a short time period?

Achievable. Shortened lengths of stay have complicated the accomplishments of most healthcare professionals. With fewer days of inpatient or even outpatient care, it is difficult and sometimes impossible to achieve the outcomes that may have been identified 5 or 10 years ago. It has been a difficult task for most therapeutic recreation professionals to narrow their scope of measurement (and programming) to fit the patient's length of stay. What can be accomplished within a patient's 2-day to 5-day stay? What is important in this person's treatment and how can it be achieved?

Demonstrable or ***documented*** (Peterson & Stumbo, 2000). If a stress management program is to produce measurable changes in the clients' behavior, attitude, or level of stress, the therapeutic recreation specialist must be able to document that change. This means having valid and reliable instruments or tools that measure the level of behavior, attitude, or knowledge targeted and how that level changed as the result of care.

Predictable or ***causal*** (Riley, 1991b). There must be a direct relationship between the intervention and the outcome. Using the same example of a stress management program, it would be unwise to measure differences in leisure attitudes as an outcome, as a change in leisure attitudes is unlikely to be directly attributable to a stress management program.

Meaningful. Even with the constraints listed, client outcomes must still be meaningful to the client and his or her recovery or health status. What important contribution does therapeutic recreation make to the client's success? What contribution does therapeutic recreation make to other services on the healthcare team? What outcome changes in the client would make the most difference in his or her life?

Peterson and Stumbo (2000, p. 65) noted that many authors in the field of therapeutic recreation have contributed to a simple set of guidelines for creating and implementing client outcome statements, which include:

- Efficiency and effectiveness of demonstrating client change
- Reasonable relationship between the services provided and the expected outcome
- Connection between the occurrence of the outcome and the timing of data collection
- Relevance to the client and society
- Goals and intent of the program
- Appropriate level of specification
- Individual client variation within any given program
- Long-term and short-term goals and objectives

- Social and home environments to which the client will return
- Behaviors that are generalizable and transferable to a variety of settings and situations

How each specialist practices therapeutic recreation matters a great deal. Sound decisions—integrating all aspects of assessment, planning, implementation, and evaluation—are paramount to being able to produce important, logical, and necessary client outcomes. These factors make the definition and measurement of outcomes a challenge. According to Aral and Peterman (1998, p. 33) "our knowledge of the effectiveness of behavioural interventions is determined by the comprehensiveness of the behavioural-intervention research that has been done, the representativeness and completeness of the published research findings, and the scientific rigour and appropriateness of the research."

DEFINING AND MEASURING OUTCOMES IN HEALTHCARE

Patient outcome research, often called effectiveness research, is an evolving research discipline that provides information about the appropriate application of healthcare practices (Powe, 1996). This information can take a variety of forms, depending on the healthcare discipline and the nature of services and patients. The method chosen may also depend on the audience or entity requesting the information (e.g., insurance company, chief financial officer, patient or his or her family, accreditation body) and what portions of the service are measurable. Each profession has different expected outcomes, and some outcomes are more definable and measurable than others. All must take into consideration the imperatives mentioned in the previous section.

Powe (1996) presented eight categories of methods used to measure healthcare outcomes: epidemiological methods, analysis of variations and outcomes in practice, formal literature reviews and metaanalyses, quality of life measurements, decision analyses, patient preference assessment, patient satisfaction assessment, and economic and cost-effectiveness analyses. These eight methods provide an overview of the majority of outcome research in healthcare. In therapeutic recreation, the efforts at outcome formation and description have been less energetic, but still important. Many of these categories overlap and can be combined—for example, measuring the economic realities of achieving various states of quality of life.

Epidemiology "is a science that studies the frequencies and distributions of disease and health conditions among population groups...comparison and contrast are used to determine whether groups of people who share a common characteristic (such as people who exercise) experience some condition (such as coronary heart disease) with the same frequency of occurrence as another group (such as sedentary people)" (Thomas & Nelson, 1996, pp. 134–135).

Analysis of variations in medical practice and outcomes demonstrate differences in patient management procedures—for example between different facilities or in different geographic regions (Powe, 1996). Formal literature reviews or metaanalyses are related but separate types of studies. *Literature reviews* make a formal attempt to synthesize written literature to find threads of common understanding on a certain procedure or practice. *Metaanalyses* perform a similar function, but do so through statistical analyses of the major data points in the sample studies (Thomas & Nelson, 1996).

Powe (1996) identified two categories of *quality of life studies*: those using global measures of quality of life that can be applied to different diseases and disease-specific measures of quality of life. The former can be used to compare between different groups of patients, the latter describes one group's more narrow experiences.

Decision analyses "involves explicit identification of treatment choices, review of evidence-based studies on factors such as prevalence of disease and incidence of complications, and quantitative comparison of those choices through the use of sophisticated computer programs...decision analysis is particularly useful for examining tradeoffs between clinical outcomes and costs" (Powe, 1996, p. 232).

Patient preference of treatment options (e.g., choosing between a lumpectomy and chemotherapy versus a mastectomy) and *patient satisfaction* are both difficult to measure. "Patient

involvement in decision making is receiving greater attention because of its potential impact on health outcomes. Patient compliance and satisfaction may be enhanced through involvement" (Powe, 1996, p. 233). Preference and satisfaction depend on a highly informed patient as a consumer of healthcare.

According to Powe (1996, p. 233) there are three basic types of *economic analyses*: cost identification studies, cost-effectiveness analyses, and cost-benefit analyses. *Cost-identification studies* measure the contribution of different types of resources to aggregate healthcare costs. *Cost-effectiveness analyses* allow for the enumeration and comparison of costs and benefits of different medical interventions. Cost-effectiveness analysis expresses costs in monetary terms. In *cost-benefit analyses* there is greater interest in clinical outcomes, such as lives saved or complications avoided. In *cost-utility analysis*, a variant of cost-effectiveness analysis, clinical benefits are commonly measured in quality adjusted life years—quality of life resulting from the use of one intervention versus another (Powe, 1996).

THERAPEUTIC RECREATION'S RESPONSE TO OUTCOMES

In 1978 Gunn and Peterson advocated a systems design approach to therapeutic recreation program planning. This goal-oriented, outcome-focused, and consumer-driven approach was very different from other program planning literature of the time and soon became the profession's basis for accountable program design."The systems approach provides a framework from which programs can logically be planned, conducted, and evaluated. The resulting programs are completely client centered. They are based on an assessment of client needs and proceed from there to the design of program content (activities) and process (method of interacting with clients), which are related to goals and outcomes behaviors" (Gunn & Peterson, 1978, p. 61). The rationale for a systems-designed therapeutic recreation program was clear: "This procedure provides a structure for evaluating how well the program is operating and allows a type of accountability not feasible in traditional program planning approaches. *Therapeutic recreators who use systems approaches can determine how well their programs facilitate behavioral improvement*" [emphasis added] (Gunn & Peterson, 1978, p. 61).

Dunn et al. (1991) noted that within the profession of therapeutic recreation a variety of terms (e.g., objectives, behavioral objectives, performance measures) have been used to define what is currently termed outcome measures. Several authors have defined outcomes measures as the documentable changes in client behavior, skills, and/or attitudes that can be attributed to active participation in the therapeutic recreation intervention program (Dunn et al., 1991; Peterson & Stumbo, 2000; Shank & Kinney, 1991; Stumbo, 1996). Therefore, in a broad sense therapeutic recreation has been focusing on outcomes for quite some time (Hood & Krinsky, 1997/98). We now define them more clearly and more succinctly, however, and specify them to external accrediting organizations. This requires a paradigm shift to ensure that outcomes are empirically based, integrated, and standardized.

METHODS OF DEFINING AND MEASURING OUTCOMES IN THERAPEUTIC RECREATION

Cost-containment, corporatization of healthcare, and consumer advocacy have demanded that only services that could be *proven* (documented) to be beneficial to the health and well-being of clients be provided. It is imperative to link the *causal relationship* between processes of intervention and end results or outcomes of intervention (Riley, 1991a, 1991b). Research must build and substantiate this link into definable, defendable outcomes that can be targeted and evaluated. These outcomes must meet two criteria (Seibert, 1991, p. 7):

1. There must be a body of empirical research, validated by repetition and rigorous peer review, that supports achievement of the desired outcome in a respectable number of cases

2. The outcomes that we intend to achieve, and demonstrate that we can achieve, must be ones that are valued by third-party payers

Those outcomes shown through documented research to be achievable by clients time after time are the strongest indicators of the accountability of the profession. These types of outcomes are best achieved through consistent and well-designed programs examined by using experimental, descriptive, or qualitative research methods. Recent examples of these types of research efforts in therapeutic recreation include Buettner (2000), Caroleo (1999), Hodges and Luken (2000), Johnson and Ashton-Shaeffer (2000), Kloseck, Crilly, and Hutchinson-Troyer (2001), Lee, Mittlesteadt, and Perkins (1999), Lee and Yang (2000), McCormack and Funderburk (2000), Russoniello (2000), Stumbo and Hess (in press), and West (2000). Efforts at gathering information concerning the desirable consequences of particular interventions such as these must be continued and expanded (Shank & Kinney, 1991).

Stumbo and Hess (2001) reviewed six efforts by therapeutic recreation researchers and practitioners that have moved the profession toward the definition and measurement of important client outcomes. Some these nationwide efforts overlap with Powe's (1996) eight categorizations. The six efforts—comprehensive literature review, development of clinical practice guidelines, use of programmatic data, such as program evaluation and performance measure statistics, ATRA's treatment networks for collaboration and research, use of theories and theories in action to provide service provision rationale, and development of research agendas—will be described briefly as to their contribution to outcome measurement in therapeutic recreation services.

One of the most well-known national *literature reviews* in therapeutic recreation was the Temple University Benefits Project—an effort "to conduct research to determine the efficacy of therapeutic recreation in rehabilitation" (Coyle, Kinney, Riley & Shank, 1991, p. i). This federally funded project resulted in a significant publication outlining findings related to six disability groupings, nested into six benefits areas: physical health and maintenance, cognitive functioning, psychosocial health, growth and personal development, personal and life satisfaction, and societal and healthcare system outcomes (Coyle, Kinney & Shank, 1991).

A second national-level project on *clinical guidelines* has been the work of the American Therapeutic Recreation Association's Protocol Committee. The efforts to date have included achieving national consensus in identifying the treatment needs of individuals involved in alcohol treatment (see Hood & Krinsky, 1997/98). With a method established (Hood, 2001), it is anticipated that additional clinical guidelines will be generated in the near future.

A third effort in therapeutic recreation has been to use *existing programmatic data* collected daily in most therapeutic recreation departments (Caldwell & Weissinger, 1993; Coyle, Kinney & Shank, 1993; Patrick, 1997, 2001; Rhodes, 1991; Shank, Coyle, Kinney & Lay, 1995; Shank, Kinney & Coyle, 1993). Systematic program evaluations and quality performance measures are two examples of existing program data that may be used to examine outcomes.

ATRA's nine *treatment networks* were established to connect members interested in specific population groups and to share information and research findings (Ancone, 2000; Jake, 2000a, 2000b). According to Jake (2000a, p. 5), these activities will assist those involved to "develop a stronger and more consistent practice" and allow for the utilization of shared "time, talent, and resources" of colleagues interested in both practice and research.

Another approach to identifying and targeting outcomes for measurement is using *theories* and *theories in action* to provide a rationale for service provision (Caldwell, 2001; Devine & Wilhite, 1999; Ellis, 1993; Gruver, 1993/94). According to Devine and Wilhite (1999, p. 29), "The application of theory to TR practice and research allows for the suggestion of relationships between phenomena so that outcomes can be generalized, understood, and explained."

Establishing *national research agendas* also identifies those areas in need of greater research efforts—for example, those leading to measuring outcomes. Advocated by a number of authors in the field (Bedini, 2001; Bullock, McGuire & Barch, 1984; Carruthers, 1997/98; Compton, 1984; Compton & Deiser, 1997; Jacobson, Carruthers & Keller, 2001; Malkin, 1993; Malkin, Coyle & Carruthers, 1998; Witt, 1988), national research agendas provide the advantage of gaining consensus on a list of topics of importance to the profession.

These six categories identify some of the nationwide efforts being undertaken to address the issues of outcome measurement. They are clearly in the early stages of development and are not as sophisticated as methods outlined by Powe (1996). However, these are starting points for developing more succinct methods of delivering quality care and measuring its outcomes. When combined with the increase in effectiveness and efficacy research currently being conducted in the field, they can make a powerful contribution to improving the status of outcomes in therapeutic recreation.

TYPICAL OUTCOMES OF THERAPEUTIC RECREATION SERVICES

Several recent efforts by therapeutic recreation professionals and researchers have provided momentum for outcomes research. The identification of outcomes is the starting point for outcomes measurement and service provision. Covey (1989) stated: "Begin with the end in mind" (p. 95). What does this mean for outcomes research? "To begin with the end in mind means to start with a clear understanding of your destination. It means to know where you're going so you better understand where you are now and so that the steps you take are always in the right direction" (Covey, 1989, p. 98). Therapeutic recreation professionals must begin with specific, targeted outcomes *prior* to all other planning and implementation activities.

These debates and reviews are critical to understanding that service provision to clients needs to be based on *something* (Mobily, 1999; Witman, 1999). When the professional therapist selects a model upon which to base his or her practice, that is a tremendously important decision. The model selected affects all services and interactions with clients, as well as the client outcomes targeted by the professional. If a leisure-based model is chosen, then leisure outcomes become important. If a wellness-based model is selected, then wellness outcomes become important. Client needs, services provided, and targeted outcomes are more likely to become integrated when a service model or philosophy is conscientiously chosen by the professional. This manual focuses on the *Leisure Ability Model* (Peterson & Stumbo, 2000; Stumbo &

Peterson, 1998) for therapeutic recreation services. Using the Leisure Ability Model, Peterson and Stumbo (2000, p. 64) provided a list of outcomes that can be targeted within therapeutic recreation services.

Functional Intervention

- Increased ability to manage anger appropriately
- Increased emotional control and healthy expression
- Increased physical endurance
- Increased ability to remain on task
- Improved adjustment to disability and/or illness
- Improved orientation to people, place, and time

Leisure Education

- Increased ability to make decisions related to leisure participation
- Increased knowledge of importance of leisure in one's life
- Improved ability to initiate and maintain conversations
- Improved ability to compromise and negotiate a solution
- Improved ability to display acceptable hygiene practices
- Improved skills in an individual leisure activity
- Increased ability to locate and utilize a community leisure resource
- Increased knowledge of leisure resources within the home

Recreation Participation

- Improved ability to express self within leisure context
- Improved ability to select and participate in an activity of choice

Selecting a practice model helps to narrow the selection of appropriate client goals and interventions. Shank and Kinney (1991, p. 76) noted:

> each time that therapeutic recreation specialists work with their clients, they make critical decisions in the course of providing care. Usually these decisions are based on and relevant to predetermined goals

[which are based on practice models and professional beliefs]. These decisions can have positive and negative consequences, and are essentially the outcomes that ought to be monitored and evaluated as the indicators for continued care and for determining quality of care.

The Leisure Ability Model focuses on the ultimate outcome of clients attaining an appropriate and satisfying leisure lifestyle. Peterson and Stumbo (2000, pp. 21–22) identified what a person with a healthy leisure lifestyle looks like. This individual:

- Has few major functional limitations that prohibit or significantly limit leisure involvement (or has learned ways to overcome these barriers)
- Understands and values the importance of leisure in the totality of life experiences
- Incorporates leisure into his or her daily life
- Has adequate social skills for involvement with others
- Can choose between several leisure activity options on a daily basis and make decisions for leisure participation
- Can locate and use leisure resources as necessary
- Has increased perceptions of choice, motivation, freedom, responsibility, causality, and independence with regard to his or her leisure

These [ultimate] outcomes are targeted through the identification of client need, provision of programs to meet those needs, and the evaluation of outcomes during and after program delivery. A therapeutic recreation specialist designs, implements, and evaluates services aimed at those outcomes (Peterson & Stumbo, 2000, p. 22).

SUMMARY

Measurement of healthcare outcomes is difficult because people who enter the system vary in significant ways. However, due to the mandates of accrediting agencies, third-party payers, and consumers, the measurement of outcomes is no longer voluntary.

This chapter presented relevant terminology and background information to increase the reader's understanding of the need for outcomes to be based on solid evidence of empirically-based, integrative, and standardized treatment. A brief comparison was made between Powe's (1996) eight categories of outcome measurements in healthcare and Stumbo and Hess's (2001) review of therapeutic recreation's outcome measurement efforts. Finally, some of the outcomes targeted through therapeutic recreation services were reviewed using the Leisure Ability Model.

REFERENCES

Ancone, D. (2000). President's message. *ATRA Newsletter, 16*(1), 1–2.

Aral, S. O. and Peterman, T. A. (1998). Do we know the effectiveness of behavioural interventions? *Lancet, Supplement STDs, 351*(9119), 33–37.

Bedini, L. (2001). Status of therapeutic recreation research. In N. J. Stumbo (Ed.), *Professional issues in therapeutic recreation: On competence and outcomes* (pp. 335–348). Champaign, IL: Sagamore.

Buettner, L. L. (2000). Gerontological recreation therapy: Examining the trends and making a forecast. *Annual in Therapeutic Recreation, 9*, 35–46.

Bullock, C., McGuire, F., and Barch, E. (1984). Perceived research needs of therapeutic recreators. *Therapeutic Recreation Journal, 18*, 17–24.

Caldwell, L. (2001). The role of theory in therapeutic recreation: A practical approach. In N. J. Stumbo (Ed.), *Professional issues in therapeutic recreation: On competence and outcomes* (pp. 349–364). Champaign, IL: Sagamore.

Caldwell, L. L. and Weissinger, E. (1993). A model for research utilization in therapeutic recreation. In M. J. Malkin and C. Z. Howe (Eds.), *Research in therapeutic recreation: Concepts and methods* (pp. 127–142). State College, PA: Venture Publishing, Inc.

Campbell, S. (1997). Outcomes-based accreditation evolves slowly with JCAHO's Oryx initiative. *Healthcare Strategic Management, 15*(40), 12–13.

CARF. (2000). *Managing outcomes: Customer-driven outcomes measurement and management systems—A guide to development and use.* Phoenix, AZ: Author.

Caroleo, O. (1999). The impact of a therapeutic recreation program on the use of coping strategies among people with AIDS. *Annual in Therapeutic Recreation, 8*, 22–32.

Carruthers, C. (1997/98). Therapeutic recreation efficacy research agenda. *Annual in Therapeutic Recreation, 7,* 29–41.

Compton, D. (1984). Research priorities for special populations. *Therapeutic Recreation Journal, 18,* 9–17.

Compton, D. M. and Deiser, R. (1997). Research initiatives in therapeutic recreation. In D. M. Compton (Ed.), *Issues in therapeutic recreation: Toward the new millennium* (2nd ed., pp. 299–326). Champaign, IL: Sagamore.

Covey, S. R. (1989). *The 7 habits of highly effective people: Powerful lessons in personal change.* New York, NY: Simon and Schuster.

Coyle, C. P., Kinney, W. B., and Shank, J. W. (1991). A summary of benefits common to therapeutic recreation. In C. P. Coyle, W. B. Kinney, B. Riley, and J. W. Shank (Eds.), *Benefits of therapeutic recreation: A consensus view.* (pp. 353–385). Philadelphia, PA: Temple University.

Coyle, C. P., Kinney, W. B., and Shank, J. W. (1993). Trials and tribulations of field-based research in therapeutic recreation. In M. J. Malkin and C. Z. Howe (Eds.), *Research in therapeutic recreation: Concepts and methods* (pp. 207–232). State College, PA: Venture Publishing, Inc.

Coyle, C. P., Kinney, W. B., Riley, B., and Shank, J. W. (1991). *Benefits of therapeutic recreation: A consensus view.* Philadelphia, PA: Temple University.

Delaney, B. C., Hyde, C. J., McManus, R. J., Wilson, S., Fitzmaurice, D. A., Jowett, S., Tobias, R., and Thorpe, G. H. (1999). Systematic review of near patient test evaluations in primary care. *British Medical Journal, 319*(7213), 824–827.

Devine, M. A. and Wilhite, B. (1999). Theory application in therapeutic recreation practice and research. *Therapeutic Recreation Journal, 33*(1), 29–45.

Dufault, M. A. and Sullivan, M. (2000). A collaborative research utilization approach to evaluate the effects of pain management standards on patient outcomes. *Journal of Professional Nursing, 16(4),* 240–250.

Dunn, J. K., Sneegas, J. J., and Carruthers, C. A. (1991). Outcomes measures: Monitoring patient progress. In B. Riley (Ed.), *Quality management: Applications for therapeutic recreation* (pp. 107–115). State College, PA: Venture Publishing, Inc.

Ellis, G. (1993). The status of recreation, leisure and therapeutic recreation as a developing science. In M. J. Malkin and C. Z. Howe (Eds.), *Research in therapeutic recreation: Concepts and methods* (pp. 43–56). State College, PA: Venture Publishing, Inc.

Gerber, L. (1994/95). Keynote address for the first annual ATRA research institute. *Annual in Therapeutic Recreation, 5,* 1–4.

Gorski, T. T. (1995). The strategic advantage perspective on outcomes. *Behavioral Health Management, 15(3),* 33–36.

Gruver, B. (1993/94). Theories and models: A heuristic analysis of therapeutic recreation practice. *Annual in Therapeutic Recreation, 4,* 1–10.

Gunn, S. L. and Peterson, C. A. (1978). *Therapeutic recreation program design: Principles and procedures.* Englewood Cliffs, NJ: Prentice-Hall.

Hatala, R., Holbrook, A., and Goldsmith, C. H. (1999). Therapeutic equivalence: All studies are not created equal. *Canadian Journal of Clinical Pharmacology, 6*(1), 9–11.

Hodges, J. S. and Luken, K. (2000). Services and support as a means to meaningful outcomes for persons with developmental disabilities. *Annual in Therapeutic Recreation, 9,* 47–56.

Hood, C. D. (2001). Clinical practice guidelines - A decision making tool for best practice? In N. J. Stumbo (Ed.), *Professional issues in therapeutic recreation: On competence and outcomes* (pp. 189–214). Champaign, IL: Sagamore.

Hood, C. and Krinsky, A. (1997/98). The use of a Delphi procedure to identify priority client treatment needs for therapeutic recreation intervention in alcoholism treatment. *Annual in Therapeutic Recreation, 7,* 74–83.

Horn, S. D. (1997). Overcoming obstacles to effective treatment: Use of clinical practice improvement methodology. *Journal of Clinical Psychiatry, 58,* 15–19.

Hudson, M. P., Christenson, R. H., Newby, L. K., Kaplan, A. L., and Ohman, E. M. (1999). Cardiac markers: Point of care testing. *Clinica Chimica Acta, 284*(2), 223–237.

Jacobson, S., Carruthers, C., and Keller, M. J. (2001). Keynote: A sociohistorical perspective on therapeutic recreation research. In N. J. Stumbo (Ed.), *Professional issues in therapeutic recreation: On competence and outcomes* (pp. 317–334). Champaign, IL: Sagamore.

Jake, L. (2000a). Announcing treatment networks openings. *ATRA Newsletter, 16*(1), 5.

Jake, L. (2000b). News from Laurie Jake, treatment network board liaison. *Treatment Networks, 1*(2), 1.

Johnson, D. E. and Ashton-Shaeffer, C. (2000). A framework for TR outcomes in school-based settings. *Annual in Therapeutic Recreation, 9,* 57–70.

Joint Commission on Accreditation of Healthcare Organizations. (1995). *1996 Comprehensive Accreditation Manual for Hospitals.* Oakbrook Terrace, IL: Author.

Kloseck, M., Crilly, R. G., Ellis, G. D., and Lammers, E. (1996). Leisure competence measure: Development and reliability testing of a scale to measure functional outcomes in therapeutic recreation. *Therapeutic Recreation Journal, 30*(1), 13–26.

Kloseck, M., Crilly, R. G., and Hutchinson-Troyer, L. (2001). Measuring therapeutic recreation outcomes in rehabilitation: Further testing of the Leisure Competence Measure. *Therapeutic Recreation Journal, 35*(1), 31–42.

Lee, Y., Middlesteadt, R., and Perkins, S. (1999). An exploratory study of the comparison of leisure functioning of people with paraplegia and quadriplegia. *Annual in Therapeutic Recreation, 8,* 12–21.

Lee, Y. and Yang, H. (2000). A review of therapeutic recreation outcomes in physical medicine and rehabilitation between 1991–2000. *Annual in Therapeutic Recreation, 9,* 21–34.

Linde, M. (1999). Theory and practice in the management of depressive disorders. *International Clinical Psychopharmacology, 14,* S15–25.

Loeffler, M. A. and Henley, S. (1997). Standards of practice: Are they relevant? In D. M. Compton (Ed.), *Issues in therapeutic recreation: Toward the new millennium* (2nd ed., pp. 419–443). Champaign, IL: Sagamore.

Malkin, M. J. (1993). Issues and needs in therapeutic recreation research. In M. J. Malkin and C. Z. Howe (Eds.), *Research in therapeutic recreation: Concepts and methods* (pp. 3–23). State College, PA: Venture Publishing, Inc.

Malkin, M. J., Coyle, C. P., and Carruthers, C. (1998). Efficacy research in recreational therapy. In F. Brasile, T. Skalko, and J. Burlingame (Eds.), *Perspectives in recreational therapy: Issues of a dynamic profession* (pp. 141–164). Ravensdale, WA: Idyll Arbor.

Margison, F. R., Barkham, M., Evans, C., McGrath, G., Clark, J. M., Audin, K., and Connell, J. (2000). Measurement and psychotherapy - Evidence-based practice and practice-based evidence. *British Journal of Psychiatry, 177,* 123–130.

McCormack, B. P. and Funderburk, J. (2000). Therapeutic recreation outcomes in mental health practice. *Annual in Therapeutic Recreation, 9,* 9–20.

Mobily, K. E. (1999). New horizons in models of practice in therapeutic recreation. *Therapeutic Recreation Journal, 33*(3), 174–192.

Olsson, R. H. (1986). The prospective payment system: Implications for therapeutic recreation. *Therapeutic Recreation Journal, 20*(1), 6–16.

O'Morrow, G. S. and Carter, M. J. (1997). *Effective management in therapeutic recreation service.* State College, PA: Venture Publishing, Inc.

Patrick, G. (1997). Making clinical research happen. In D. M. (Ed.), *Issues in therapeutic recreation: Toward a new millennium* (2nd ed., pp. 327–346). Champaign, IL: Sagamore.

Patrick, G. (2001). Perspective: Clinical research: Methods and mandates. In N. J. Stumbo (Ed.), *Professional issues in therapeutic recreation: On competencies and outcomes* (pp. 401–418). Champaign, IL: Sagamore.

Peterson, C. A. and Stumbo, N. J. (2000). *Therapeutic recreation program design: Principles and procedures* (3rd ed.). Needham Heights, MA: Allyn and Bacon.

Petryshen, P. M. and Petryshen, P. R. (1993/94). Managed care: Shaping the delivery and healthcare and creating an expanded role for the care giver. *Annual in Therapeutic Recreation, 4,* 108–114.

Powe, N. R. (1996). Measuring effectiveness and outcomes of interventions for renal disease. *Current Opinion in Nephrology and Hypertension, 5*(3), 230–235.

Reitter, M. S. (1989). Third party payers: Are we getting our share? In D. Compton, (Ed.), *Issues in therapeutic recreation: A profession in transition* (pp. 238–256). Champaign, IL: Sagamore.

Rhodes, M. (1991). The use of patient satisfaction data as an outcome monitor in therapeutic recreation quality assurance. In B. Riley (Ed.), *Quality management: Applications for therapeutic recreation* (pp. 83–106). State College, PA: Venture Publishing, Inc.

Riley, B. (1991a). Introduction. In C. P. Coyle, W. B. Kinney, B. Riley, and J. W. Shank (Eds.), *Benefits of therapeutic recreation: A consensus view* (pp. 1–3). Philadelphia, PA: Temple University.

Riley, B. (1991b). Quality assessment: The use of outcome indicators. In B. Riley (Ed.), *Quality management: Applications for therapeutic recreation* (pp. 53–67). State College, PA: Venture Publishing, Inc.

Russoniello, C. (2000). Recreation therapy and behavioral medicine: Outcomes and cost effectiveness. *Annual in Therapeutic Recreation, 9,* 71–78.

Scalenghe, R. (1991). The Joint Commission's "Agenda for change" as related to the provision of therapeutic recreation services. In B. Riley (Ed.), *Quality management: Applications for therapeutic recreation* (pp. 29–42). State College, PA: Venture Publishing, Inc.

Schyve, P. M. (1996). The evolving role of the Joint Commission on the Accreditation of Healthcare Organization. *American Journal of Medical Quality, 11*(1), 54–57.

Scott, S. J. (1984). The Medicare prospective payment system. *The American Journal of Occupational Therapy, 38*(5), 330–334.

Seibert, M. L. (1991). Keynote. In C. P. Coyle, W. B. Kinney, B. Riley, and J. W. Shank (Eds.), *Benefits of therapeutic recreation: A consensus view* (pp. 5–15). Philadelphia, PA: Temple University.

Shank, J. W., Coyle, C. P., Kinney, W. B., and Lay, C. (1995). Using existing data to examine therapeutic recreation services. *Annual in Therapeutic Recreation, 5,* 5–12.

Shank, J. W. and Kinney, W. B. (1991). Monitoring and measuring outcomes in therapeutic recreation. In B. Riley (Ed.), *Quality management: Applications for therapeutic recreation* (pp. 69–88). State College, PA: Venture Publishing, Inc.

Shank, J. W., Kinney, W. B., and Coyle, C. P. (1993). Efficacy studies in therapeutic recreation research: The need, the state of the art, and future implications. In M. J. Malkin and C.Z. Howe (Eds.), *Research in therapeutic recreation: Concepts and methods* (pp. 301–336). State College, PA: Venture Publishing, Inc.

Stumbo, N. J. (1996). A proposed accountability model for therapeutic recreation services. *Therapeutic Recreation Journal, 30*(4), 246–259.

Stumbo, N. J. (2000). Outcome measurement in healthcare: Implications for therapeutic recreation. *Annual in Therapeutic Recreation, 9,* 1–8.

Stumbo, N. J. and Hess, M. E. (2001). On competencies and outcomes in therapeutic recreation. In N. J. Stumbo (Ed.), *Professional issues in therapeutic recreation: On competence and outcomes* (pp. 3–20). Champaign, IL: Sagamore.

Stumbo, N. J. and Hess, M. E. (in press). The status of client outcomes in selected programs as measured by adherence to the therapeutic recreation accountability model. *Annual in Therapeutic Recreation.*

Stumbo, N. J. and Peterson, C. A. (1998). The leisure ability model. *Therapeutic Recreation Journal, 32*(2), 82–96.

Thomas, J. R. and Nelson, J. K. (1996). *Research methods in physical activity* (3rd ed.). Champaign, IL: Human Kinetics.

Thompson, G. T. (2001). Reimbursement: Surviving prospective payment as a recreational therapy practitioner. In N. J. Stumbo (Ed.), *Issues in therapeutic recreation: On competence and outcomes* (pp. 249–264). Champaign, IL: Sagamore.

Touchstone, W. (1997). The administrators speak: Real issues we face daily—An interview. In D. M. Compton (Ed.), *Issues in therapeutic recreation: Toward the new millennium* (2nd ed., pp. 141-148). Champaign, IL: Sagamore.

United Kingdom Clearing House on Health Outcomes. (1997). About health outcomes. Available online: http://www.leeds.ac.uk/nuffield/infoservices/UKCH/about.html

Vorderer, L. H. (1997). Healthcare in America: Containing costs while expanding access. In D. M. Compton (Ed.), *Issues in therapeutic recreation: Toward the new millennium* (2nd ed., pp. 121–140). Champaign, IL: Sagamore.

Waise, A. (1999). Clinical audit and the contribution of the laboratory to clinical outcome. *Clinica Chimica Acta, 280*(1–2), 47–57.

West, R. E. (2000). Outcome measurement as an aspect of recreational therapy practice management. *Annual in Therapeutic Recreation, 9*, 79–86.

Witman, J. (1999). Letter to the guest editors of the practice model series. *Therapeutic Recreation Journal, 33*(4), 342–343.

Witt, P. (1988). Therapeutic recreation research: Past, present, and future. *Therapeutic Recreation Journal, 22*(1), 14–23.

CHAPTER 2
WRITING GOALS
FOR LEISURE
EDUCATION*

Therapeutic recreation services comprise three major categories of programs:

1. Functional intervention—to improve clients' functional abilities

2. Leisure education—to improve clients' knowledge, attitudes, and skills related to their own leisure involvement

3. Recreation participation—to improve participants' ability to self direct and participate in leisure activities of their choice

This chapter focuses primarily on leisure education services and how to write program and client goals related to these types of services.

> In many ways, the leisure education component appears to be the most important program service area within therapeutic recreation for most clients. This component contains the essential knowledge and skills necessary to develop an appropriate and meaningful leisure lifestyle. Regardless of the disabling condition and the limitations or barriers it presents, the individual has the right to experience leisure involvement and satisfaction. This opportunity, however, is dependent upon sufficient leisure-related attitudes, knowledge, and skills. Programs emerging from the leisure education concept and models provide for an understanding of leisure and the acquisition of participatory abilities and skills. (Peterson & Stumbo, 2000, p. 53)

WHAT IS LEISURE EDUCATION?

Leisure education focuses on the development and acquisition of various leisure-related skills, attitudes, and knowledge. The establishment and ex

pression of an appropriate leisure lifestyle depends on the acquisition of diverse knowledge and skills, as well as a cognitive understanding of leisure, a positive attitude toward leisure experiences, various participatory and decision-making skills, and the ability to utilize resources. These leisure education content areas can be operationalized into programs that have as their purpose the acquisition of appropriate leisure-related skills, knowledge, and attitudes. **Figure 2.1** (p. 20) displays a model that organizes this conceptualization of leisure education content (Peterson & Stumbo, 2000, p. 38).

Although leisure is acknowledged as a basic right and need of all individuals, many people require some assistance in developing an appropriate and satisfying leisure lifestyle. Barriers to a satisfying and healthy leisure lifestyle are common among both children and adults. The Protestant work ethic still exerts a strong influence on many people. In many ways, individuals with illnesses or disabilities are most often victimized by this influence. The disabling condition often removes individuals from socially defined productive activities (work) and leaves them without identifiable contributory roles. Unfortunately, a lingering view of leisure involvement is that leisure is earned as a reward for work, and thus, the individual is not entitled to leisure benefits or enjoyment if he or she is not contributing to society in some recognized manner. Within our contemporary society, and with the influence of more humanistic theories, this previous attitude has largely been rejected. The individual is seen as valuable and significant because he or she exists. The individual has rights and responsibilities like anyone else. Our human service system structure and legislative mandates support and reinforce this philosophy. However, the fact remains that many individuals with illnesses and disabilities are negatively impacted by previous attitudes and values of the society.

Because leisure is a significant component of contemporary life, it also must be viewed as a necessary aspect of existence for individuals with illnesses and disabilities. The concept of quality of life closely relates to the opportunities available for leisure involvement and expression. Individuals with disabling conditions, however, may need assistance in the development and expression of an independent leisure lifestyle. The leisure education

---

*Adapted from: Peterson and Stumbo, 2000

component of therapeutic recreation services addresses this need in a direct and comprehensive manner.

Since the development and expression of an appropriate leisure lifestyle is an important aspect of the human condition, there appears to be substantial reason for therapeutic recreation specialists to intervene. Even if the individual is not concerned about leisure, and in the absence of widespread concern by other medical and health professionals, the profession of therapeutic recreation plays a significant role in the total living experience of the individual, independent of its recognition by others.

NATURE OF LEISURE EDUCATION SERVICES

Leisure education services utilize an educational model, as opposed to the medical model. The educational model operates on the assumption that behavior can change and improve as the individual acquires new knowledge, skills, attitudes, and abilities. These changes occur through a learning process. The client is an active participant in the process, sharing responsibility for the targeted change or growth. Although illness or disability must be considered both in the content to be

learned and the process through which learning takes place, the illness or disability is not the primary concern at this point. Behavioral growth and change are sought independent of the condition. In leisure education, the focus of learning (or desired area of behavioral change) is leisure ability.

CONTENT OF LEISURE EDUCATION SERVICES

Four components have been conceptualized to identify the major aspects of leisure education content. These four components—leisure awareness, social interaction skills, leisure activity skills, and leisure resources—comprise the Leisure Education Content Model (**Figure 2.1**), as proposed by Peterson and Stumbo (2000).

LEISURE AWARENESS

An important aspect of leisure lifestyle and involvement appears to be a cognitive awareness of leisure and its benefits, including a valuing of the leisure phenomenon and a conscious decision-making process to activate involvement. These cognitive aspects seem to be what was missing in past recreation and therapeutic recreation programming. The historical assumption seemed to be that individuals only needed to acquire recreation

LEISURE AWARENESS
1.1 Knowledge of leisure
1.2 Self-awareness
1.3 Leisure and play attitudes
1.4 Related participatory and decision-making skills

SOCIAL INTERACTION SKILLS
2.1 Communication skills
2.2 Relationship-building skills
2.3 Self-presentation skills

LEISURE RESOURCES
4.1 Activity opportunities
4.2 Personal resources
4.3 Family and home resources
4.4 Community resources
4.5 State and national resources

LEISURE ACTIVITY SKILLS
3.1 Traditional
3.2 Nontraditional

Figure 2.1 Leisure Education Content Model

activity skills and from there they would apply those skills in some meaningful pattern of leisure involvement. That approach did not positively influence the leisure involvement of most clients beyond the actual participation in the segmented agency-sponsored programs. The more contemporary approach, which focuses on some understanding of leisure, better facilitates the development and expression of an appropriate leisure lifestyle. Regardless of whether or not the individual immediately responds to the content of leisure education programs, they are still exposed to knowledge and information that may be useful to them at some later point.

Within the component of leisure awareness, four content areas can be identified that facilitate the development and expression of an appropriate leisure lifestyle:

1. Knowledge of leisure
2. Self-awareness
3. Leisure and play attitudes
4. Related participatory and decision-making skills

Knowledge of leisure can address a variety of topics that have been found to be useful with many populations, including:

- Leisure and its relation to quality of life
- Difference between leisure behaviors and other behaviors
- Benefits and outcomes of leisure involvement
- Barriers to leisure involvement
- Forms of leisure involvement
- Leisure as a context to learn new skills, meet new people, experience new events
- Leisure lifestyle
- Balance between leisure, work, and other obligations
- Personal responsibility for leisure lifestyle

A second area, *self-awareness*, focuses on a more personal understanding of leisure and the individual. The following are possible topic areas for inclusion in this content area:

- Actual and perceived abilities and skills that impact leisure involvement
- Actual and perceived limitations that impact leisure involvement

- Effects of a disability or illness on leisure behavior
- Past leisure and play patterns and activities
- Current leisure involvement and satisfaction
- Areas for future discovery and involvement
- Personal resources for leisure involvement
- Goals areas for development through leisure
- Effects of family and friends on personal leisure development

Leisure and play attitudes is the third content area. Within this area, existing attitudes about play and leisure can be explored. This is often a critical point in terms of redirecting or moving toward change in leisure lifestyle development. Typical topics might include:

- Past, current, and future societal attitudes related to leisure
- Origin of one's personal beliefs and values about leisure
- Relationship between attitudes and behavior
- Appropriateness of former leisure attitudes with regard to current life situation
- Relationship between leisure attitudes, values, and life satisfaction
- Impact of leisure attitudes on current and future leisure lifestyle
- Evolution of attitudes about leisure throughout the life span

The fourth content area, *related participatory and decision-making skills*, also identifies a variety of topics and processes for content inclusion in this area, including:

- Decision-making skills with regard to leisure involvement
- Leisure-planning skills
- Problem-solving techniques for daily use
- Long-term coping and adaptation strategies
- Creating and evaluating options for leisure participation
- Reducing and managing stress through conscious planning and decision making

Many of these topics are generic. Several decision-making and problem-solving models emphasize a general step-by-step approach, but they can be applied specifically to leisure participation. These processes may require substantial time for learning; however, these skills are essential if meaningful changes are to take place in the individual's leisure lifestyle and involvement related participatory and decision-making skills also include topics that may vary considerably depending on the specific population being served by the program. Consider the following three examples:

Rehabilitation Center for Individuals with Spinal Cord Injuries

- Ask appropriate questions about physical accessibility of recreation facilities
- Ask for assistance when necessary
- Locate information about resources available to individuals with spinal injuries
- Interact with nondisabled people in leisure participation (friends, staff, strangers)
- Decide in which activities to participate
- Make long-term adjustments to a personal leisure lifestyle

Psychiatric Inpatient Unit

- Plan for leisure involvement postdischarge
- Use leisure to counter the affects of living with stressful situations
- Make appropriate decisions with regard to leisure involvement
- Make daily choices for leisure on the unit
- Decide which leisure skills the individual would like to learn
- Plan for leisure participation, considering fatigue levels, interest, and availability

Group Home for Individuals with Developmental Disabilities

- Review options for leisure involvement
- Plan for involvement in leisure events
- Examine consequences of participation or nonparticipation
- Make choices about leisure involvement and participation
- Decide which leisure activities are most enjoyable
- Reduce barriers to leisure involvement

These examples are for illustration only—none of the lists of possible related participatory skills or topics is complete. In addition, many other populations and settings were not included at

all. Readers are encouraged to develop such topic areas as needed.

Aspects of these four areas are generally combined into one leisure education program structure. The selection of topics is based on the specific population and their leisure-related information needs. In most cases, however, the information and skills found in the first component are not part of previously acquired knowledge. Thus, the conceptualization of the actual content for programs related to this component is at the discretion of the therapeutic recreation specialist designing the program.

SOCIAL INTERACTION SKILLS

Social interaction is a major aspect of leisure lifestyle, particularly adult leisure involvement. In many situations, the social interaction is more significant to the participants than the activity itself. The activity may be the reason to be together, but it is the social interaction that has real meaning for the people involved—for example, social dancing (e.g., ballroom, disco, rock). In other situations, the activity has significant meaning to the participants, but interaction abilities are essential for successful involvement. Playing bridge, which requires interaction between partners as well as bidding against others, illustrates this point. Most team sports also require interaction between and among team members for successful participation. Some group-oriented leisure activities require little social interaction, but the participation and enjoyment seem to be heightened by social interaction—for example, square dancing or bowling. Within the comprehensive concept of leisure lifestyle, there are many leisure participation situations that do not involve traditional activities at all. An exclusively verbal social encounter could be considered a leisure experience depending on the motivation, content, and outcomes. This type of social interaction takes place frequently for most individuals without disabilities and is a very important consideration. Simply stated, social interaction among adults may be the most frequent form of leisure participation and appropriate social interaction skills are necessary for satisfactory participation.

Since social interaction appears to be such a significant aspect of leisure participation and lifestyle, it is included as a component of leisure education. The skills and abilities involved in social interaction can be learned and conceptualized into program structures. More importantly, they can be learned through involvement in various recreation and leisure activities and take on a more dynamic, action-oriented dimension. Acquiring social interaction skills in the context of activities allows for more realistic learning and application. Generally, learning interaction skills through activity involvement is enjoyable for the client as well. Fortunately, traditional recreation activities have within their structures all the various and basic interaction patterns normally required within our society. Careful assessment of the client's existing social interaction skill level and analysis of additional interaction skills needed can be conducted. Activities that have the appropriate inherent interactional requirements to facilitate the acquisition of the designated social interaction skills can then be selected. Activity analysis provides valuable information related to the process of activity selection for the development of social interaction skills.

The acquisition of social interaction skills, like any other skill acquisition, requires the planning of specific programs designed to facilitate the learning of the designated behavior. Depending on the population and setting, social interaction skill development may be a significant aspect of the comprehensive leisure education and therapeutic recreation mission. For example, individuals with moderate mental retardation may need specific programs to develop appropriate social interaction skills. Individuals in substance abuse programs or in short-term psychiatric facilities, however, may need only to have appropriate social interaction skills reinforced through other types of therapeutic recreation programming.

For the purposes of leisure education, social interactions skills have been divided into three categories: communication skills, relationship-building skills, and self-presentation skills. This section does not intend to discount or ignore, however, those leisure activities and experiences that the individual engages in and enjoys while alone. Indeed, there is a great need to assist individuals in developing a repertoire of activities and interests that can be done alone. Likewise, helping them to understand the need for, and develop a positive attitude toward solitary leisure appears to be a significant aspect of an overall leisure lifestyle.

Communication Skills. Clear and honest communication is a necessity in all aspects of everyday life, including leisure. For many client groups an improvement in communications skills would enable them to participate more appropriately with others in a variety of leisure pursuits. A host of skills may be taught in this area, including:

- Assertiveness skills
- Negotiation, disagreement, conflict, and compromise skills
- Conversational skills
- Active listening skills and responsive behavior skills
- Skills for expressing feelings and thoughts
- Information-seeking and information-giving skills
- Empathy and perspective taking skills

Relationship-Building Skills. Relationship building skills address those areas that assist an individual in locating, maintaining, and developing friendships and other relationships. Significant others play important roles in most people's lives, and many skills are needed to maintain and sustain healthy relationships. Social networks and social support are important to most individuals, and leisure pursuits provide many opportunities to develop these aspects. Some client groups will need more work in the social skills area than others. Some typical skills that might be taught in this area include:

- Greeting and initiation skills (e.g., locating leisure partners)
- Friendship development skills
- Self-disclosure and privacy issues
- Cooperation and competitive skills
- Developing and maintaining social networks
- Reciprocal social support (expressing care and concern for others and vice versa)

Self-Presentation Skills. For communication skills and relationship-building skills to be utilized, the individual also must maintain some basic social etiquette rules. Some clients groups will need more training in this area than others, but all will need to exhibit fundamental skills. Often, the lack of these skills prevents an individual from being accepted and becoming friends with or meeting other individuals. Examples of these skills include:

- Politeness, etiquette, and manners (e.g., taking turns, sharing)
- Hygiene, health, and grooming skills
- Appropriate attire and dressing
- Responsibility for self-care

Social interaction ability is an essential aspect of successful leisure involvement and lifestyle. Since the behaviors and skills involved can be learned and for the most part are independent of illness or disability itself, social interaction skills are included as a component of leisure education. If clients need to develop interaction skills, then appropriate programs should be conceptualized and implemented. The absence of adequate interaction ability can be as much a barrier to leisure involvement as the absence of activity skills or knowledge of leisure and its significance.

LEISURE SKILLS DEVELOPMENT

Expressing a satisfying leisure lifestyle implies that the individual has a sense of freedom and choice in leisure involvement. A repertoire of leisure activities and related interests is necessary for meaningful experiences, but the issue is not simply one of acquiring as many leisure skills as possible. It seems more important to assist the individual in selecting and developing adequate skills in a number of activities that potentially will be a source of enjoyment and personal satisfaction for the individual across the lifespan.

Developing an appropriate leisure lifestyle shifts responsibility to the individual for ongoing leisure expressions. Once leisure skills are acquired, it is expected that they will become a meaningful aspect of the individual's leisure lifestyle. Some of the activities may be participated in through an organized delivery program (e.g., bowling league, ceramics program, photography club) but many of the skills will be utilized independent of any agency. These skills will be engaged in through commercial leisure opportunities, at home (or in the facility) alone, or with others in a social situation.

In the past, most skill development programs have focused on traditional recreation activities—ones commonly identified as recreational and sanctioned by the society. They have been promoted and programmed by the leisure and recreation profession. Countless classification and categorical systems have been developed to iden-

tify them. The following list includes examples of activities frequently referred to within the traditional recreation category.

Traditional Categories of Commonly Identified Forms of Recreation
- Sports
- Dance
- Aquatics and water-related activities
- Drama
- Outdoor activities
- Music
- Arts and crafts
- Other expressive arts
- Mental games and activities
- Hobbies

There is nothing inherently wrong or inappropriate with activities that fall under the label of traditional recreation. Indeed, individuals with disabling conditions may need and want activity skills from the traditional categories. The problem, however, is the assumption that these activities, and only these activities, are important or appropriate. When we accept the concept of leisure lifestyle, we recognize a multitude of leisure experiences and interests that extend far beyond traditional recreation activities. Observing what adults actually do with their leisure results in very different list of activities and events. The following list identifies by category the nontraditional types of adult leisure pursuits and involvements common in our culture. These are in addition to the traditional activities previously identified.

Nontraditional Categories of Adult Leisure Involvement
- Social interaction
- Spectating and appreciating
- Leadership and community service
- Fitness
- Relaxation and meditation
- Eating
- Food preparation
- Shopping
- Home improvement and maintenance
- Living things maintenance—pet care and plant care
- Self-development

- Education
- Computer and Internet activities
- Travel
- Fantasy and daydreaming
- Intimacy and sexually related activity
- Substance use—alcohol, drugs, tobacco
- Nothing
- Interaction with family and friends
- Telephone/e-mail conversations

Involvement in these leisure activities more adequately represents the content and nature of adult leisure lifestyles. Many of the actions are engaged in alone or with significant others as opposed to organized activity-centered groups and are less structured with fewer exact procedures or rules. Most often the environment for participation is the home or some general environment as opposed to a specific recreation activity or facility. The dimension of time is also different for many of the activities. Nontraditional activities are less likely to require a specific amount of time or time scheduled by someone else. Another difference between these activities and traditional recreation activities is the absence of a program structure by a leisure service delivery agency.

Leisure involvements and activities identified as nontraditional do require various skills, knowledge, and participatory abilities. Many people engage in these leisure pursuits without specific programmed instruction; however, it is possible to analyze these activities and develop programs that address the acquisition of various skills. Individuals with disabling conditions may need this specific form of leisure skill development. If leisure lifestyle development and expression are the concern of therapeutic recreation services, then the understanding, selection, and programming of skills related to these leisure pursuits may take precedence over the traditional forms of recreation.

Assisting the client in developing appropriate leisure skills takes on new dimensions when using this leisure lifestyle approach. The concern shifts from focus on the skills of a specific traditional activity to broader participatory abilities that include knowledge of leisure possibilities, selecting and learning appropriate leisure activities, and integrating leisure involvement within the total life situation. This does not mean that specific leisure skills are not part of the total programming focus. It merely means that specific activity skills must be viewed and selected within a broader context. More attention must be paid to the individual and the development of leisure skills and related participatory abilities for a unique lifestyle and situation.

In clinical and community settings, there is a need for leisure skills development programs for individuals with disabling conditions. Many clients lack specific and general leisure activity skills appropriate for a meaningful ongoing leisure lifestyle. The task of the therapeutic recreation specialist is to select appropriate content for these leisure skill development programs. The concept of leisure lifestyle and the previously identified lists of activity categories may be useful in the selection process. The following list presents some of the criteria for selecting leisure skills to be taught to clients.

Additional Criteria for Selecting Leisure Skills

- Choice by the individual (selected from a range of options)
- Within functional ability and interests of the clients (evaluated through activity analysis)
- Feasible for clients' resources (money, equipment, access to facilities)
- Compatible with the overall life situation of the individual
- Compatible with leisure interests of those with whom the individual lives
- Age-appropriate but with opportunities for continued development and involvement at later life stages
- Demographic considerations (place of residence, socioeconomic status, educational level, ethnicity, and religion)
- Opportunity for continuing leisure involvement rather than a short-term focus
- Transfer of responsibility for leisure involvement to clients
- Helping clients define and prepare for a leisure lifestyle independent of the current agency program structure
- Nature and mandate of the agency delivering the services

It is difficult to determine how many and what kinds of leisure activity skills an individual needs—no absolutes or established standards can be applied. The absence of such global absolutes should be respected. The concept of an individualized leisure lifestyle and activity repertoire deserves to be protected. Professional knowledge and judgment of the therapeutic recreation specialist, with input from the client, becomes the basis for decision making related to the development of a leisure skill repertoire of a given client. A well-developed comprehensive scheme or model of leisure lifestyle that includes leisure skills can be very useful in the assessment and programming efforts related to this component of leisure education.

LEISURE RESOURCES

The *leisure resources* component adds another important dimension to program content. Knowledge of leisure resources and the ability to utilize these resources appear to be significant in the establishment and expression of a leisure lifestyle. All too often professionals assume that clients have a basic knowledge of information acquisition and utilization. In other cases, therapeutic recreation specialists have not processed the importance of identifying resources and assisting the client in acquiring the ability to be independent through the use of such resources. The concept of an independent leisure lifestyle requires that the client be able to seek out information and use it appropriately.

Leisure is not a well-understood phenomenon in our society. Thus, it is not unusual that many people, both those with and without disabilities and/or illnesses, are not aware of leisure resources and how to use them. Individuals with some disabling conditions may be at an even greater disadvantage, in that they may have been protected or isolated from resource information utilization. A well-planned, comprehensive leisure education program must include information and utilization skills development related to the topic of leisure resources. Such programming gives to clients the tools for their own exploration, expansion, and participation in leisure involvement. Independent leisure involvement likely is not possible without such knowledge and ability.

Leisure resources can be identified and categorized in many ways. They target five areas: activity opportunities, personal resources, family and home resources, community resources, and state and national resources.

Activity Opportunities. Many clients may need information regarding the vast number of different leisure activities available. Thus, identifying possible leisure activities could be a valuable area of program content. Helping clients to understand the wide range of activities available allows them choice and freedom in decision making. Increased knowledge of the potential of diverse activities translates into increased opportunities for selecting intrinsically motivating, interesting, and challenging options. Not to be confused with the actual development of activity skills, knowledge of activity opportunities means that the individual understands that the list of possible activities for participation may be limitless. The individual cannot be responsible for choice and self-selection of activities that he or she knows nothing about. The intent here is both to expand the clients' awareness of leisure opportunities as well as to assist them in identifying preferences for possible inclusion in their personal repertoire.

Personal Resources. Because leisure is not well-understood, many individuals may have limited awareness of possible leisure involvements already within their ability and experience. Identifying these resources can expand individuals' leisure repertoire considerably by merely bringing attention to the opportunity. Examples of this might be verbal and interaction ability that can be used for leisure enjoyment. For the person who is ambulatory, walking and jogging are possible leisure activities. Characteristics such as finances, educational level, athleticism, creativity, and past leisure experiences can be explored for possible current and future leisure involvement. This category also can be expanded to identify functional abilities and limitations that influence leisure.

Family and Home Resources. The people with whom one lives (family members, partners, friends, or individuals in the facility) can be considered leisure resources. Thus, the identification of leisure interests of others can expand the repertoire of leisure possibilities for a given client. The home, whether it is the client's own house or a facility in which he or she lives, is another source of potential leisure involvement. Since most people spend a considerable amount of time in the place of residence, the home becomes an important leisure resource. Assistance frequently is needed to help the client identify various aspects of the home that are possible leisure resources. Obvious ones, such as television, books, magazines, and games are easily identified; however, there are many others. Newspapers, the kitchen, the garage, plants, and pets often are overlooked as leisure resources. When engaged in such discussion, identifying what is can be supplemented with what could be. How objects or places could be used for leisure involvement is an interesting and expanding experience, especially for those individuals for whom the home may be the primary environment for leisure involvement.

Community Resources. Most communities have a variety of agencies, commercial enterprises, and facilities that are leisure resources. It cannot be assumed that a given client is aware of these opportunities. Some aspect of programming must focus on identifying these leisure resources, as well as considering the participatory requirements. Most commonly recognized recreation resources would include the pubic recreation programs, services, and facilities, such as a city's recreation department or park district; programs offered through the school district, often listed as adult education or community education; and the voluntary, nonprofit agency programs and facilities, such as the YMCA, YWCA, scouting, Campfire, and Boys' and Girls' clubs. Commercial recreation plays a major role in the leisure involvement of most people. Bowling alleys, movie theaters, billiards centers, dance studios, golf courses, game arcades, and skating rinks are a few examples of commercial recreation activity establishments. Swim clubs, racquet clubs, health spas, and fitness centers are additional examples of commercial leisure involvement. Commercial transportation options may be another area of concern for clients. The commercial category can be extended to a wide variety of other establishments. For example, arts and crafts stores, in-line skate rental facilities, and photography stores often sponsor classes and other group participation opportunities. Within most communities, a large number of nonagency-sponsored clubs exist, such as square dance, bridge, motorcycle, or model airplane clubs. Youth and social and service organizations and clubs also are considered part of the leisure resource network. Thus, groups like Soroptomists, Lions, and

Rotary International need to be identified for possible leisure resources. Multiple opportunities for volunteer work or service can also be viewed as a leisure opportunity. Newer additions to the list may include Internet sites, chat rooms, electronic bulletin boards, Web television, and the like.

State and National Resources. In addition to the home environment and community resources, leisure opportunities on a state and national level may be appropriate to introduce to clients. This area can be conceptualized many ways, since there are multiple public and commercial resources and opportunities.

Knowledge and awareness of leisure resources is only one aspect of this component of leisure education. Equally important are utilization skills related to resources. Of primary significance is assisting clients in being able to identify and locate leisure resources on their own. This information, along with the knowledge of various participatory and utilization aspects, is vital in the process of facilitating an independent leisure lifestyle. For most individuals, obtaining and being able to utilize these skills require the opportunity to practice them in natural settings. Utilizing skills in naturalized situations parallel to future independent involvement typically increases the transferability and generalizability of the skills learned. Clients are most successful later in the community when they have had ample opportunity to practice and use a set of skills under the guidance of a specialist. Professionals should consider allowing clients adequate experiences to gain mastery of skills necessary for projected involvement.

The nature and amount of leisure resources content to be programmed depends on several factors. Consider the type of clients being served, their resource information needs, and their processing skills. Wide variability exists in the populations being served by therapeutic recreation. Since the leisure resource category is very cognitive in nature, programming approaches and processes need to reflect the abilities and limitations of the specific individuals or groups. For example, an individual with mild to moderate mental retardation may have difficulty processing information about resources and their utilization. Thus, programming may need to be substantial to assist in the acquisition of the information. An individual with a college degree who has recently acquired a spinal cord injury may be able to acquire information about leisure resources quickly—for example, through the Internet—and immediately apply this information to the community after rehabilitation. An individual residing in a long-term healthcare facility on a permanent basis has a different kind of leisure information need. In this case, the information may be centered on resources of the facility and the individual's own personal resources. Programming needs to reflect these differences in the clientele being served.

Other areas of client need also must be addressed through the various therapeutic recreation programs. Total available programming time must be balanced among the diverse areas of client need. Leisure resource knowledge and utilization skills are important, but must be analyzed and selected within the context of total programming concerns. Leisure resource content can be programmed in many different ways. Specific and separate programs can be structured to focus exclusively on this content; however, the content is most often presented in combination with other areas of the leisure education model. The content can be compatible with information and content from the leisure awareness category, or it can be combined with leisure skills development programs. In the latter case, resources generally relate directly to the leisure skills being taught.

As in all other components of leisure education and therapeutic recreation programming, objectives must be specified and content and process descriptions delineated to facilitate the acquisition of the leisure resource information. An understanding of clients' informational needs and a sound conceptual scheme related to leisure resources is fundamental to this type of program development.

WRITING GOALS

Because goals play a major role in determining program content and direction, they should be developed carefully and with attention to alternatives, resources, and interpretation of the mission statement. Content, format, and wording of the statement are significant. The following steps should be useful in deriving and stating goals:

Process for Deriving and Stating Goals

- Review the statement of purpose

- Review the characteristics and needs of the population
- Review the nature and purpose of the agency, resources, and constraints
- Brainstorm possible goal areas
- Determine the appropriateness of goal areas for the specific population
- Develop goal statements
- Analyze goal statements

This process will help make better goals, and this in turn will help develop better, more targeted programs. A criteria list follows that may be used for this final check of goal appropriateness and technical quality.

Criteria for Judging Goal Statements

- The statement clearly delineates the goal area
    - The statement focuses directly on key concept words
    - The surrounding wording does not change possible interpretations of the goal statement
- The statement has an appropriate level of generality and specificity
    - The statement excludes material that describes actual implementation concerns and strategies
    - The statement avoids levels of generality that are too broad to direct the reader to specific content
- Statements are parallel in style and general level of content
    - Statements are consistent in wording and format
    - Statements are consistent in nature of content presented
- Statements are appropriate and feasible for population and agency
    - Goals can be substantiated through professional knowledge for development or performance expectations
    - Goals reflect the philosophy and nature of the agency and are feasible within time, budget, and staffing constraints

- Statements reflect the nature and intent of the statement of purpose.
- Program goals focus on program intention, not client goals or client outcomes.

Each agency or unit should develop its own goal statements, reflecting the needs of its population, the nature of its setting, and the philosophy of its staff. Generally the content for goal statements reflects the three functions of therapeutic recreation service (functional intervention, leisure education, and recreation participation) or subcomponents of them (leisure awareness, social skills, leisure activity skills, and leisure resources)

WRITING GOALS FOR LEISURE EDUCATION PROGRAMS AND CLIENTS

Four levels of goals and objectives become important to a comprehensive therapeutic recreation program: comprehensive program goals, specific program goals, client goals, and client objectives. While functional intervention and recreation participation service are important and viable, goals and objectives for all four levels will concentrate on leisure education content.

Each of these levels help the therapeutic recreation specialist to conceptualize and define the content and outcomes of the leisure education program. Each level is related to the other levels, from the most global program measures (comprehensive program goals) to the most specific client measures (client objectives). (See Peterson and Stumbo 2000 for a more in-depth explanation of how these levels of goals and objectives fit into the overall planning process of therapeutic recreation.)

COMPREHENSIVE PROGRAM GOALS

Comprehensive program goals are developed only after a complete analysis of the community and its resources, the agency, the profession, and the clientele so the programs will meet the expectations and needs of all these groups. After this analysis, a statement of purpose or mission statement is cre-

ated for the department or program, which speaks in broad terms about how the overall program will function and to which ends or outcomes it subscribes.

Once a statement of purpose or mission statement has been derived, the next step is to develop comprehensive goals, which describe aspects of the statement of purpose in greater detail and develop the comprehensive program's purpose. Usually goals are idealistic yet capable of being put into operation through program components. Goals are not directly measurable; they are statements of intent..

The following suggestions for goal content within leisure education are offered merely as a stimulus to the program developer. The areas are generic and not related to specific illness, disabilities or settings. Each is presented as a content area and is not a fully developed program goal statement. The focus is on the program and what it intends to deliver to clients.

Leisure Education Program Goals

- To provide services that improve clients' awareness of leisure and its significance
- To help clients increase self-awareness in relation to recreation and leisure
- To provide activities that help clients identify personal barriers to leisure
- To assist clients in exploring and developing leisure attitudes and values
- To help clients develop and utilize problem-solving abilities in relation to leisure
- To increase clients knowledge of leisure resources in their home and neighborhood
- To increase clients knowledge of local leisure opportunities
- To help clients develop self-directed, self-expressive leisure behavior
- To provide direction for clients to develop a personal leisure philosophy
- To provide activities that increase clients' social interactional skills
- To improve clients' comfort level in social situations
- To improve clients' cooperative and competitive skills in leisure situations
- To provide a variety of activities that help clients develop nontraditional leisure skills

- To improve clients' personal repertoire of leisure skills

- To provide clients with exposure to new leisure skill areas

- To provide instruction in advanced leisure skills development

These suggested goal areas can be made more precise once a specific population and setting are identified. For example, if a population is composed of children with severe mental retardation, a general physical goal might become more definitive—for example, "to provide a series of activities that develop physical coordination and basic body movements." The program planner makes these refinements when selecting and developing goal statements. A vast number of goal areas related to therapeutic recreation programs are not mentioned here because of their uniqueness to a given setting, population, or approach. For example, a goal area for a long-term healthcare facility might deal with the reduction of disoriented behaviors. The planner can be concerned with the particular population and at the same time refer to general lists such as the ones provided.

Goals clearly delineate an area of behavioral improvement, acquisition, or expression, but they do not indicate *how* this will be accomplished. The next stage of comprehensive program development will address this issue. Goals identify majors areas of focus. They are brief, concise statements written to define and further clarify the intent of the statement of purpose. Generally, there will be from five to ten goals for a comprehensive therapeutic recreation program.

Consider the following examples of comprehensive goal statements—one for chemical dependency and one for physical rehabilitation. The focus areas are indicated in brackets.

Example 1. Chemical Dependency Facility (McGowen, 1997)

1.0 To provide programs that increase clients' functional abilities in the physical, emotional, social, and cognitive areas. [functional intervention focus]

2.0 To provide programs that assist clients in utilizing previously acquired leisure skills or acquire new leisure skills appropriate to their limitations and future lifestyles. [leisure skills focus]

3.0 To provide programs to increase clients' knowledge of leisure resources for current and future sober utilization. [leisure resources focus]

4.0 To promote and foster the development of a personal awareness of leisure and its value. [leisure awareness focus]

5.0 To provide programs that increase clients' ability to interact with peers in an appropriate manner, in sober environments. [social interaction skills focus]

6.0 To provide opportunities for the client to participate in recreation activities in order to maintain and expand existing skills and interests. [recreation participation focus]

Example 2. Physical Medicine and Rehabilitation Center (Hess, 1997)

1.0 To provide programs that improve clients' deficits in the areas of physical, emotional, cognitive, and social functional abilities. [functional intervention focus]

2.0 To provide services that promote an awareness of the importance of a successful leisure lifestyle. [leisure awareness focus]

3.0 To provide programs that promote knowledge and utilization of leisure resources within the home and community. [leisure resources focus]

4.0 To provide programs that improve social skills necessary to function successfully in a variety of leisure environments. [social interaction skills focus]

5.0 To provide information and resources pertaining to physical and architectural barriers commonly found in the environment. [leisure barriers focus]

6.0 To provide services in which clients are actively involved in the community in order to promote independence when returning to the home community. [community reintegration focus]

7.0   To provide programs in a variety of leisure skill development areas. [leisure activity skill focus]

These comprehensive goal statements show the broad categories of therapeutic recreation departments. At the chemical dependency facility, major categories of therapeutic recreation programming include:

- Functional intervention skills
- Leisure skills
- Leisure resources
- Leisure awareness
- Social interaction skills
- Recreation participation

At the physical rehabilitation facility, major categories of therapeutic recreation include:

- Functional intervention skills
- Leisure awareness
- Leisure resources
- Social interaction skills
- Leisure barriers
- Community reintegration
- Leisure activity skills

The therapeutic recreation specialists at these two facilities selected these areas after a careful analysis of the community, the agency, the therapeutic recreation profession, and the clients.

SPECIFIC PROGRAM GOALS

After determining a comprehensive statement of purpose and goal statements for a therapeutic recreation unit or agency, the specialist must develop specific programs. Specific programs put the comprehensive goals and purpose into motion. Agency or unit goals must be translated and transformed into actual operational programs. These specific programs need to be developed and described in a very specific manner, so that desired outcomes relate directly to planned interventions and activities. A *specific program* can be defined as:

> A set of activities and their corresponding interactions that are designed to achieve predetermined goals selected for a given group of clients. The specific program is implemented and evaluated independently of all other specific programs. (Peterson and Stumbo, 2000, p. 106)

Each specific program identifies and addresses some major aspect of functional intervention, leisure education, or recreation participation. One specific program usually cannot focus adequately on all of these areas of client need. Thus, specific programs are selected and developed that relate to different categories of client need. Some programs will address various functional intervention concerns; others will be developed to focus on the diverse aspects of leisure education; still others will center on recreation and leisure participation opportunities.

Specific programs need to be developed and described so that they can be implemented by the specialist in a consistent manner. This allows the program to be repeated by the same implementer, or implemented by someone else. The thorough written description is also of value for the purpose of evaluation. Additionally, it allows the agency to maintain a high level of accountability in that all programs are documented before, during, and after implementation.

The therapeutic recreation specialist must, for every program designed, understand what content is important, how it will be facilitated, what steps must be taken, what activities will be offered, what resources are needed, and what outcomes are expected. The steps assist the specialist in determining the answers in a systematic, logical way. When the system used to create and implement the programs is well-thought-out, connected, and systematic, this enhances the ability to produce predictable, reproducible client outcomes.

Consider the following examples of specific program goals, using the previously mentioned rehabilitation facility.

Example 2. Physical Medicine and Rehabilitation Center (Hess, 1997)

2.0   **To provide services that promote an awareness of the importance of a successful leisure lifestyle. [leisure awareness focus]**

2.1   To provide programs that improve participants' knowledge of leisure and its importance to an overall balanced lifestyle [knowledge of leisure]

2.2   To provide services that improve participants' self-awareness in relation to leisure [self-awareness]

2.3 To provide programs that improve participants' understanding of their own personal leisure and play attitudes [leisure and play attitudes]

2.4 To provide programs that enhance participants' leisure participatory and decision-making skills [leisure participatory and decision-making skills]

3.0 To provide programs that promote knowledge and utilization of leisure resources within the home and community. [leisure resources focus]

3.1 To provide programs and service that improve participants' understanding of the wide range of activity opportunities available for leisure [activity opportunities]

3.2 To provide programs and services to enhance participants' understanding and utilization of personal resources for leisure [personal resources]

3.3 To provide programs and services that improve participants' understanding and utilization of family and home resources for leisure [family and home resources]

3.4 To provide programs and services to improve participants' understanding and utilization of community resources available for leisure [community resources]

4.0 To provide programs that improve social skills necessary to function successfully in a variety of leisure environments. [social interaction skills focus]

4.1 To provide programs that improve participants' communication skills in relation to leisure [communication skills]

4.2 To provide programs and activities that improve participants' relationship building skills as necessary for leisure participation [relationship building skills]

4.3 To provide programs and services that improve participants' self-presentation skills in relation to leisure [self-presentation skills]

Specific programs and their goals represent the major areas of content derived from the comprehensive program design. Each of these examples pinpoints the intent of the program in clear and concise language. Specific program goals state what content the program intends to cover. It is written from the point of view of the sponsoring agency or unit. The language used states what the program is intended to provide. Note also that the specific program goals do not state how the program will accomplish this. The remainder of the program design will delineate the "how" and the "who."

To address the diverse goals delineated by the therapeutic recreation agency, unit, or department, the therapeutic recreation specialist generally selects a variety of specific programs. These combined statements provide the overall operational definition of the previously delineated agency's or unit's goals. At this point, the specialist can verify that the more generalized intent of the comprehensive goals has been reflected in actual programming efforts.

Once the general topic of a specific program is selected, client goals and objectives will be derived and stated. These goals objectives will be delineated for a given group of clients (usually a subgroup of the total population served by the agency). Activities then will be developed that relate directly to the identified objectives and are appropriate for the designated clients. "Activities" in this context does not mean just traditional recreation or leisure activities. It implies a broader category of actions or program content, which can include such areas as discussions, lectures, and written or cognitive exercises as well as traditional or nontraditional recreation activities. Thus, the term *activity* refers to the action, content, or media presented to the clients to address the objectives and, it is hoped, to achieve the desired outcomes.

Similarly, specific interactions will be designed to be used with those activities for that particular set of clients. The program is designed to be implemented for that particular set of clients, independently of other programs. Its objectives, activities, and interventions have their own timelines, staff, resource allocations, and designated evaluation mechanism. A given client is placed or referred to one or more specific programs based on the client's need and the program's designed ability to address that need. This method of programming enables the individual leisure-related needs of clients to be met. It also allows for specific programs to be added, deleted, or changed as clients' needs dictate. Because each specific program has its own focus, it can be evaluated based on its contribution to the overall mission of the therapeutic recreation unit, agency, or department. Likewise, the progress of an individual client can be carefully monitored, based on achievement and participation within each assigned or designated program.

Note that some agencies or units may not be using a comprehensive approach to therapeutic recreation program planning. Even if an agency does not advocate to do so, it is still possible and desirable for an individual therapeutic recreation specialist to develop programs in a logical, systematic, and accountable method. Systems design procedures provide such a method. (See Peterson and Stumbo 2000 for an explanation of systems design.)

CLIENT GOALS

Client goals and objectives represent the participant's perspective. What should the participant be able to do, state, or think by the end of the program? What are outcomes are expected as the result of participant in the program? Comprehensive and specific program goals consider content from the *programmer's* perspective; client goals and objectives take the *participant's* perspective.

Examples of vague or inappropriate client goals as well as measurable, appropriate goals might include:

Sample Client Goals (inappropriate)

- To improve self-concept
- To improve socialization
- To increase responsible use of leisure

Sample Client Goals (appropriate)

- To give and receive constructive criticism
- To give and receive compliments
- To maintain eye contact
- To verbalize personal responsibility for own actions
- To initiate/sustain a conversation with a peer
- To make a leisure decision when given a choice between two options

- To identify leisure resources available in the community

The appropriate goals can be measured, although they are not yet written in fully measurable terms. One major difference is that the second set of goals begins with an *action verb*. Professionals and clients can *see* what action will be expected to prove the client has achieved the goal, which helps with measurement. In addition, it becomes clearer what types of programs the client needs to be involved to achieve the goal. Client goals and objectives, which result from proper client assessment, serve as the bridge between the program being offered and the client's participation in it. Increased specification helps keep the specialist and client focused on the outcomes that will be anticipated from involvement.

Consider the following examples of client goals related to the physical rehabilitation facility example:

Example 2. Physical Medicine and Rehabilitation Center (Hess, 1997)

4.0 To provide programs that improve social skills necessary to function successfully in a variety of leisure environments. [social interaction skills focus]

4.1 To provide programs that improve participants' communication skills in relation to leisure [communication skills]

- *The client will engage a peer in conversation.*
- *The client will listen to a peer and respond with an appropriate question.*
- *The client will maintain eye contact.*
- *The client will ask for needed information.*

4.2 To provide programs and activities that improve participants' relationship building skills as necessary for leisure participation [relationship building skills]

- *The client will locate a leisure partner with similar leisure interests.*
- *The client will determine the amount of personal information to disclose to a friend.*

- *The client will express care and concern for another individual.*
- *The client will cooperate with other participants within a small group activity.*

Client goals help define the outcomes expected of participants at the end of the program. They provide the content that the client is to learn while participating in the activity or set of activities within the total program. Client goals are further delineated into client objectives.

CLIENT OBJECTIVES

The most common type of objective is the *behavioral objective*. The purpose of behavioral objectives is to specify the exact behavior that will provide evidence that the intent of the objective has been met. As such, the conditions under which the behavior is expected to be performed, the representative behavior, and the criteria for judging whether the behavior has occurred are all extremely important. One of the major reasons for writing and designing client involvement to achieve the objectives is to increase accountability and improve services. Client behavioral objectives help keep the client and specialist focused on the important aspects of behavior, and the intended outcomes of participation.

One method for evaluating behavioral objectives is to ask the following questions, which should be answered affirmatively:

- Can you readily identify the behavior that is to be demonstrated by the client to show that he or she has achieved the objective?
- Can you readily identify the conditions under which the behavior will be demonstrated?
- Can you readily identify the standard to which the client's behavior must conform?
- If two staff members looked at this behavioral objective and a client's performance, could they agree whether the standards and limits had been achieved?

Writing and reading behavioral objectives are enhanced by using a standard format. It is highly recommended that the sequence of the parts by the same for all behavioral objectives. The most common format arranges the parts in the following sequence: conditions, behavior, and criterion. The phrase "as judged by" appears as the last line. The format allows all readers to identify the various

parts easily. Behavioral objectives are usually very specific and contain a condition, behavior, and criterion.

Condition. A *condition* is the circumstance under which the desired behavior will occur. Phrases that indicate common conditions include:

- *On request...*
- *When given the necessary equipment...*
- *When given a choice of three activities...*
- *With an opponent of equal ability...*
- *With Level 4 minimal assistance...*
- *On a written examination...*
- *After completion of the program...*
- *After one week of active participation...*

Conditions can be specific to a situation, setting, population or program. For example:

- *While involved in a trip in the community with the therapeutic recreation specialist and after completing the program of assertiveness training, the client will...*

Conditions of a behavioral objective set the stage by identifying necessary equipment, activities, timelines, or other events essential to the performance of the desired behavior. Normally, the condition is the first phase of the behavioral objective. It starts with a preposition and is set off from the rest of the behavioral objective by a comma. Occasionally, the conditions are scattered throughout the behavioral objective. Conditions occur throughout the following behavioral objective and are italicized for identification. For example:

- ***On request***, *the client will play a game of checkers* ***with an opponent of equal ability***, *staying on task throughout the activity as evidenced by continuous attention to the game and completion of the game within a reasonable amount of time, as judged by the therapeutic recreation specialist.*

In this example, some conditions are not mentioned but implied. The checkers game itself is not specified. How the game is played doesn't matter—the important point is staying on task. Often, when a condition is obvious, it can be eliminated to reduce the length of the complete behavioral objective.

Behavior. The *behavior* identified in the behavioral objective is the central focus. This phrase identifies what action the client will demonstrate to prove he or she has achieved the desired knowledge, skills, or ability. The behavior must be *observable* and *measurable* to meet this requirement. Some examples of the behavioral component include:

- *...the client will name leisure resources in the home...*

- *...the client will walk....*

- *...the client will explain the difference between work and leisure...*

- *...the client will plan a weekend trip....*

- *...the client will serve an overhand tennis shot...*

- *...the client will converse...*

- *...the client will verbalize the actions needed to get from the center to downtown...*

Note that the wording always includes the phrase "the client will," followed by an action verb. The challenge for the therapeutic recreation specialist is to select the most important, representative behavior that would indicate that the client has achieved the targeted outcome. One difficulty of writing good objectives is to stay focused on the important behavior, while making it specific enough to measure it well.

Some agencies also stress that the behavior should be stated in *positive terms*, rather than negative. For example, an objective might read "client will keep hands to self" rather than "client will not hit peer." Just like other aspects of the behavioral objective, this positive focus often requires practice in writing.

Criterion. The *criterion* in the behavioral objective delineates the exact amounts and nature of the behavior that can be taken as evidence that the objective has been met. A criterion is a precise statement or standard that allows individuals to make judgments based on the observable, measurable behavior. Good criterion statements are so clear that two or more different evaluators have no problem making the same decision about whether the desired behavior occurred.

The criterion section defines more specifically the exact act or representation of the behavior stated, along with standards of form, frequency, or other behavioral descriptions. Writing criterion statements requires selecting representative behaviors and then describing the amounts and nature of those behaviors. Selecting the most appropriate kind of criterion directly relates to the nature of the knowledge or skill identified in the behavior

portion. Criteria may take a number of forms, including number of trials, level of accuracy, amount of time, percentages and fractions, form, or procedures and characteristics. Criteria specify the quality of behavior desire. Consider the following examples:

Number of Trials. Some behaviors occur by chance, and thus the criteria need to be written in the standard format, "x out of y attempts." For example, hitting a target with darts or catching a ball or executing a Ping-Pong serve can occur by chance if just one trial or attempt is called for. In situations such as these, number of trials can be used as criterion. For example:

- *On request the client will serve a legal Ping-Pong serve three out of five times, as judged by the instructor.*

It is unlikely that the client can serve the ball three out of five times by chance. Note that the word "legal" designates a criterion. There is a standard definition of a legal serve, and thus the criterion does not need further definition.

- *When asked to groom himself for the afternoon activity group, the client will brush his teeth two out of three times, as judged by the instructor.*

In this case, the number of trials may be decreased as the client improves behavior. For some clients in this situation, it may also be necessary to include whether the client completed the behavior with or without prompts from the staff.

Level of Accuracy. Certain behaviors require a criterion of accuracy to be useful. Ability to throw a baseball, putt a golf ball, or bowl usually is judged by a degree of accuracy. For example:

- *After completion of the community reentry program, the client will estimate the cost of dinner and a movie within three dollars.*

- *Given a putting green with a circle one yard in radius drawn around the hole, upon request, the client will putt six out of ten golf balls into the circle as judged by the instructor.*

Note that this behavioral objective combines accuracy and number of trials.

Amount of Time. Some behaviors are best judged by utilizing time as a criterion. For example:

- *On request, the client will dress in appropriate clothing for a community outing within ten minutes.*

- *On request, the client will run the 100-yard dash within 20 seconds, as judged by the instructor.*

Note that this behavior may not need the number of trials. The client either can or cannot run that fast. The same can be said for such activities as bike riding or swimming. A client either can or cannot do the activity. It would be unlikely that the behavior could occur by chance alone. Thus, increasing the trials only increases the amount of evaluation time required.

Percentages and Fractions. Certain behaviors are valid only if maintained over time, but all activities are not consistent in terms of time required for action or number of opportunities available. A percentage criterion allows for such variation. For example:

- *While engaged in a basketball game, the client will make 25% of the attempted field shots, as judged by the instructor.*

- *By completion of the activity, the client will write down information about 25% of the resources in the "My Community Directory" notebook, as judged by the specialist.*

Form. Some behavioral objectives require the specification of form to be appropriate. This is often the case when dealing with activity skills that include an aspect of physical performance, such as sports and dance. For example, form is important in executing a forehand shot in tennis, a specific stroke in swimming, or a golf swing. Likewise, form is vital to ballet, gymnastics, and many other motor skills activities. This can be described in two ways:

1. Relate the behavioral objective to an existing, known standard that is generally respected and accepted. For example:

   - *On request, the client will swim 25 yards using the side stroke as described in the Red Cross manual, as judged by the instructor.*
   - *At the restaurant, the client will use proper table manners, as outlined in the Manners and You program, as judged by the specialist.*

2. Judgment of an expert. A good golf instructor knows and can judge form with reliable and valid consistency. In this case, the behavioral objective might read:

   - *On request, the client will drive a golf ball a minimum of 100 yards with acceptable form, as judged by the instructor.*

Note that this behavioral objective combines form and distance for a thorough criterion.

- *When given the choice of two pieces of leisure equipment, the client will select which product represents the best value for her dollar, as judged by the specialist.*

Note that in this case, the answer of which product has the most value is not clear-cut and will need to be interpreted by the specialist.

Procedures and Characteristics. Many behavioral objectives for therapeutic recreation programs deal with content and behavior that are not adequately specified by criterion statements using form, number of trials, percentages, or accuracy. Countless situations exist where the best criteria would be statements developed to describe the specific procedure or characteristics of the representative behavior itself. These characteristic statements are appropriate, valid, and reliable. They can be observed and measured. In most cases, they enhance the quality of the behavioral objective because of their specificity and direct application to the behavior being addressed in the particular behavioral objective. Behavioral objectives using the procedures and characteristics criteria use the phrase "as characterized by" immediately following the identified behavior and then list in narrative form the selected statements. The following behavioral objective illustrates this type of criteria use. Note that other types of criteria often are used in combination with this approach. For example:

- *During the evening meal, the client will converse with another patient during the meal, as characterized by:*

  - *Initiating a conversation with another resident*

  - *Listening to the other resident's response*

  - *Continuing conversation on an appropriate topic*

  - *Speaking in acceptable tone and at an appropriate volume*

  - *Maintaining appropriate eye contact and body positioning throughout*

  - *Concluding the conversation in an appropriate manner, as judged by the therapeutic recreation specialist*

Most often, when these types of criteria are used, they also require the use of the phrase "as judged by" as a necessary aspect of the criteria. The phrase indicates that some knowledge and expertise are held by the person making the judgment. In the preceding behavioral objective, a variety of appropriate topics, tones, volumes, and completions of the conversation may fulfill the specified criteria. The specialist makes these judgments based on experience, acceptable behaviors, and common sense. The criteria in the example are loose, but they serve as adequate guidelines for judging whether the client has acquired the desired behaviors.

Two other examples of behavioral objectives that use the procedure and characteristic criteria:

- *Upon request, the client will take own pulse rate as characterized by the following:*

  - *Placing second and third fingers on neck*

  - *Finding pulse and maintaining finger position*

  - *Counting number of beats for thirty seconds*

  - *Doubling that number to get heart rate, as judged by the therapeutic recreation specialist.*

- *Upon request, the client will name personal preference for leisure activities as characterized by:*

  - *Completing an appropriate leisure education activity in writing,*

  - *Verbally describing a preferred leisure activity for each section depicted in the form as judged appropriate by the therapeutic recreation specialist.*

The use of procedures and characteristics criteria is very common in the writing of behavioral objectives for therapeutic recreation programs. The value of this criteria cannot be overemphasized. This approach allows the therapeutic recreation specialist to focus on the behavioral descriptions that capture the essence of the desired representative behavior in the most precise and meaningful way possible.

Regardless of the type of behavior and criteria used, all behavioral objectives must be viewed and judged by someone. Although it may appear tedious to place this phrase in all behavioral objectives, it is a necessary aspect of most behavioral objectives. In most of the examples the criteria is explicit, and almost anyone could view the behavior and make the judgment based on the criteria. This is most often true of behavioral objectives that involve physical skills. However, there are many behavioral objectives where this is not true, where the judgment by an expert is an essential part of the criteria itself. Many of the programs in therapeutic recreation that deal with improved functional behavior and leisure awareness will require this judgment by an expert to make the behavioral objective credible. However, the specialist must be forewarned that professional judgment alone, without other stated criteria, defeats the purpose of behavioral objectives. Observable and measurable behavioral descriptions are by definition a necessary part of the behavioral objective.

Several examples of poor behavioral objectives may help to illustrate how vague the behavioral objective is without criteria for the desired behavior. They also show how nebulous the behavioral objective is when only the judgment of the therapeutic recreation specialist is stipulated.

Poor Examples of Client Objectives

- *Upon request, the client will demonstrate increased endurance, as judged by the therapeutic recreation specialist.*

- *Upon request the client will demonstrate awareness of leisure preferences and patterns, as judged by the therapeutic recreation specialist.*

- *At the end of the program, the client will have improved self-esteem, as judged by the therapeutic recreation specialist.*

- *By the time of discharge, the client will have improved social skills, as judged by the therapeutic recreation specialist.*

The absence of the representative behaviors and criterion for judgment in each of the foregoing examples makes these behavioral objectives useless.

SUMMARY

This chapter provided a brief overview of the four content components of the Leisure Education Content Model (Peterson & Stumbo, 2000) and a summary of how to write goals and objectives. Examples of comprehensive program goals, specific program goals, client goals, and client objectives using leisure education content were illustrated. This material intends to aid the reader in better utilizing the activities contained in this manual as well as to improve their ability to develop and implement leisure education programs and activities that produce measurable client outcomes.

REFERENCES

Hess, M. (1997). *Physical medicine and rehabilitation center*. Unpublished manuscript, Illinois State University Normal.

McGowen, A. (1997). *Chemical dependency facility*. Unpublished manuscript, Illinois State University, Normal.

Peterson, C. A. and Stumbo, N. J. (2000). *Therapeutic recreation program design: Principles and procedures* (3rd ed.). Needham Heights, MA: Allyn and Bacon.

CHAPTER 3 DESIGNING GAMES AND ACTIVITIES FOR LEISURE EDUCATION

The first chapter of this manual discussed the need for therapeutic recreation specialists to identify important client outcomes and implement programs to help clients achieve those outcomes. The second chapter addressed leisure education program content as well as how to develop program and client goals and objectives. This chapter provides a structured way to develop and evaluate leisure education games and activities to ensure they meet their intended goals and help clients achieve their intended outcomes.

The four components of leisure education content (leisure awareness, social interaction skills, leisure activity skills, and leisure resources) are often introduced to participants through a game or activity format. In this way, the participant can gain knowledge of complex subject matter in a fun and challenging manner. Leisure education often uses this "learning while playing" approach. This manual presents several ideas for activities or games for use in a diversity of settings. It is acknowledged, however, that a specialist may not find the right activity appropriate for the clients or setting in which he or she works. Therefore, this chapter also provides a framework for specialists to create their own activities through a systematic design process.

Games and activities provide a stimulating and novel situation in which participants may learn specified knowledge and/or skills in a nonthreatening environment. They can provide an opportunity for people to gain new ideas, see other people's reactions, understand their own values, and experience winning and losing without directly threatening who they are or what they know. This situation allows the participants to interact freely within a controlled environment, without the hazards of rejection or embarrassment from a situation that might arise in reality. The gaming format is protective, yet it allows the participant to become knowledgeable of how situations might occur, to develop and explore alternatives, and to choose a course of action without dire consequences.

ADVANTAGES TO USING GAMES AND ACTIVITIES

There are eight major advantages to using game or activity format for leisure education programs:

1. Ability to induce changes
2. Flexibility and relevance to real-life situations
3. Group cohesiveness
4. Depth of involvement
5. Level of motivation
6. Receptiveness
7. Responsibility
8. Safe environment

All eight factors point to the usefulness of leisure education games and activities when working with participants. Together, they provide distinct advantages that are not found in other program formats.

ABILITY TO INDUCE CHANGES

Games and activities can be powerful tools for changing participant behavior. They allow participants to view various alternatives for behavior, distinguish between socially appropriate and inappropriate behaviors, and determine logical consequences for behavioral actions. A participant may be more likely to accept suggestions to change his or her behavior during a game rather than through a direct confrontation. Since most activities require that the participant explore alternatives, the natural course would be for the participant to examine and practice options that are more suitable during the game, and then apply these alternatives during real-life interactions.

FLEXIBILITY AND RELEVANCE TO REAL-LIFE SITUATIONS

One of the best features of leisure eduction games and activities is that they can correspond with whatever leisure education content is being introduced and they can be customized to a specific group of participants and their needs. Leisure education games and activities can be modified according to participant skill level, needs, disability, or home or community situation. The limitless possibilities for adapting activities allow the specialist to create the "perfect" activity for a specific group of clients. Not only can this flexibility and relevance help the specialist target directed participant outcomes, it allows for several basic activities to be repeated within a program cycle without being repetitious for participants.

GROUP COHESIVENESS

Most games or activities require participation by a small group of people. Cooperation, rather than competition, is often stressed to achieve the final outcome of the game. Each player must make some kind of contribution to the larger whole to ensure success. These cooperation requirements can inspire a sense of camaraderie, cohesiveness, and equality among participants.

DEPTH OF INVOLVEMENT

Most people easily become engaged in an activity when it has a clear purpose and an interesting format. Rather than simply lecture, counsel, or provide written materials, the specialist can often get the message across more quickly and deeply when games and activities are used. Being involved in a situation that parallels reality but lacks its immediate consequences helps to entrench clients in its play.

LEVEL OF MOTIVATION

Because games are conducted within a short time span and involve several players, each participant can maintain a relatively high level of motivation and enthusiasm. Some activities may examine attitudes, others may teach new knowledge, while others allow the participant to practice new skills. Whatever direction they take, well-designed activities tend to hold the participant's attention and allow for high motivation. We have grown up with all types of games (e.g., Candyland, Monopoly, Battleship, Dodgeball) and are accustomed to the general rules of play. Most people want to continue to play until the end of the activity to see what the outcome will be.

RECEPTIVENESS

Games and activities provide an environment for the participant to reduce defenses used in everyday life. The specialist can help the participant examine certain behaviors or attitudes that may be blocking fuller participation in a game situation in a nonthreatening way. This may help the participant voice opinions or concerns that otherwise could not be spoken. Participants also seem more willing to accept constructive criticism and look for alternatives during activities than in real-life situations.

RESPONSIBILITY

Most leisure education activities require that the participants take responsibility for their actions. Unlike staff-controlled treatment programs, leisure education activities attempt to shift the responsibility from the specialist to the participant. This includes taking responsibility for making personal decisions and learning the consequences of making those decisions. Through leisure education games and activities, the participant can learn what the probable and potential consequences of his or her decisions will be. Many leisure education activities can help the participant learn planning and decision-making skills in relation to his or her leisure lifestyle, enabling the participant to become solely responsible for his or her own level of comfort and satisfaction.

SAFE ENVIRONMENT

Since many leisure education activities are at least partial simulations of real life, they can provide a meaningful but sheltered environment in which to learn and experiment with new behaviors and choices. Games can provide a controlled, safe environment in which skills can be practiced. Participants often find it useful to practice new knowledge or skills in a less threatening setting before actually being called upon to do so in front of strangers. Because of the sheltered setting, participants may feel free to experiment with new choices and behaviors that they can use later.

GENERAL RULES FOR CONSTRUCTING GAMES

The following are general rules for creating and designing new leisure education games and activities:

1. Decide the overall purpose and goal
2. Write specific, intended objectives for outcomes related to participation
3. Select the general format
4. Develop the rules
5. Gather or create the necessary materials
6. Play the game
7. Revise if necessary

The Leisure Education Activities Planning worksheet found at the end of this chapter (adapted from Levy, 1989) also will help guide in the creation of new activities and games.

DECIDE THE OVERALL PURPOSE AND GOAL

Most creators design activities because they have a specific purpose in mind and have not yet found another activity that meets this purpose. The purpose of the game must be clear-cut. The selection of the overall goal depends on the focus area, the general abilities of the participant group, and how much time can be spent on the activity. For example, a social skills activity for a half-hour session with people who have traumatic brain injury may be more narrow in focus than a social skills activity for an hour session for people with substance abuse problems. The specialist may find that throughout the creation process, the overall goals may need to be revised as the activity develops.

Some sample overall purposes for leisure education activities include:

- To teach participants how to locate and use leisure resources in the community
- To increase participants' understanding of the importance of leisure in a balanced lifestyle
- To increase participants' awareness of appropriate self-disclosure in social situations

- To improve participants' ability to examine options and select the best alternative
- To improve participants' ability to access state leisure resources
- To increase participants' understanding of the need for leisure planning
- To teach participants a process for examining choices/options and making decisions
- To teach participants about how to locate low-cost activities and events in the community

Each activity or program has a focused purpose that relates to a specific area of leisure education content (see **Figure 2.1**, p. 20).

WRITE SPECIFIC, INTENDED OBJECTIVES FOR OUTCOMES RELATED TO PARTICIPATION

The participant objectives guide the development of the activity and keep the designer focused on what the activity is meant to do. They should include measurable objectives aimed at specific behaviors when possible. The development of three to five measurable objectives aids the specialist in evaluating the effects of the activity on the participants and helps in documenting client outcomes (e.g., treatment plans, progress notes, participation records). Participant outcome objectives are important to the activity development process and should not be overlooked.

For example, participant objectives for the overall goal "to teach participants how to locate and use leisure resources in the community" may include:

- At the conclusion of the activity, the participant will identify three sources of community leisure information (e.g., newspaper, program brochures, telephone directory) with 80% accuracy.
- At the conclusion of the activity (using the information sources provided) the participant will identify two community leisure resources in which he or she is interested in participating in the next month, with 100% accuracy.

- At the conclusion of the activity, the participant will contact the two identified community leisure facilities in which they are interested in registering for programs.

- Within the next month, the participant will arrange the necessary transportation and finances to participate in the two identified community leisure activities.

- Within the next month, the participant will participate in the two identified community leisure activities.

From these objectives, it becomes clear that the activity should target the participant behaviors of identifying and using leisure resource information, selecting activities of interest to the participant, contacting agencies for additional information when needed, making transportation and financial arrangements, and following through with the leisure plan.

The level of specificity of the participant objectives depends on the abilities of the participants. How much do they know before the activity begins (e.g., about bus schedules, city maps, making change)? How quickly can they be expected to learn new information within the activity? How will this activity relate to other leisure education activities and other therapies? The nature and pace of the activity should match the participants' abilities. Once the specialist has identified general participant abilities and measurable participant objectives, an activity or game can be developed further.

SELECT THE GENERAL FORMAT

Determining the general structure of the activity is the next step in further defining how it will be created. Will the activity consist of a board game, a paper and pencil exercise, a discussion group, an initiative game, a community outing, a one-to-one session, or a take-home exercise? Selecting the format depends on what kind of environment or setting is required to learn the content of the participant objectives. For example, a board game can teach both cooperative and competitive skills and may allow for individual input; a paper and pencil exercise can be used to have individuals think about his or her responses before sharing with the

group; a discussion group allows for all individuals to communicate and have input and may be used to brainstorm ideas.

Selecting the activity structure depends on participant abilities, activity goals and objectives, and activity content. Because several leisure education activities use a game board format, some have been included at the end of this chapter.

DEVELOP THE RULES

The rules should be detailed but not confining. Complex games that present complicated rules are often not as fun or as easy to learn as those that can be played without prior knowledge. In most instances, the creator should attempt to develop a game that another person could lead easily without the creator having to be there. Look at the rules included in other published games (e.g., Yahtzee, Uno, Scattergories, Scruples, Monopoly) to see how they describe play. Also, adapt commonly played, familiar games so that most participants are already familiar with how the activity is played. In that way, start up time is reduced and the content becomes the focus of play.

GATHER OR CREATE THE NECESSARY MATERIALS

This step includes gathering the materials needed for the game, developing the activity sheets or game board, and making playing pieces. Activity sheets, game boards, playing pieces and the like can either be made by the creator or taken from existing games. The activity may require spinners, dice, game cards, game pieces, or tokens. Game materials should be durable and visually appealing, relate well to the intent of the game, and reflect real life as much as possible.

PLAY THE GAME

After the game is finished, playing it with people unfamiliar with it will help to detect problem areas. This will determine how others react to the game board and rules and what kinds of questions they have. There may be a question or situation where the participants are expected to respond or act one way, but when others play the game, they interpret the question or situation in a different way. Every rule or situation within the game should be aimed at participants achieving the objectives and being able to translate the information for use in real life.

A Leisure Education Activity Evaluation worksheet (adapted from Malik, 1991) is provided at the end of this chapter to assess newly created games or activities. Each player may complete this form after finishing with the activity or game, so the designer gets different perspectives on how others view it. The evaluation sheet contains 12 areas and those that receive fair or poor ratings should be redesigned.

REVISE IF NECESSARY

Based on the previous test of playing the game and the results of the evaluation sheet, the creator may have to revise the intent of the game or some aspect of the game itself. This ensures that the outcomes of the game match the intended goals and objectives.

SUMMARY

Although this manual intends to provide ready-made leisure education activities, many therapeutic recreation specialists will need to develop new games and activities to meet the needs of a particular group. This chapter provided information on how to structure as well as evaluate these new activities.

REFERENCES

Levy, J. (1989). *Leisure education activity planning.* Unpublished manuscript, Bloomington, IL.

Malik, P. (1991). *Leisure education activity evaluation.* Unpublished manuscript, Illinois State University, Normal.

LEISURE EDUCATION ACTIVITY PLANNING

Name of Game/Activity: _____ Designer: _____

1. What is the overall goal of the activity? What area of leisure education content is to be addressed? What is the object of the game?

2. What are the participant objectives for the activity? At the end of the activity or game, what should they have gained?

3. What format will be used to play or participate in the activity?

4. What are the rules of the activity?

    a. How will play start?
    Roll of the dice?
    Specific person in the group?

    b. Are the players in teams or as individuals?
    If teams, how selected?

    c. How do players move around the game board?
    Moves correspond to dice numbers or a spinner?
    Each person moves one space per turn?

    d. How will participants score or gain points?
    By landing on the "right" squares?
    By answering questions?
    By accumulating points?
    By making certain decisions?

    e. Will a score sheet be used?
    What does it look like?
    Who records on it?
    How is the score kept?

f. How does someone win or finish?
   First player to reach finish line?
   End of 10 minutes?
   Play to the score of 50?
   Does there have to be a winner?

g. What does the player get for winning or finishing?
   Tokens?
   Prizes?

h. How much can the players vary the rules of the game?
   Do they have to play by the book?
   Can they create their own rules as they go?

5. What kinds of adaptations can be made for various participant groups?

6. What other kinds of activities or games can be created that use similar (or the same) materials, but have a different intent or overall goal?

Adapted from J. Levy, 1989

LEISURE EDUCATION ACTIVITY EVALUATION

Name of Game/Activity: _____ Designer: _____

Rate each leisure education game/activity on the following 12 points. Modify any part of the game/activity that receives a 3 or 4 rating.

EXCELLENT = 1   GOOD = 2   FAIR = 3   POOR = 4

_____ 1. **GOAL APPROPRIATENESS**

    Purpose and goals are appropriate for leisure education games/activities

_____ 2. **CONTENT APPROPRIATENESS**

    Content covered in the game/activity meets the stated purpose and goals within the description of the game/activity

_____ 3. **SIMULATION OF REALITY**

    Content, rules, consequences. reflect reality as much as possible

_____ 4. **FACILITATION TECHNIQUES**

    Suggestions for facilitating game/activity (e.g., discussion questions) are included

_____ 5. **DURABLE**

    Game can be used repeatedly by participant groups

_____ 6. **FEASIBLE**

    Game/activity is age-appropriate and ability-appropriate for intended participant(s)

_____ 7. **SELF-EXPLANATORY**

    Play could start easily; instructions are clear and easy to understand

_____ 8. **SELF-CONTAINED**

    All equipment and/or supplies are included in game/activity package

_____ 9. **ATTRACTIVE**

    Game board, cards, and playing pieces are visually pleasing, neat, and "invite" players to play

_____ 10. **ADAPTATIONS/MODIFICATIONS**

    Suggestions for how game could be adapted for other settings or participant group are included, as appropriate

_____ 11. **CHALLENGE**

    Appropriate level of challenge for target participants (i.e., not too easy, not too hard)

_____ 12. **GAME IS FUN TO PLAY**

    Beyond learning content, participants are likely to enjoy playing or being involved in the game/activity

Adapted from P. Malik, 1991

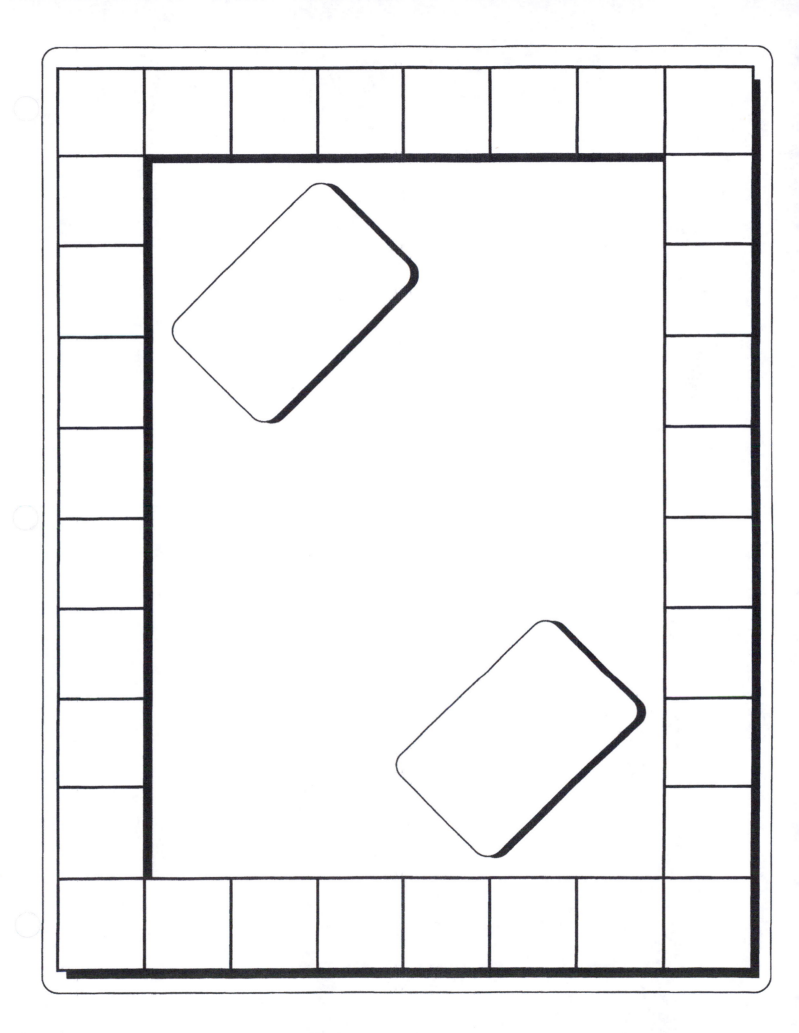

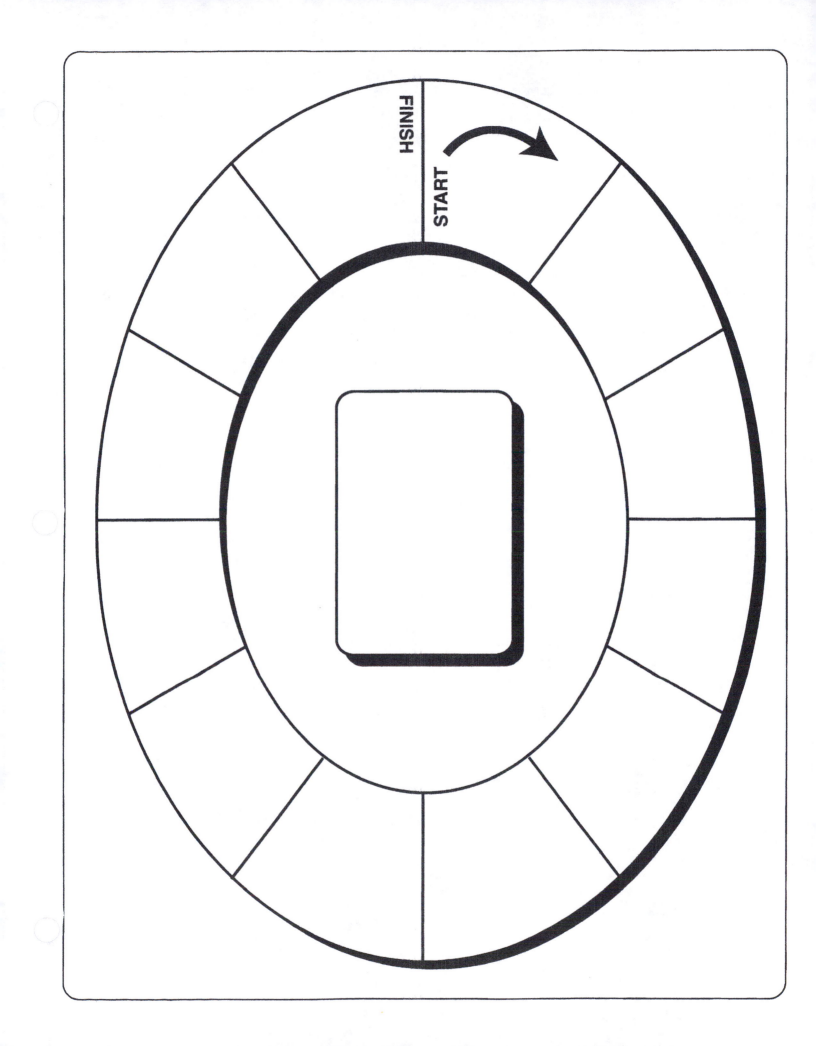

FINISH

START

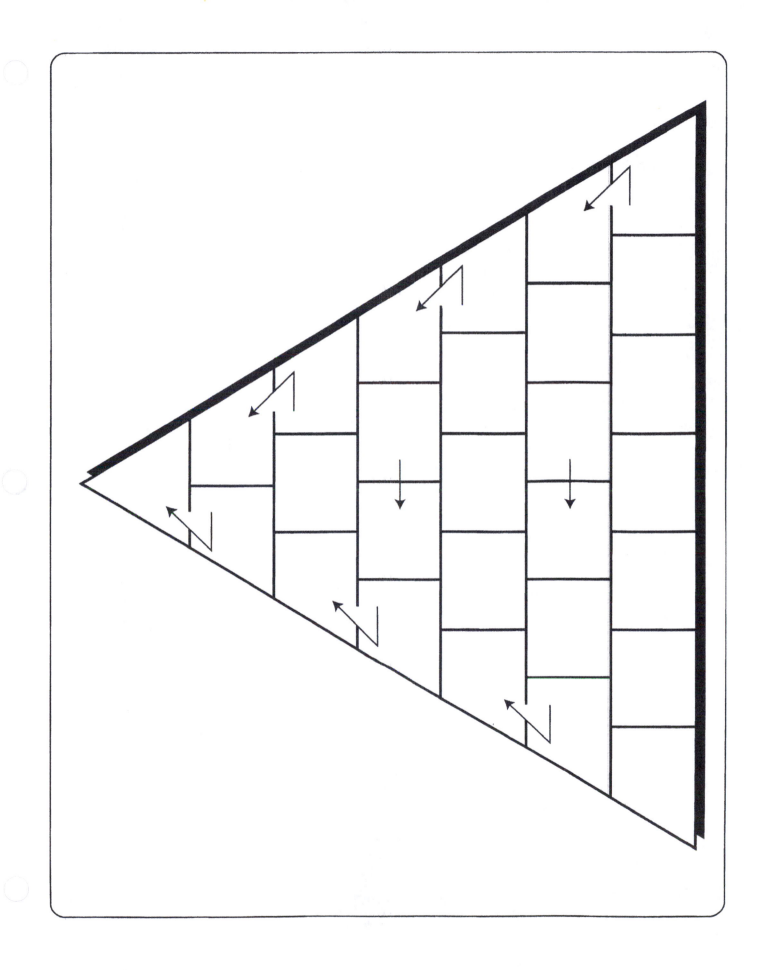

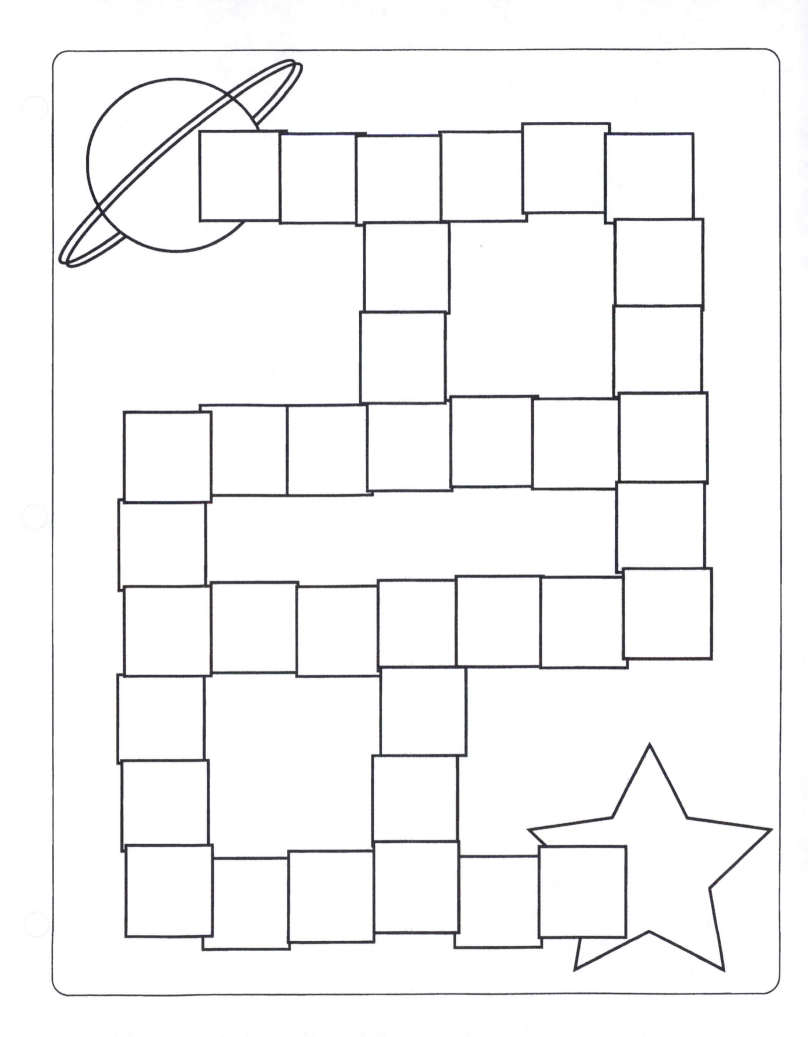

LEISURE AWARENESS ACTIVITIES

PLAYGROUND ACTIVITIES

SPACE REQUIREMENTS

Classroom or activity room

MATERIALS

Chalkboard and chalk or whiteboard and marker

GROUP SIZE

Small group

GOALS

1. To improve participants' awareness of activities available on a playground.
2. To improve participants' awareness of the characteristics of activities on a playground.

PREPARATION

Gather materials

ACTIVITY DESCRIPTION

Have the group gather around a table or sit in a circle. Introduces the purpose of the activity. Ask the group to think of their favorite playground activities and list them on the board. As each activity is listed ask the participants why this is a favorite activity. Some of the activities listed might be swinging, sliding, playing games, seesawing, and playing on a jungle gym.

Ask each child to choose his or her favorite activity and pantomime how it is played. Have the person to pretend he or she is the piece of equipment used in his or her favorite activity and show how the piece of equipment looks and moves. For example, a child pantomiming a seesaw might spread his or her arms to the side and raise and lower them in opposition, or stand in a wide forward and back stride position and shift weight from one foot to the other. To illustrate a baseball, the child might roll on the floor, or stand up and spin about as he or she travels forward, showing "spin" on the ball.

Have participants who have chosen the same or similar activities group themselves together and work out movements to show how the activity is performed and how the equipment looks and moves. The participants may accompany their movement by chanting sounds or words related to the activity. For example, if the activity were skipping rope, accompaniment might consist of some of the chants children use in skipping rope, or it might consist of a sound, such as "whish, whish" indicating how the rope sounds when it is turned. Allow 2–3 minutes.

Return to the larger group, alternating the circle with individuals from different groups and ask them to perform their movements and their sounds within the larger group. Allow 2–3 minutes.

Close with a discussion about the activities and their characteristics.

DEBRIEFING QUESTIONS

1. What are some of your favorite playground activities?
2. What are some other playground activities that we didn't mention today?
3. Think about the activities we talked about today. Which can you do alone? Which requires two or more people? Which requires you to go high off the ground? Which requires the most time? Which requires you to be fast? to be strong? to work as a team?

LEADERSHIP CONSIDERATIONS

1. Most appropriate for younger children.
2. Encourage creativity from participants.

VARIATIONS

1. After this activity take participants to a playground and allow free play.
2. Start the activity by allowing the participants to draw pictures of playground equipment or construct models out of dough or erector sets.

CONTRIBUTOR

Norma J. Stumbo

GET THE PICTURE

SPACE REQUIREMENTS

Classroom or activity room

MATERIALS

Pictures (e.g., from magazines) of leisure activities in different settings

GROUP SIZE

Small group

GOALS

1. To improve participants' awareness of leisure activities.
2. To improve participants' awareness of the characteristics of leisure activities.

PREPARATION

Gather materials
May want to laminate pictures for durability

ACTIVITY DESCRIPTION

Have the group gather around a table or sit in a circle. Introduce the purpose of the session. Ask each participant to describe his or her favorite activity.

Hold up a picture of a leisure activity (e.g., golfing, hiking, exercising, horseback riding, gardening, fishing, stamp collecting, weightlifting, pet care). Ask participants to pantomime the activity shown in the picture, individually or in a group. For example, if the picture is fishing, the participant(s) can pantomime putting a worm on the hook, casting, and reeling in a big fish.

After each picture is shown and pantomimed, ask participants to discuss the activity. Where can you participate in this activity? How much does it cost? Does it require special skills? equipment? Do you have to be a certain age to do it? Can you do it alone or with other people? Does it require strength? endurance? speed? flexibility? Where can you do to learn this activity?

Discussion continues for each activity. At the end of the pictures, pantomimes, and individual activity discussion, close the session with following debriefing questions.

DEBRIEFING QUESTIONS

1. Name the activities that we mentioned today.
2. In which of these activities have you participated?
3. What are some of the common characteristics of the activities discussed today?
4. Which activities required special equipment? other people? a special location?
5. Why is it important to know about different leisure activities?
6. How can knowing about a lot of different leisure activities help you when you're bored?
7. What did you learn about leisure activities and their characteristics today?

LEADERSHIP CONSIDERATION

1. Use a variety of pictures.

VARIATIONS

1. Have the participants gather the pictures from magazines.
2. Have the participants draw their favorite activities.

CONTRIBUTOR

Norma J. Stumbo

I AM THE CAMERA

SPACE REQUIREMENTS

Classroom or activity room

MATERIALS

Paper, markers or crayons

GROUP SIZE

Small group

GOALS

1. To improve participants' awareness of leisure activities.
2. To improve participants' awareness of the characteristics of leisure activities.

PREPARATION

Gather materials

ACTIVITY DESCRIPTION

Have the group gather around a table or sit in a circle. Introduce the purpose of the session. Ask participants to name as many leisure activities as possible within 2 minutes.

Ask each individual to close their eyes and think of a favorite leisure activity, including the environment in which it usually takes place. Each person pretends he or she is a camera, takes a "picture" of the activity in his or her mind, and then draws it on paper. The drawing should include each item required for the activity (e.g., people and equipment). Allow 10–15 minutes.

Ask each individual to share information about the leisure "picture" including where it is located and what people are included. Encourage participants to ask each other questions about their leisure activity.

After all participants have shown and discussed their pictures, close with a discussion using the following debriefing questions.

DEBRIEFING QUESTIONS

1. Discuss the activities mentioned today, including skills, people, and equipment required.
2. What characteristics do most of the activities have in common?
3. What were some less common activities mentioned today?
4. How easy or difficult was it to think of and then draw your activity?
5. When was the last time you participated in this activity?
6. When do you plan to participate next in this activity?
7. Summarize what you've learned about leisure activities and their characteristics today.

LEADERSHIP CONSIDERATIONS

1. Encourage creativity and expression, rather than drawing abilities.
2. Be descriptive to help participants to create in their mind's eye the picture they would like to draw.

VARIATIONS

1. Depending on the purpose of the activity, a theme can be used for the pictures, such as low-cost activities, activities done at holidays, or activities done on family vacations.
2. May be used as an introduction session to leisure education program.

CONTRIBUTOR

Norma J. Stumbo

ACTIVITY ALPHABET

SPACE REQUIREMENTS

Classroom or activity room

MATERIALS

Handout, pencils

GROUP SIZE

Small group

GOALS

1. To improve participants' awareness of leisure activities.
2. To improve participants' awareness of the characteristics of leisure activities.

PREPARATION

Gather materials
Make one copy of the handout for each participant

ACTIVITY DESCRIPTION

Have the group gather around a table or sit in a circle. Explain purpose of the session. Ask participants to describe "leisure" and what it means to them.

Distribute a copy of the handout and a pencil to each individual. Ask participants to list as many leisure activities as possible that start with each letter of the alphabet. (e.g., A—alpine skiing, aerobics). Each person should work independently. Allow 10–15 minutes.

Ask one person to list all the activities he or she has written. Other participants mark through any duplicate activity they have on their sheets. The next person says all of his or her remaining activities, and again each person marks through any duplicate activities. Each person should say only those activities not mentioned by anyone else in the group.

Close the discussion with the following debriefing questions.

DEBRIEFING QUESTIONS

1. How easy or difficult was it to list different activities according to the alphabet?

2. What were some of the most common activities listed?
3. What were the least common activities listed?
4. Which of these activities can be done alone? with no or little cost? in your backyard? on water? in the air? with family or friends?
5. Does everyone consider the same activities to be "leisure?"
6. What determines whether someone considers an activity "leisure" or not?
7. What are some of the characteristics of your favorite leisure activities?
8. What did you learn about leisure activities and their characteristics today?

LEADERSHIP CONSIDERATIONS

1. Encourage participants to be creative in making their lists.
2. May need to determine whether certain activities qualify for being included on the list.

VARIATIONS

1. Divide the group into smaller groups that each take only parts of the alphabet, and then share when back in the larger group.
2. Have participants select only 1 activity per letter.

CONTRIBUTOR

Norma J. Stumbo

ACTIVITY ALPHABET

A_____

B_____

C_____

D_____

E_____

F_____

G_____

H_____

I_____

J_____

K_____

L_____

M_____

N_____

O_____

P_____

Q_____

R_____

S_____

T_____

U_____

V_____

W_____

X_____

Y_____

Z_____

TOY LAND

SPACE REQUIREMENTS

Classroom or activity room

MATERIALS

Participants bring their favorite toys to the activity

GROUP SIZE

Small group

GOALS

1. To improve participants' awareness of toys as a leisure resource.
2. To improve participants' awareness of different ways to play with and explore toys.

PREPARATION

Prior to the activity, ask participants to bring their favorite toys to the session

ACTIVITY DESCRIPTION

Have the group gather around a table or sit in a circle. Explain the purpose of the activity and tell participants that they will be doing a variety of grouping and movement activities with their toys. Let each individual briefly describe the toy he or she brought and why it was chosen. Ask each participant to talk about how he or she plays with his or her toy, how often, and in what context.

Ask individuals with similar toys to group themselves by similarity of toys (e.g., dolls, construction toys, games). For each grouping, have participants describe the toys within that group. For example, are they heavy? square? rounded? Do they need batteries? Are they specific colors? Repeat this for every grouping of toys. Ask participants to then use overall comparisons: Which group is the heaviest? Which group is the most colorful? Which group has the most parts per toy? Which toys are smoother?

Next, ask participants to remain in their groups and create a group movement using their toys. The movements might show the action of the toys, such as digging, dancing, or building. Let each group show their movement for 1–2 minutes.

Next, ask participants to form one large circle alternating people from each group. Participants

perform their original movement, within the larger group. Let the movements continue for 1–2 minutes.

Close with a discussion about toys as leisure resources and how there are many ways to appreciate and play with toys.

DEBRIEFING QUESTIONS

1. How similar or dissimilar was your toy to others in the group?
2. Why did you select this toy to bring today?
3. Describe some of the ways that toys are different from one another.
4. How does your toy compare to other toys brought today? Is it smoother? lighter? taller?
5. Describe the movement chosen by your group to represent your toys.
6. How did the movements within the larger group compare to one another?
7. What are other creative ways that you can play with your toy?
8. When are good times to play with your toys?

LEADERSHIP CONSIDERATIONS

1. Have some extra toys on hand in case participants forget to bring their own.
2. Make sure the movements are safe and that participants are spaced apart.

VARIATIONS

1. Supply toys for each individual rather than having them bring their own.
2. Create a mini-play with participants using their toys as props and actors.
3. For adolescents or adults, substitute leisure equipment for toys.

CONTRIBUTOR

Norma J. Stumbo

ALPHABET GUESS

SPACE REQUIREMENTS

Classroom or activity room

MATERIALS

None needed

GROUP SIZE

Small group

GOALS

1. To improve participants' awareness of leisure activities.
2. To improve participants' awareness of the characteristics of leisure activities.

PREPARATION

None needed

ACTIVITY DESCRIPTION

Have the group gather around a table or sit in a circle. Explain the purpose of the activity. Select three individuals from the group. These individuals are the actors, and they stand in front of the group. The leader will whisper a letter of the alphabet to the three individuals (all the same letter), and they will pantomime a leisure activity beginning with that letter. For example, for "S" one person may pantomime "skiing," one may choose "sledding," and one person may choose "surfing."

The three individuals pantomime the actions to the rest of the group, who shout out guesses until someone guesses the right letter. Three new individuals are chosen and a different letter of the alphabet is whispered in their ears, and they pantomime activities that start with that letter. Continue for 10–15 minutes.

Closes the session with a discussion about leisure activities and their characteristics.

DEBRIEFING QUESTIONS

1. How easy or difficult was it to think of different activities according to the alphabet?
2. What were some of the most common activities pantomimed?
3. What were some of the least common activities pantomimed?
4. Which of these activities can be done alone? with no or little cost? in your backyard? on water? in the air? with family or friends?
5. Does everyone consider the same activities to be "leisure?"
6. What determines whether someone considers an activity "leisure" or not?
7. What are some of the characteristics of your favorite leisure activities?
8. What did you learn about leisure activities and their characteristics today?

LEADERSHIP CONSIDERATIONS

1. Encourage participants to be expressive in their pantomimes.
2. The focus of the activity should be the discussion following the pantomimes.

VARIATIONS

1. Ask participants not only to guess the letter, but also to guess each of the three activities being pantomimed.
2. Have the three individuals agree on one activity to be pantomimed.
3. Have the three individuals present a short skit that includes the activity.

CONTRIBUTOR

Norma J. Stumbo

ACTIVITY MARCH

SPACE REQUIREMENTS

Classroom or activity room

MATERIALS

CD or tape player and upbeat music

GROUP SIZE

Small group

GOALS

1. To improve participants' awareness of leisure activities.
2. To improve participants' awareness of the characteristics of leisure activities.

PREPARATION

Gather materials

ACTIVITY DESCRIPTION

Have the group gather around a table or sit in a circle. Introduce the purpose of the activity.

Have participants form a double circle with equal numbers in the inside and outside circles. The outside moves to the right (counterclockwise) and the inside moves to the left (clockwise).

Play music while participants begin moving in the given direction. When the music stops, each participant in the outside circle faces a partner in the inside circle. The leader calls out a type of activity (e.g., winter activity, activity that requires water, free activity, family activity). The partners decide on an activity that matches the description and pantomime their selected activity. Allow 1 minute.

When the music starts again, participants move around the circle until the music stops. When the music stops, each person faces a new partner and the leader calls out a new type of leisure activity. The partners decide on an activity which fits the category and pantomimes that activity. Allow 1 minute. Continue 6–7 times.

Close the activity by using the following debriefing questions.

DEBRIEFING QUESTIONS

1. For each of the categories, what activity did each group pantomime?
2. Were the activities chosen for the pantomimes similar to or different from one another?
3. How do pantomimes allow you to see the actions of the activity?
4. What were some of your favorite activities to act out?
5. In how many activities do you participate in regularly?
6. Why is it important to know a variety of leisure activities?
7. What are some options for activities to participate in when you're bored?
8. Describe what kinds of activities you like best.
9. Summarize what you've learned about activities and their characteristics today.

LEADERSHIP CONSIDERATIONS

1. Make sure each participant has adequate room to move around.
2. Encourage creativity from the participants in thinking of leisure activities as well as acting them out.

VARIATIONS

1. Different forms of movement can be used to move around the circle, such as galloping, hopping, or jumping.
2. Have one set of partners decide the activity that each set of partners will pantomime for each category.

CONTRIBUTOR

Norma J. Stumbo

ACTIVITY TRIANGLE

SPACE REQUIREMENTS

Classroom or activity room

MATERIALS

None needed

GROUP SIZE

Small group

GOALS

1. To improve participants' awareness of leisure activities.
2. To improve participants' awareness of the characteristics of leisure activities.

PREPARATION

None needed

ACTIVITY DESCRIPTION

Have the group gather around a table or sit in a circle. Explain the purpose of the activity. Ask the group to describe some of their favorite activities.

Divide into groups of three. Have each group form a triangle with each side about 6 feet long and stand at one point (Point A, B, or C). Person A will pantomime an activity (e.g., Ping-Pong) while moving to point B. Person B will pantomime a different activity (e.g., swimming) while moving to point C. Person C will pantomime an activity (e.g., reading) while moving to point A. When they arrive at the new corner, different activities are given to each person and he or she pantomimes that activity while moving to the next corner. After each person has moved around the triangle twice, the direction of movement is reversed and new activities are given.

Close the session by using the following debriefing questions.

DEBRIEFING QUESTIONS

1. What are some of the activities we mentioned today?
2. Which are some of your favorite activities?
3. Which of these can you do on a rainy day?
4. Which of these can you do with your family?
5. Which require a considerable amount of skill?
6. Which can be done for free?
7. Which was the most fun activity to move to?
8. Which of these activities would you like to learn?
9. Summarize what you've learned about activities and their characteristics today.

LEADERSHIP CONSIDERATIONS

1. Have an easy system to divide into teams of three.
2. Pick activities that can be expressed easily with movement.
3. Encourage participants to be creative when acting out the activities.

VARIATIONS

1. After the first round make different groups of three.
2. Choose an activity and have each side of the triangle pantomime one aspect of the activity. For example, for swimming person A could dive, person B could do the breaststroke, and person C could do the backstroke.

CONTRIBUTOR

Norma J. Stumbo

LEISURE STRETCH ALPHABET

SPACE REQUIREMENTS

Classroom or activity room

MATERIALS

None needed

GROUP SIZE

Small group

GOALS

1. To improve participants' awareness of leisure activities.
2. To improve participants' awareness of the characteristics of leisure activities.

PREPARATION

None needed

ACTIVITY DESCRIPTION

Have the group stand in a circle. Explain the purpose of the activity. Ask each individual to make sure he or she has at least an arm's length between their body and the next person.

Ask one of the group members to name a leisure activity (e.g., rock climbing). The individual then comes to the front and leads the group in spelling the word individually with their bodies (similar to the YMCA song). The person would lead the group in spelling rock climbing with their full bodies, stretching and bending into the letter shapes.

Ask a second person to name a different leisure activity. That person then leads the group in spelling the activity, and so on. The activity continues until all individuals have chosen a word and led the group.

Close the discussion by using the debriefing questions provided.

DEBRIEFING QUESTIONS

1. What were some of the activities mentioned?
2. Which were the best activities to make "body letters" out of?
3. What were some similarities of the activities used today?
4. What were some of the activities that stood out as being different?
5. Do you consider all of the activities to be something you could do in your leisure?
6. Which of these activities would you like to try in the future?
7. What did you learn about leisure activities and their characteristics today?

LEADERSHIP CONSIDERATION

1. This can be an excellent warm-up to a leisure awareness session.

VARIATIONS

1. Have the individual lead the spelling without telling the name of the activity. Have the other participants guess the activity.
2. Choose "theme" words (e.g., vacation, holiday, family, choice, decision making).
3. Form small groups of 6–7 people. The small group chooses a word and each individual spells out one letter for the rest of the large group to guess the entire word.
4. The individual makes the letter on the floor by walking the outline and individuals have to guess the letter drawn on the floor.

CONTRIBUTOR

Norma J. Stumbo

LEISURE IMAGINATION

SPACE REQUIREMENTS

Classroom or activity room

MATERIALS

Drawing paper, markers, CD or tape player and classical or instrumental music (optional)

GROUP SIZE

Small group

GOALS

1. To enable participants to feel comfortable in using and expressing their imagination.
2. To increase the participants' awareness of the personal desires for leisure.

PREPARATION

Gather materials

ACTIVITY DESCRIPTION

Have participants sit in comfortable chairs with their eyes closed. Tell them to imagine themselves participating in a leisure activity. Have them imagine the location, who they are with, whether they are indoors or outside, and any sensory experiences such as smell, taste, or touch. While the group participants are imagining the leisure experience, the group facilitator may play background music (see leadership considerations). Give participants ample time to experience their leisure setting and activity.

Next, have the group members draw what leisure experiences they imagined. Give ample time to complete this part of the activity.

When everyone has finished, have the group members take turns explaining their drawings. Discussion questions could center around whether they have ever participated in the leisure activity they imagined, and if not, what has stopped them from doing so. They may also include whether or not the drawing included other people, the time of day the activity occurred, whether special equip-

ment was needed for the activity, and how difficult it was to share their drawing with the group.

DEBRIEFING QUESTIONS

1. Have you been able to participate in the activity in your drawing?
2. If not, what has prevented you from doing so? What barriers have you encountered?
3. Describe this leisure experience in terms of the people, cost, resources, and facilities that it requires.
4. Do you have access to these things?
5. If you can't participate completely in the desired activity, what are parts that you can carry to another activity?
6. How often do you think about this ideal activity?
7. Describe the details of this activity that make it desirable to you.
8. What plans would you need to make to participate in this activity?

LEADERSHIP CONSIDERATIONS

1. Clients who have participated in this group experience reported that the music assisted them in feeling comfortable using their imaginations. This is an optional part of the activity.
2. If doing this activity with clients who have schizophrenia and are currently having difficulties with hearing voices or feeling delusional, the group leader may want to talk the group through the experience by using guided imagery.
3. Do not focus on the techniques of drawing. Emphasize that how well participants draw is not the issue—the group is using drawing as a means of expressing their imagined experience.

VARIATION

1. Have the group members write about their leisure experiences they imagined rather than to draw the experience.

CONTRIBUTOR

Lois Witt Nilson

PANTOMIME POEM

SPACE REQUIREMENTS

Classroom or activity room

MATERIALS

Poem that contains action and leisure words

GROUP SIZE

Small group

GOALS

1. To improve participants' awareness of leisure activities.
2. To improve participants' awareness of the movements of selected leisure activities.

PREPARATION

Gather materials

ACTIVITY DESCRIPTION

Have the group gather around a table or sit in a circle. Introduce the purpose of the activity. Read a poem to the participants that suggests certain movements. The participants decide what kinds of movements will be portrayed for each part of the poem. Several practice sessions might be needed depending on the complexity of the poem and actions. Close the activity using the debriefing questions.

SAMPLE POEM

Hide-and-Seek by Janet Felshin
    A game of hide-and-seek is fun.
    We need a lot of space,
    Someone's It while we all run
    To find a hiding place.
    It's best to play it just at dark
    Finding them is hard
    But you can play it in the park
    Or in a large backyard.
    The one who's It will hide his eyes
    The rest of us start running,
    One person hides but stands and spies
    To warn if It is coming.
    If It gets looking far from home
    And someone looks to see,
    He'll wait until he's all alone
    Then run and call "home free."

SUGGESTED MOVEMENTS

A game of hide-and-seek is fun. (broad smile)

We need a lot of space, (outstretch arms and wiggle)

Someone's It while we all run (run in place)

To find a hiding place. (cover head with hands)

It's best to play it just at dark (peek between hands)

Finding them is hard (hand over brow looking)

But you can play it in the park (arm outstretched to the right)

Or in a large backyard. (arm outstretched to the left)

The one who's It will hide his eyes (cover eyes with hands)

The rest of us start running, (run in place)

One person hides but stands and spies (peek between hands)

To warn if It is coming. (hands cupped around mouth)

If It gets looking far from home (marching in place)

And someone looks to see, (hand over brow looking)

He'll wait until he's all alone (look to both sides)

Then run and call "Home free." (run in place, hands in air)

DEBRIEFING QUESTIONS

1. What leisure activity was the poem mainly about?
2. How often have you participated in this activity?
3. How closely did our movement resemble the actual activity?
4. What the most prominent feature of this activity?
5. How does it differ from other leisure activities?
6. What new things did you learn about this leisure activity today?

LEADERSHIP CONSIDERATIONS

1. Choose the poem and movements based on the age and abilities of the group.
2. Teach the poem and movements in parts and the put the whole poem and all the movements together.

VARIATION

1. Choose the poem based on the topic of the leisure education program.

CONTRIBUTOR

Norma J. Stumbo

LEISURELY LIVING

SPACE REQUIREMENTS

Classroom or activity room

MATERIALS

Magazines, paper, markers, staplers, scissors

GROUP SIZE

Medium to large group

GOALS

1. To increase participants' awareness of appropriate leisure activities.
2. To develop participants' decision-making skills as well as to learn to co-operate with other participants on a group project.
3. To develop and enhance participants' interaction skills.

PREPARATION

Gather materials

ACTIVITY DESCRIPTION

Ask participants to gather around a table. Place supplies in the center of the table. Discuss the variety of leisure activities available. Ask the group members to name some common leisure activities. Discuss the concepts of satisfaction, freedom of choice, and other factors that distinguish leisure.

Participants will be selecting or drawing pictures that will be placed on a bulletin board. Each participant will cut out or draw specific leisure activities. Group may choose a theme for the bulletin board (e.g., spring, outdoor activities,) or just make a general activity board. When finished decide as a group which pictures will be used and where on the bulletin board they will be placed. At the end the group can choose a title or slogan for the board and label if desired.

Discussion may focus on who chose what activity and why. Promote participants' interactions with one another (e.g., asking each other about activities, where they can find that activity, and the abilities needed to participate).

DEBRIEFING QUESTIONS

1. Describe the activities chosen.
2. How did the group decide on the activities to be included?
3. Who had input into these decisions? Did everyone in the group have equal input?
4. When you look at the bulletin board, what message does it represent?
5. How many activities are new to you?
6. How many of these activities would you like to participate in?
7. Where can we go to participate in these activities?

LEADERSHIP CONSIDERATIONS

1. If participants are unable to use scissors, allow them to glue or staple pictures.
2. Encourage participants to work alone to gather more activities.
3. Do not label any activity as incorrect; however, keep in mind appropriateness.

VARIATIONS

1. If working with individuals who are physically disabled, leader can cut pictures out that participant chooses. Leader can also paste picture on poster board, if working one-on-one.
2. If participants have various functioning levels, have participants team up and work together; however, encourage both to play equal roles.

CONTRIBUTOR

Michelle DelGuidice

HELP YOURSELF

SPACE REQUIREMENTS

Classroom or activity room

MATERIALS

Handout, pencils

GROUP SIZE

Small group

GOALS

1. To improve participants' awareness of self in relation to leisure.
2. To improve participants' ability to plan for leisure participation.

PREPARATION

Gather supplies
Make one copy of the handout for each participant

ACTIVITY DESCRIPTION

Have the group gather around a table or sit in a circle. Introduce the session by explaining the purpose of the activity. Discuss how leisure may provide an opportunity to learn about yourself and help to make a transition in our lives a bit easier. Ask participants if they've ever thought about using leisure in this way, and what examples they might have.

Distribute a copy of the handout and a pencil to each participant. Explain that each of the 10 ideas may be ways that they can explore their own strengths and weaknesses and develop plans to put their leisure to use during this transition. Encourage participants to be realistic as they are filling out the worksheet. Allow 10–15 minutes.

Ask each person to share 1 or 2 items and the steps necessary to complete the tasks. Encourage others to ask questions and make suggestions. Focus the discussion on self-awareness and leisure planning.

DEBRIEFING QUESTIONS

1. What did you learn or have reinforced about yourself?
2. How likely are you to succeed at 1 of these activities this week? What would help you to succeed? What might prevent you from succeeding?
3. How often do you plan for your own leisure?
4. What are some planning skills that you use? What skills do you need to learn?
5. What did you learn from this activity today?

LEADERSHIP CONSIDERATIONS

1. Have 1 or 2 examples ready to present to participants.
2. Allow participants to choose new categories if these are not of interest.

VARIATIONS

1. Ask participants to generate ideas for what they would like to do next month.
2. Use partners to help generate ideas and then report back to the group.

CONTRIBUTOR

Norma J. Stumbo

HELP YOURSELF

Directions: Select at least three of the choices. Note what you'd like to do and the first 2–3 steps it will take to get there. For example: *Keep a journal. Write down thoughts that will encourage my success. I need to buy a journal and set a date to start writing in it.*

1. Keep a journal. _____

_____

_____

2. Write a letter to yourself to suggest ways for self-improvement. _____

_____

_____

3. Eat right and exercise. _____

_____

_____

4. Talk to people who know you and care about you. _____

_____

_____

5. Do something pleasurable. _____

_____

_____

6. Take care of something other than you._____

_____

_____

7. Try one new activity this week. _____

_____

_____

8. Go to one new place this week. _____

_____

_____

9. Learn one new skill this week. _____

_____

_____

10. Try one new healthy food this week._____

_____

_____

LEISURE USING VERSUS LEISURE SOBER

SPACE REQUIREMENTS

Classroom or activity room

MATERIALS

Large sheets of paper, magazines, glue, scissors, pencils

GROUP SIZE

Individuals, small group, or large group

GOALS

1. To improve participant's ability to identify how his/her leisure is affected by use and can change in sobriety.

2. To increase participant's knowledge of sober leisure alternatives.

3. To increase participants' insight into own leisure fears.

PREPARATION

Gather materials

ACTIVITY DESCRIPTION

Ask participants to gather around a table or sit in a circle. Explain that the object of this activity is to create a collage that represents "using" leisure and "sober" leisure.

Have participants divide a large sheet of paper into two halves. Have them mark one side "using" and one side "sober." Ask participants to create a collage for each half, one representing their "using" leisure, and one representing their "sober" leisure. Allow 10–15 minutes.

Have group members share their collages with the group. Allow participants to give and receive feedback and discuss any discoveries. Process the overall activity using the following debriefing questions:

DEBRIEFING QUESTIONS

1. Describe your "using" leisure.

2. Describe your "sober" leisure.

3. What are the major differences between your using and sober leisure?

4. What are the perks and drawbacks of each?

5. What do you think your family would say are the differences between your using and sober leisure?

6. What insights did you gain from exploring using vs. sober leisure?

7. If you could write a moral to the story, what would it be?

8. What did you learn from this activity?

9. What decisions does this help you to make?

10. What strategies can you use to help in your sober leisure?

11. Who might help you with these strategies?

LEADERSHIP CONSIDERATIONS

1. Consider individuals' hesitancy in creating a collage and sharing with the group.

2. Be prepared to facilitate discussion with specific questions about the differences between the two halves, the types of feelings that they have when participating in both types of leisure, and strategies for coping with sober leisure.

3. Keep in mind that larger groups take additional time for processing and discussion, and vary the time given for individual presentations accordingly.

VARIATION

1. Collage topic could be "using" or "sober" self-image.

CONTRIBUTOR

Pat O'Dea-Evans

LEISURE BARRIERS

SPACE REQUIREMENTS

Classroom or activity room

MATERIALS

Handout, pencils

GROUP SIZE

Small group

GOALS

1. To improve participants' awareness of barriers to their leisure.
2. To improve participants' awareness of ways to remove barriers to their leisure.

PREPARATION

Gather materials
Make one copy of the handout for each participant

ACTIVITY DESCRIPTION

Have the group gather around a table or sit in a circle. Ask participants to identify some barriers to leisure they have encountered (e.g., not enough money, stairs in a restaurant, not feeling like participating).

Distribute a copy of the handout and a pencil to each individual. Ask each individual to fill in one barrier in each of the 4 columns that matches with the environment. For example, "L" barriers may include *lighting* of parking lot, no *leisure* partner, or *lack* of equipment. Encourage participants to name as many as possible. Allow 5–10 minutes.

On the second line under each environment, ask each individual to fill in one way to reduce or eliminate that leisure barrier. For example, the "lighting of parking lot" barrier may be eliminated by "going during the day." (The suggestions for removing the barriers does not have to begin with the letter.) Encourage participants to name as many as possible. Allow 5–10 minutes.

Ask each individual to share his or her responses as the word "leisure" is spelled out. Have individuals write down others' suggestions for removing barriers. Draw similarities between answers and close with the following debriefing questions.

DEBRIEFING QUESTIONS

1. What were some of the common barriers experienced?
2. What were some of the least common barriers?
3. How often do you experience barriers to your leisure?
4. Are these barriers increasing or reducing in number or intensity?
5. What are some of the common ways to remove or reduce barriers to leisure?
6. What do these solutions have in common?
7. What are two ways to reduce or remove your most "drastic" barrier to your leisure?
8. What actions do you need to take or changes that you need to make to reduce or remove that barrier?
9. What would be the consequences if you were able to remove or reduce that barrier?
10. Are any of your barriers put up by you (e.g., attitude, lack of motivation)?
11. Who is in charge of removing or reducing barriers for you?
12. Summarize what you learned about barriers and their removal today.

LEADERSHIP CONSIDERATIONS

1. Allow a wide range of answers for barriers and their removal. Not all barriers will be physical or environmental.

VARIATIONS

1. Change the word down the left hand side to coincide with the theme of the rest of the leisure education program.
2. Change the locations across the top according to the age and needs of the participants.

CONTRIBUTOR

Norma J. Stumbo

LEISURE BARRIERS

Directions: On the first line under each heading, write one barrier to leisure you experience in that environment. On the second line under each heading, write one way to remove or reduce that barrier to your leisure.

	HOME	NEIGHBORHOOD	COMMUNITY	VACATION

L

_____

_____

E

_____

_____

I

_____

_____

S

_____

_____

U

_____

_____

R

_____

_____

E

_____

_____

MY FAVORITE THINGS

SPACE REQUIREMENTS

Classroom or activity room

MATERIALS

Large sheets of paper, markers, public transportation information, access books, adaptive equipment, community resources information

GROUP SIZE

Small group

GOALS

1. To improve participants' ability to identify possible barriers to leisure interests.
2. To improve participants' abilities to problem solve with regard to leisure involvement.
3. To increase participants' awareness of community resources for leisure.
4. To determine participant referral needs

PREPARATION

Gather materials

ACTIVITY DESCRIPTION

Ask participants to gather around a table or sit in a circle. Discuss leisure barriers (e.g., types of barriers, what new barriers are encountered because of disability, how to overcome barriers through problem solving). Ask participants to identify premorbid leisure interests. List interests (15–20) on large sheet of paper. Both active and passive activities may be listed.

When all participants have contributed to the list, review with the participants each activity in the following format:

1. Identify current barriers to participation.
2. Patients problem solve ways to continue participation in both the hospital and community.
3. Introduce adaptive equipment and resources information.

Discussion may center around ways to overcome barriers, the usefulness of problem solving and examining options, the variety of community resources available, and the needs and interests of the participants upon discharge. Participant responsibility should be stressed throughout and during final discussion.

DEBRIEFING QUESTIONS

1. What kinds of barriers to leisure were mentioned today?
2. What ways were mentioned to overcome these barriers?
3. Were any of the barriers impossible to overcome or reduce?
4. What are two options for you to participate in community activities?
5. What information do you need to know to participate in these activities?
6. What barriers might be present at any of these activities?
7. What are ways to overcome or reduce these barriers?
8. What did you learn today from this activity?
9. How might you use this information now or when you are discharged?

LEADERSHIP CONSIDERATION

1. Be prepared with specific local community resource information pertaining to program participants.

VARIATION

1. May focus on specific themes (e.g., family resources, low-cost resources).

CONTRIBUTORS

Cynthia Rodgers, Marilyn Tense

LEISURE QUOTES

SPACE REQUIREMENTS

Classroom or activity room

MATERIALS

Paper, pencils, quotes, envelopes, scissors

GROUP SIZE

Small group

GOALS

1. To increase participants' awareness of personal meaning of leisure.
2. To improve participants' ability to share personal values within a small group situation.

PREPARATION

Gather materials
Make one copy of the quotes for each participant

ACTIVITY DESCRIPTION

Ask participants to gather around a table or sit in a circle. Explain the purpose of the activity.

Hand out paper, a pencil, and a copy of the leisure quotes to each participant. Have the group members read each of the leisure quotes.

Divide participants into groups of 3–4 and have each individual pick one of the quotes that best describes how he or she individually views his or her own leisure. Then have each individual write down the leisure quote he or she has selected, explaining why the quote was chosen, and how it describes his or her leisure. Each participant shares his or her quote and explanation with the group.

Discussion may center around how important leisure is in the participants' lives, what they would like to change, or what prevents them from doing what they want.

DEBRIEFING QUESTIONS

1. Did any two people in the group choose the same quote?
2. Which quote represented the most people in the group?
3. What do your quotes tell you about how you value leisure in your lives?
4. Where does leisure fit into the rest of your life priorities?
5. How has the value of leisure changed for you over your lifetime?
6. What does leisure enable you to think, feel, experience that no other life activity can?
7. What would happen if all your leisure time were taken away from you?
8. Do you give leisure a high priority or a low priority? Why?

LEADERSHIP CONSIDERATIONS

1. Choose quotes that reflect the group's values.
2. Allow ample time for participants to read the leisure quotes.
3. Encourage acceptance and respect of individuals' concept of leisure.

VARIATIONS

1. Activity can be done individually or in large group.
2. Allow participants to choose one quote they feel best describes their leisure and one quote they feel disagrees with their views and discuss reasons why.
3. Choose one quote at a time for discussion.
4. Once the participant has chosen the quote that describes his/her leisure, have the participant write a short paragraph describing a leisure experience that relates to the quote chosen.

CONTRIBUTORS

Denise Berry, Jerri L. Harding, Barbara Kolb, Julie Burns, Lisa Stretch-Dodson

LEISURE QUOTES

Across the fields of yesterday he sometimes comes to me, a little lad just back from play...the lad I used to be. I wonder if he hopes to see the man I might have been.
Thomas Samual Jones, Jr.

All work and no play makes Johnny a dull boy.
Anonymous

Only a person who can live with himself can enjoy the gift of leisure.
Henry Greber

To be able to fill leisure intelligently is the last product of civilization.
Arnold Toynbee

Leisure tends to corrupt, and absolute leisure corrupts absolutely.
Edgar A. Shoaff

All happiness depends on a leisurely breakfast.
John Gunther

Most people say that as you get old, you have to give up things. I think you get old because you give things up.
Theodore Green

The best games of children are timeless, and there seems to be nothing more natural than play.
Sports Illustrated, 1960

Your mental health will be better if you have lots of fun outside the office.
Dr. William Menninger

Be temperate in your work, but don't carry the practice over into your leisure hours.
Monty Woolley

Most people spend most of their days doing what they do not want to do in order to earn the right, at times, to do what they may desire.
John Brown

You can learn more about a person in an hour of play than in a lifetime of conversation.
Plato

A man will live thus, not to the extent that he is a man, but to the extent that a divine principle dwells within him.
Aristotle

People with the greatest life satisfaction have been able to maintain a sense of playfulness.
Anonymous

Idleness is the enemy of the soul, and work is one's salvation.
St. Benedict

Time is money.
Benjamin Franklin

Idleness is the devil's playground.
Anonymous

Every man is a builder of a temple, called his body...We are all sculptors and painters, and our material is flesh and blood and bone.
Thoreau

We listen too much on the telephone and we listen too little to nature...Everybody should have his personal sounds to listen for, sounds that will make him exhilarated and alive, or quiet and calm.
Andre Kostelanetz

LEISURE QUOTES

Sport is working its changes on them and the atmosphere in which they live. A banker rounding a buoy, a stenographer on horseback, a mechanic in a duck blind can all savor—even in the age of the desk, the lathe, the tractor, and the split-level-with mortgage—that expansiveness of spirit, that sense of the uniqueness, which have always been the hallmarks of a full and satisfying life.

Paul O'Neil

Baseball is for the leisurely afternoons of summer and for the unchanging dreams.

Roger Kahn

Here is no sentiment, no contest, no grandeur, no economics. From the sanctity of this occupation, a man may emerge refreshed and in control of his own soul. He is not idle. He is fishing, alone with himself in dignity and peace. It seems a very precious thing to me.

John Steinbeck

I do not think that winning is the most important thing. I think winning is the only thing.

Bill Veeck, President, Chicago White Sox

Work and love—these are the basics. Without them there is neurosis.

Dr. Theodore Reik

Don't be afraid to enjoy the stress of a full life nor too naive to think you can do so without some intelligent thinking and planning. Man should not try to avoid stress any more than he would shun food, love or exercise.

Dr. Hans Selye

You gotta be a man to play baseball for a living but you gotta have a lot of little boy in you, too.

Roy Campanella

If you watch the game, it's fun. If you play it, it's recreation. If you work at it, it's golf.

Bob Hope

More free time means more time to waste.

Robert Hutchins

There is no leisure time today except for the totally shiftless living in a shack with a hound dog.

Margaret Mead

If you spend your free time playing bridge, you will be a good bridge player; if you spend it in reading, discussing and thinking of things that matter, you will be an educated person.

Sidney Smith

Life is precious to the old person. He is not interested merely in thoughts of yesterday's good life and tomorrow's path to the grave. He does not want his later years to be a sentence of solitary confinement in society. Nor does he want them to be a death watch.

Dr. David Allman

Striving to outdo one's companions on the golf course, on the tennis court, or in the swimming pool constitutes several socially acceptable forms of suicide.

Dr. George Griffith

The art of leisure lies, to me, in the power of absorbing without effort the spirit of one's surroundings; to look without speculation, at the sky and sea; to become part of a green plain; to rejoice, with a tranquil mind, in the feast of colour in a bed of flowers.

Dion Calthrop

LEISURE QUOTES

Those who decide to use leisure as a means of mental development, who love good music, good books, good pictures, good plays, good company, good conversation—what are they? They are the happiest people in the world.

William Lyon Phelps

Leisure is a beautiful garment, but it will not do for constant wear.

Anonymous

If the world were not so full of people, and most of them did not have to work so hard, there would be more time for them to get out and lie on the grass, and there would be more grass for them to lie on.

Don Marquis

CHOICES VERSUS SHOULDS

SPACE REQUIREMENTS

Classroom or activity room

MATERIALS

Chalkboard and chalk or whiteboard and markers, paper, pencils

GROUP SIZE

Small group, even number works best

GOALS

1. To increase participants' awareness of personal choice in their lives.

2. To increase participants' awareness of the anticipated consequences of their choices.

3. To increase participants' awareness of the possible consequences to one's leisure involvement of not evaluating one' own choices.

PREPARATION

Gather materials

ACTIVITY DESCRIPTION

Ask participants to gather around a table or sit in a circle. Explain the purpose of the activity. Inform participants that they will be exploring their "shoulds" and "oughts" during the session and that these messages can have an impact on the quality of their lives, including leisure.

Have participants form pairs and give each pair paper and pencil. Instruct the participants that they will take turns serving as a speaker and recorder, and to choose which partner will go first (speaker). The speaker then takes 5 minutes to tell the recorder everything that they "should," "ought," or "have to" do in their lives. The recorder writes down everything the speaker says.

When the speaker has finished, the two members reverse roles. After all of the responses have been generated, ask the participants their feelings associated with all those "shoulds," "oughts," and "have tos."

After a brief discussion participants are given their own lists by their partners (their recorder). Instruct each person to read each of the statements out loud, replacing the word "should," "ought," or "have to" in each statement with "choose to," "want to," or "will" and the reasons for their choice or desire. For example, a participant may have initially said, "I should work harder." Out loud, she will now say "I choose to work harder, so that I can be promoted." Another example of substitution would be, "I have to lose weight" which could be converted to "I want to lose weight, so that I can have more energy to do more things." Participants go through all of the items on the list, and make the appropriate substitution for each statement.

Discussion focuses on the feelings engendered by owning responsibility for personal choices. Leader asks the participants if the feelings were different after the substitutions. Second, discussion may address the roots of the shoulds, oughts and have tos and whether these messages serve them well or result primarily in guilt. Lastly, discussion may focus on the impact of "shoulds," "oughts," and "have tos" that relate to work and perfection in one's leisure, relationships, and self-acceptance.

DEBRIEFING QUESTIONS

1. How many shoulds or oughts or have tos did your list have?

2. Do these originate from parents? teachers? friends? society?

3. How often do you stop to reflect whether these statements are actually true?

4. What feelings or thoughts are produced by these statements?

5. How did it feel to replace these statements with a greater focus on personal responsibility?

6. How easy or difficult was it for you to use the "I choose" type of statements?

7. What would result if you took total responsibility for your life and lifestyle?

8. What did you learn from this activity that you can apply to your life?

LEADERSHIP CONSIDERATIONS

1. If one person in the pair cannot read or write, the other person writes down both of their responses. When it is the turn of the person who cannot read/write to substitute, their partner reads each statement out loud, and the person replaces wording and provides reasons.

2. Emphasize that it is not the purpose of the activity to tell the participants what to choose, only to look at personal choices, and the consequences of choices on their lives.

3. This activity would ideally be included as one segment of a more comprehensive leisure education program. The comprehensive leisure education program would sequentially address a number of goals.

VARIATIONS

1. This activity may be preceded by an activity that asks participants to explore how much choice/control they think they have in different areas of their lives and leisure. For example, have the participants rate how much control (on a scale of 1–10) they have over the energy they expend, what they choose to do or not do, or with whom they participate. This variation is a good lead-in to discussion of choice.

CONTRIBUTOR

Cynny Carruthers

LEISURE OUTBURST

SPACE REQUIREMENTS

Classroom or activity room

MATERIALS

List of categories, dice, 1-minute timer

GROUP SIZE

Small group

GOALS

1. To increase participants' awareness of the variety of leisure activities.
2. To provide an opportunity to enable participants to learn about leisure activities in a game environment.

PREPARATION

Gather materials

ACTIVITY DESCRIPTION

Ask participants to gather around a table or sit in a circle. Introduce the activity by explaining that the game involves naming as many activities as possible under the headings on the attached lists. The objective is to brainstorm and name as many of the activities on the list as possible within 1 minute.

The participants are divided into 2 teams of equal numbers. One member of each team rolls the dice. The team with the highest number starts first. Select a topic and give it to the first team, then starts the 1-minute timer.

The team has 1 minute to "outburst" as many answers as possible that fit the category. Answers must be identical to the answers on the list. The leader checks off correct answers as team members shout them out. Only those answers found on the list count. When the time runs out, the leader adds the correct responses and awards 1 point per correct response (maximum of 10 points for each round).

Continue play by alternating teams. At the end of the game (when all 12 lists have been used), the team with the most points wins. Discussion may center around various leisure activities available

for the participants, both within the hospital and the community.

DEBRIEFING QUESTIONS

1. How easy or difficult was it to think of activities under a time constraint?
2. How many of the activities mentioned were new to you?
3. Describe the similarities and differences of activities mentioned today.
4. Which of the activities have you participated in?
5. Which of the activities would you like to participate in?
6. Given the large range of activities available, why do some people have trouble finding activities they like?
7. Who is responsible for your leisure participation?
8. What did you learn from this activity today?

LEADERSHIP CONSIDERATIONS

1. Explain that the team not "outbursting" should remain quiet to not give away any clues or additional answers.
2. Ground rules should be set that only answers identical to those found on the list will be accepted, to minimize confusion and favoritism, OR that partial or full credit will be given for close answers.

VARIATION

1. A variety of lists may be constructed, depending on the topics the leader wants to cover (e.g., low-cost activities, activities that require partners, activities that require equipment).

CONTRIBUTOR

Maureen Cullerton

LEISURE OUTBURST

WATER SPORTS/ACTIVITIES

Water-skiing
Scuba diving
Swimming
Snorkeling
Wind surfing
Canoeing
Sailing
Fishing
Water polo

CARD GAMES

Poker
Uno
Rummy
Crazy 8s
War
Go fish
Old maid
Bridge
King's corner
Hearts

COMPETITIVE SPORTS

Football
Golf
Polo
Tennis
Basketball
Hockey
Volleyball
Baseball
Soccer
Ski racing

PICNIC GAMES

Sack races
Egg toss
Water balloon toss
Softball
Volleyball
3-legged race
Pie-eating contest
Horseshoes
Croquet
Watermelon-eating contest

OUTDOOR ACTIVITIES

Hiking
Boating
Camping
Sunbathing
Bike riding
Jogging
Horseshoes
Kite flying
Fishing
Swimming

WINTER SPORTS/ACTIVITIES

Downhill skiing
Ice skating
Tobagganing
Sledding
Snowmobiling
Cross-country skiing
Building a snowman
Snowball fights
Ice hockey
Ice fishing

PASSIVE ACTIVITIES

Reading
Watching television
Spectator sports
Meditating
Sitting in the park
Stargazing
Listening to the radio
Watching videos
Listening to music
Praying

ACTIVITIES THAT TAKE TWO

Tennis
Checkers
Ping-Pong
Chess
Teeter totter
Boxing
Water skiing
Ballroom dancing
Talking on the telephone
Singing a duet

BOARD GAMES

Checkers
Chess
Life
Monopoly
Sorry
Backgammon
Candyland
Trivial Pursuit
Clue
Scrabble

SOLITARY GAMES/ACTIVITIES

Reading
Solitare
Watching television
Listening to the radio
Sewing
Walking
Crafts
Cooking or baking
Painting or drawing
Writing letters

GAMES PLAYED WITH A BALL

Basketball
Volleyball
Football
Tennis
Racquetball
Handball
Ping-Pong
Billiards
Croquet
Soccer

EXERCISE

Aerobics
Walking
Jogging
Weightlifting
Bike riding
Swimming
Rowing
Sit-ups or push-ups
Jumping rope
Yoga

THE YARN GAME

SPACE REQUIREMENTS

Classroom or activity room

MATERIALS

Yarn, scissors

GROUP SIZE

Small or medium group

GOALS

1. To improve participants' ability to express leisure interests in front of a group.
2. To improve participants' ability to respond to and discuss others' leisure interests.

PREPARATION

Gather materials

ACTIVITY DESCRIPTION

Ask participants to gather around a table or sit in a circle. Instruct participants to pass around the yarn and scissors and take as much yarn as they wish. Each person wraps the yarn around his or her hand.

After all participants have taken some yarn, explain that each individual is to tell something about him/herself in leisure for each time he/she unwraps one circumference of the yarn from around the hand. Remind other participants to listen well so that they may discuss each person's leisure interests at the close of the activity.

Discussion may focus on the different types of activities each person discussed, how many people they discussed, the amount of information they shared or learned about each other, and whether this was an easy topic for them to disclose.

DEBRIEFING QUESTIONS

1. Describe the leisure interests of the person to your right.
2. Who in the group has the most unusual leisure interests?
3. Who in the group has the most diverse leisure interests?
4. Who in the group shared common leisure interests?
5. Name some of the activities that depended on including other people.
6. Name some of the activities that required expensive equipment.
7. What did you learn about other participants in the group today?
8. How easy or hard was it to discuss your leisure interests within the group?
9. How easy or hard was it to discuss others' leisure interests?

LEADERSHIP CONSIDERATION

1. Individuals with poor fine motor skills or paralysis may require physical assistance from the group leader for unwrapping the yarn; however, they should be able to communicate information about themselves.

VARIATIONS

1. Provide a list of leisure education questions available for those participants who do not know what to say. Prompts may be necessary.
2. Activity may be played with roll of toilet paper. Each person is instructed to take as much as they want for an upcoming out-trip. For each square that they have taken off, they must tell about one activity.

CONTRIBUTORS

Diane Wagner, Gail Alexander, Sue Myers

DRAW YOUR LEISURE

SPACE REQUIREMENTS

Classroom or activity room

MATERIALS

Newsprint, markers, 3x5 cards, stop watch or 1-minute timer.

GROUP SIZE

Small or large group

GOALS

1. To increase participants' personal awareness of leisure choices.
2. To increase participants' knowledge and awareness of leisure activities and options.

PREPARATION

Gather materials
Write leisure activities on 3x5 cards (see suggested list)

ACTIVITY DESCRIPTION

Ask participants to gather around a table or sit in a circle. Divide participants into groups of 3–4. Each team will take turns choosing a card and sending a teammate to the drawing board. The person who is drawing chooses a card and then draws a picture of the word written on the card.

The rest of the team members have 1 minute to guess what the word is on the card. The team members can continuously be calling out guesses throughout the minute. If the team guesses correctly within 1 minute, it earns two points; no points are given for an incorrect answer.

Repeat the process for all teams. Depending on the group, minimize the competitive aspect by emphasizing correct answers and group participation. Close the session using the debriefing questions below.

DEBRIEFING QUESTIONS

1. How many activities were mentioned today?
2. How easy or difficult was it to guess the activity from the drawing?
3. What do these activities have in common?
4. How many of these leisure activities have you participated in?
5. Name your top three favorite activities.
6. We mentioned lots of activities. How do we make the choice to participate in one over another?
7. Do we always have a choice of what activities we participate in?
8. How do we go about making those choices?
9. How satisfied are you with the choices you make for your leisure?
10. What would you change about the choices you make for your leisure?

LEADERSHIP CONSIDERATIONS

1. Have cards prepared ahead of time or ask participants to write leisure activities on the cards as part of the program.
2. Encourage participants to draw simple drawings.
3. Have participants start another drawing if their teammates are not guessing correctly, by placing an X through the old drawing.
4. Give suggestions or ideas to the participant for what they can draw.

VARIATIONS

1. Have one card that states that all teams will draw at the same time. The team that guesses first can receive two points. If no team guesses correctly, the next team will take its turn.
2. More leisure topics or activities can be added to the game.

CONTRIBUTOR

Penelope J. Levenberry

SUGGESTIONS FOR "DRAW YOUR LEISURE" CARDS

Reading
Bird watching
Doing puzzles
Walking on the beach
Knitting
Watching television
Gardening
Playing video games
Painting
Listening to music
Cooking
Eating
Dancing
Napping/sleeping
Taking pictures
Talking on the telephone
Making crafts
Playing a guitar
Singing
Playing the piano
Playing an instrument
Ping-Pong
Walking
Playing chess
Swimming
Playing cards
Hiking
Drawing
Baseball
Running
Football
Aerobics
Soccer
Golfing
Basketball
Tennis
Going to a play
Bowling
Going to the movies
Hockey
Camping
Riding a bicycle
Shopping
Flying a kite
Being with friends
Working with clay
Roller skating

Ice skating
Collecting coins/stamps
Attending religious services
Travelling
Sewing
Sightseeing
Water skiing
Boating
Snow skiing
Canoeing
Rock climbing
Sledding
Horseback riding
Frisbee
Sunbathing
Stargazing
Weightlifting
Fishing
Going out to eat
Snowshoeing
Backpacking
Motorcycle riding
Riding a roller coaster
Skydiving
Weaving

GAME IN A BAG

SPACE REQUIREMENTS

Classroom or activity room

MATERIALS

Paper bag filled with miscellaneous objects that would be useful in the development of a game (e.g., a writing utensil and paper for the development of rules, a larger piece of paper for a game board, and other objects that can be used as game pieces). May want to use game boards in 3rd chapter of this manual.

GROUP SIZE

Small group

GOALS

1. To increase participants' ability to create activities and games.
2. To increase participants' ability to make decisions within a small group.

PREPARATION

Gather materials
May want to make copies of the game boards found in chapter 3

ACTIVITY DESCRIPTION

Ask participants to gather around a table or sit in a circle. Give the group the bag of supplies and instruct them to use every object in the bag to create a new game that they will have the opportunity to play during subsequent activity groups.

First have participants develop the type of game they will create and give it a name. Then have them develop a list of rules (each person must suggest one rule and have one rule accepted, and each rule must be agreed on by 75% of the group). Allow the group to make necessary decisions with little intervention.

Once the game is completed (named, rules developed, process the experience with the group, noting areas specific to the program goals. For example, discussion could focus on whether the group cooperated toward the common goal of creating a game, how decisions were made and by whom, and how much the group communicated

with one another. The discussion may also cover whether the new game resembles one already on the market, and whether the participants think it will be fun to play.

DEBRIEFING QUESTIONS

1. How did your group choose the type of game or activity?
2. How were rules of the game or activity decided?
3. How easy or difficult was it to ensure that each group member participated equally?
4. What could have improved communication within the group?
5. How were problems solved within the group?
6. Describe the game or activity your group created.
7. Is it like any other game or activity on the market?
8. Why would people want to play your game or activity?
9. What did you learn from creating this game or activity?
10. What do you most look forward to when you play it?

LEADERSHIP CONSIDERATIONS

1. More intervention may be necessary depending on the ages and functioning levels of the group.
2. Volatile situations may occur during the activity that may require stopping the activity and processing immediately rather than waiting until the end.
3. Types and numbers of items in the bag should reflect the level and abilities of the participants.

VARIATION

1. For larger groups divide the group in half, giving each group identical bags and then allowing each group to play the other group's game at the end.

CONTRIBUTOR

Cheryl Gordon

LEISURE BINGO

SPACE REQUIREMENTS

Classroom or activity room with tables and chairs

MATERIALS

Bingo cards, pictures, bingo chips, scissors, glue, caller's list

GROUP SIZE

Small group

GOALS

1. To increase participants' ability to recognize pictures of leisure activities and correlate to another sheet.

2. To increase participants' ability to differentiate between work or obligated activities and leisure or free time activities.

PREPARATION

Gather materials
Make one copy of the bingo card and pictures for each participant

ACTIVITY DESCRIPTION

Ask participants to gather around a table or sit in a circle. Give each participant a bingo card, a copy of the leisure pictures, and several bingo chips. Have participants create their own bingo cards by cutting the pictures and pasting them onto the card in the order of their choosing. Call out leisure activities one at a time and if participants have a corresponding picture on their bingo card, they will cover that square with a bingo chip.

Play continues until a player wins by having a whole row (horizontal, vertical, or diagonal) covered with bingo chips. When player's win is confirmed, all players remove all bingo chips from their sheets and play starts again. Prizes may be given or competition can be minimized by emphasizing cooperation and the leisure activities.

Discussion may focus on the types of leisure activities represented on the sheets, whether players have participated in these activities, or where they could participate in these activities. Debriefing questions follow that may be used to close the activity.

DEBRIEFING QUESTIONS

1. Name five activities that were familiar to you.

2. Name three activities that you have participated in.

3. Name three facilities or locations you have participated in these activities.

4. How do leisure activities differ from work activities? What feelings accompany leisure?

5. On a typical day, do you participate in more leisure or work activities?

6. When may work be leisure and when may leisure be work?

7. Does leisure always have to be an activity?

8. Summarize what you've learned from this activity today.

LEADERSHIP CONSIDERATION

1. The pictures need to be shown to the participants before starting the game to determine if the participants understand what leisure activity is being depicted.

VARIATIONS

1. Participants can take turns being bingo caller.

2. Use more or different pictures, depending on cognitive level of participants.

3. Pictures of leisure-related equipment (e.g., tennis racquets, softballs, playing cards) may be substituted for leisure activities.

CONTRIBUTOR

Julie Robbins

LEISURE BINGO CALLER'S LIST

Billiards	Darts
Archery	Basketball
Gardening	Football
Bowling	Skating
Soccer	Traveling
Baseball	Sailing
Cycling	Skiing
Golf	Tennis

LEISURE BINGO

LEISURE BENEFITS

SPACE REQUIREMENTS

Classroom or activity room

MATERIALS

Handouts, pencils

GROUP SIZE

Individuals, small group

GOALS

1. To improve participants' ability to identify benefits of leisure and how they relate to the group.
2. To improve participants' ability to discuss attitudes about leisure.
3. To increase participants' ability to process leisure values with peers.

PREPARATION

Gather materials
Make one copy of the handout for each group

ACTIVITY DESCRIPTION

Ask participants to gather around a table or sit in a circle. Explain that the object of this activity is for participants to identify specific leisure attitudes, values, and benefits. Divide participants into groups of 3–4. Give each group a copy of the handout and a pencil.

Have participants in each group brainstorm a combined list of at least 20 leisure benefits. Then instruct each group to discuss the list and rank the top 10 from the most important to the least important. The group must reach agreement by consensus (rather than just voting), so encourage participants to discuss their opinions and to use persuasion.

Have each group present their list to the larger group and discuss how they came to decisions about the order. Also discuss their ability to work together as a group going by consensus rather than voting. Discussion should focus on the usefulness of leisure for a variety of purposes or benefits.

DEBRIEFING QUESTIONS

1. What were the common benefits of leisure named by all groups?
2. Have you experienced these benefits yourself?
3. Give an example of a leisure activity and a benefit you gain from participating in it.
4. Give an example of a different activity that holds a different benefit for you.
5. What do your attitudes toward leisure have to do with the benefits you get?
6. Is your overall attitude toward leisure positive? negative? unsure?
7. How are your values expressed in leisure? For example, does leisure have to be productive or earned? Does leisure have to involve family?
8. In your list of life priorities, where does leisure come on that list?
9. Summarize what you've learned about your leisure attitudes, values, and benefits.

LEADERSHIP CONSIDERATIONS

1. Encourage participants to brainstorm by allowing even the silliest or impractical ideas to be recorded.
2. Encourage participants to recall their own leisure experiences and the benefits they derived from them.

VARIATIONS

1. Could provide a list of 20 benefits of leisure activities for a beginning group.
2. Larger group can be split into smaller groups so this activity could be appropriate for any size group.

CONTRIBUTOR

Pat O'Dea-Evans

LEISURE BENEFITS

Brainstorm 20 benefits of leisure.

1. _____

2. _____

3. _____

4. _____

5. _____

6. _____

7. _____

8. _____

9. _____

10. _____

11. _____

12. _____

13. _____

14. _____

15. _____

16. _____

17. _____

18. _____

19. _____

20. _____

Rank the the top 10 benefits from the most important (1) to the least important (10).

1. _____

2. _____

3. _____

4. _____

5. _____

6. _____

7. _____

8. _____

9. _____

10. _____

LEISURE THROUGH THE YEARS

SPACE REQUIREMENTS

Classroom or activity room

MATERIALS

Flip chart and markers or chalkboard and chalk

GROUP SIZE

Small group

GOALS

1. To increase participants' awareness of various leisure activities and identify past participation patterns.
2. To improve participant's ability to create one goal related to leisure.

PREPARATION

Gather materials

ACTIVITY DESCRIPTION

Ask participants to gather around a table or sit in a circle. Introduce the activity and provides a brief definition of "leisure." Explain that each member is to recall three separate periods of time in their life and share with the group a leisure activity they participated in during that time.

Give examples of time periods to help the group members recall past experiences (e.g., grade school, high school, college years, early marriage, when children were young, when children moved away from home, last month, last week).

As group members share their past leisure activities, encourage them to expand by asking: What did you like most about the activity? Can or do you still do this activity now? If not, why not?

If it would be helpful to the group, write the shared leisure activities in chronological order under each person's name. Have group members look at their leisure activities through the years and try to determine how and why their leisure activities have changed. Discuss why leisure activity participation changes due to the following:

- Physical skills (flexibility, strength, endurance, function, vision)
- Monetary resources (retirement, unemployment, promotions)
- Social interaction patterns (divorce, addition of family members, death of spouse/ friends)
- Value/awareness of the importance of leisure participation

Close by asking each member to share with the group a leisure activity they would like to participate in during the next month. Encourage the group to state a new activity or a past activity they have not engaged in over the past few years.

DEBRIEFING QUESTIONS

1. Of all the activities named today, which is your favorite?
2. Summarize how your leisure activities have changed over the years.
3. What specific things have changed your leisure patterns?
4. Have these choices been by chance or by choice?
5. What types of leisure activities do you foresee in your future?
6. Name one activity that you will participate in in the next month that may be related to or different from your past activities.
7. What did you learn today from exploring your past and looking at your future leisure?

LEADERSHIP CONSIDERATIONS

1. Determine the comfort level of the group in deciding whether to write participants shared experiences on a flip chart or chalkboard.
2. Encourage all group members to actively participate.
3. Maintain control of the group to redirect participants to task as needed.
4. Allow participants enough time to think about their responses and not be rushed.

5. Sometimes writing down the examples results in participants not thinking for themselves but rather agreeing with other group members.

VARIATIONS

1. Vary the number of "time periods" participants are to address depending on the skills of the group.

2. Use for the first session of a weekly program. Each week have a member of the group instruct the other members on a leisure activity.

3. Have participants complete a leisure contract to encourage follow-through with leisure activity participation goal.

CONTRIBUTOR

Ruth Roeder

HOBBY FEVER

SPACE REQUIREMENTS

Classroom or activity room

MATERIALS

Hobby books, examples of hobby/collectable items, paper, pencils

GROUP SIZE

Small group

GOALS

1. To improve participants' knowledge of hobbies as a leisure option.
2. To improve participants' understanding that the positive aspects of hobbies may be a replacement for less constructive behaviors.

PREPARATION

Gather materials

ACTIVITY DESCRIPTION

Ask participants to gather around a table or sit in a circle. Show a rare coin, baseball card, or stamp, and discuss its economic value. Proceed with a series of 30–40 minute classes depending upon the number of participants and interest level. Suggested unit plans that focus on time use and hobbies as positive leisure interests include:

Free time: How do you use it? Is it good? Is it bad? What makes free time either good or bad? Explore a variety of free time options that relate to hobbies. Where did the name "hobby" originate? (See a dictionary for a simple history on how "hobby" is a derivative of the word "hobbyhorse.")

Contrast negative and positive addiction. Is the term "addiction" always negative? Have people ever been obsessed or preoccupied with good "addiction?" Give examples of athletes who have struggled to overcome injury or economic disadvantage and have made it to superstar status (e.g., Jackie Robinson, Isaiah Thomas, Bo Jackson). Have the group write down the positive results of coin collecting, developing an interest and skills in sports, baseball and basketball collecting, a handicraft skill. (Read examples from the lists.) Now turn the sheet over and list the negative results of excessive watching of TV, overeating, being lazy,

excessive alcohol and drug use. Those working in childcare agencies might ask youth to further discuss how their choices in the use of free time have been a factor in their "problems"?

Provide examples of a wide variety of hobbies. Invite hobbyists to bring their collections and hobby items to share with the group to generate interest and the options available. Also focus on what gives economic value to hobby collections (rareness, condition of the objects, popularity, hype.) Encourage youth to express an interest or choice of a specific hobby he or she might like to learn more about.

DEBRIEFING QUESTIONS

1. What hobby was discussed that might be of interest to you?
2. List 4 positive aspects related to hobbies.
3. Name 4 people you know and their hobbies.
4. How many people in the group share a hobby with you?
5. What are ways you can learn more about a hobby?
6. What new hobby would you like to try?
7. Summarize what you have learned in this activity.

LEADERSHIP CONSIDERATIONS

1. The class should be approached as a time of serious reflection yet provide enough materials and invited guests to maintain the interest of the youth.
2. Do not lecture. Use an interactive teaching and discussion technique.
3. Take a field trip to a hobby store to stimulate interest.

VARIATION

1. Adapt for use with the elderly by omitting the unit on positive and negative addiction. Replace it with a unit that focuses on a utilitarian view of the use of leisure time and work ethic issues that reflect the leisure participation patterns of many older adults.

CONTRIBUTOR

Anita Magafas

UNFINISHED SENTENCES

SPACE REQUIREMENTS

Classroom or activity room

MATERIALS

3x5 cards, unfinished sentences, small bag or bowl

GROUP SIZE

Small or medium group

GOALS

1. To improve participants' awareness of the need to plan for leisure involvement.

2. To increase participants' awareness of leisure lifestyle skills and barriers upon discharge and offer resources and suggestions for participation.

3. To encourage participants' positive focus toward the rehabilitation program and benefits of therapy.

PREPARATION

Gather materials
Write unfinished sentences on 3x5 cards and place in bag or bowl

ACTIVITY DESCRIPTION

Ask participants to gather around a table or sit in a circle. Introduce the purpose of the activity. Ask questions that will help them examine what they think will happen after discharge. Encourage participants to be honest, but as positive as possible.

Explain that the bag or bowl is going to be passed around the circle, and each participant is to take one card from it. Each participant will then read the sentence aloud and finish it accordingly. Once this is completed, collect the cards, pass the bag or bowl again, and repeat the activity until all the cards have been used.

Discussion may include how similar or different answers were, what general themes of the answers were, and areas where participants were positive or negative. Participants may be encouraged to give feedback to each other, or help solve potential problems as necessary.

DEBRIEFING QUESTIONS

1. What were two common themes to the groups' answers today?

2. Who is responsible for planning your leisure after you are discharged?

3. How do you feel about taking responsibility for your own leisure?

4. What areas do you feel most optimistic about?

5. What areas are you most worried about?

6. What barriers do you think you might face?

7. How will you overcome these barriers?

8. Who can help you solve some of those problems?

9. How has rehabilitation helped you to overcome or reduce those barriers?

LEADERSHIP CONSIDERATION

1. Encourage sharing between group members, especially if some individuals have been on the unit for a longer time.

VARIATIONS

1. Read the sentences aloud, one at a time, and allow each participant the opportunity to respond.

2. After a few rounds are played, have the participants come up with questions to put in the bag or bowl for others to draw.

CONTRIBUTORS

Diane Wagner, Gail Alexander, Sue Myers

UNFINISHED SENTENCES

One positive thing about rehabilitation is . . .

My favorite time of day is . . .

My best memory of therapy is . . .

After discharge the first thing I am going to do is . . .

When I feel down I will . . .

One positive thing I gained from my hospital stay is . . .

My favorite activity in recreation therapy was . . .

When I need exercise I will . . .

My biggest obstacle is . . .

My greatest achievement in rehabilitation was . . .

One activity I will pursue after discharge is . . .

I benefited others during my stay by . . .

My favorite person to talk to when I am sad is . . .

One skill I learned from recreation therapy is . . .

The best thing I heard from my doctor was . . .

LEISURE WORD GAME

SPACE REQUIREMENTS

Classroom or activity room

MATERIALS

None needed

GROUP SIZE

Small group

GOALS

1. To increase participants' awareness of the wide variety of leisure activities.

2. To improve participants' cognitive skills by working on sequencing, memory, and letter and word recognition.

3. To improve participants' social interaction through cooperative group work.

PREPARATION

None needed

ACTIVITY DESCRIPTION

Have the participants sit in a circle. Instruct the participants that one person will start and state a leisure activity. The next person is to think of a leisure activity that begins with the last letter of the word previously given. For example, one person might say "skiing", the next person must come up with a leisure activity that starts with a "g" and says "golf." The next person must come up with an activity that starts with "f."

Start the activity by giving the word "leisure." The person to the right must come up with an activity that begins with "e." If a participant cannot think of a leisure activity that begins with the appropriate letter, he or she moves to the center of the circle. Play continues until there is only one person left and that person is the winner.

Closing discussion may focus on the wide variety of activities available for leisure participation, what activities were named that participants engage in or would like to try, or what new activities were named.

DEBRIEFING QUESTIONS

1. How many different activities were named today?

2. Which 3 activities do you like to participate in most?

3. Which 3 activities are the most unfamiliar to you?

4. How would you describe the variety of activities mentioned today?

5. With whom in the group do you share common interests?

6. How easy or difficult was it to think of an activity that started with your letter?

LEADERSHIP CONSIDERATIONS

1. Encourage creativity by naming nontraditional activities on your turn.

2. Encourage participants to come up with activities not ending in "ing."

3. Remind each person to wait for his/her turn.

4. Watch participants for signs of frustration or boredom and end the game when appropriate, even if a winner has not been named.

5. Activities should not be repeated by participants. Each activity named must be new to the session.

VARIATIONS

1. Do not have people sit in the center if they cannot come up with a word. Their turn can be skipped and play continues with the person to their right.

2. Make the game noncompetitive by having the participants be able to ask for assistance if they are stuck on a word.

CONTRIBUTOR

Jean Folkerth

A BLAST TO THE PAST

SPACE REQUIREMENTS

Classroom activity room

MATERIALS

3x5 cards, list of blast to the past statements, small bag or bowl

GROUP SIZE

Small to medium group

GOALS

1. To improve participants' ability to reminisce on past events and memories, especially in childhood.
2. To improve participants' memory recall regarding prominent lifetime events.
3. To increase participants' ability to examine life patterns and values, especially with regard to leisure.

PREPARATION

Gather materials
Write blast to the past statements on 3x5 cards and place in bag or bowl

ACTIVITY DESCRIPTION

Ask participants to gather around a table or sit in a circle. Introduce the activity by explaining to the participants that the focus will be on their memories of their childhood years, especially positive events. Have participants take turns choosing a card and reading the question aloud. Allow each participant the opportunity to respond.

The discussion may focus around similarities and differences among group members, similarities throughout each person's lifetime (e.g., best friend as child and as an adult), and whether the most pleasant memories involved leisure experiences. The discussion may also center around whether they adhered to the same leisure patterns throughout their lives. What changed? What stayed the same? Why?

DEBRIEFING QUESTIONS

1. What was a common event that has happened in most of your lives?
2. What were a few of the unusual events that happened for group members?
3. What has been your most memorable leisure event in your life so far?
4. How has your pattern of leisure changed over your life?
5. What has impacted those changes in your leisure patterns?
6. What has remained much the same in your leisure patterns?
7. What do you see happening in your near future regarding a significant or meaningful life event that involves leisure?
8. Summarize in one phrase your leisure patterns over your lifetime.

LEADERSHIP CONSIDERATIONS

1. Encourage each person to respond to each question, although each person has the right not to respond.
2. Focus on drawing out similarities between people and individual life events (e.g., family has always been important to an individual, two participants both like to take drives in the country).

VARIATIONS

1. Pass out index cards to participants in the group. Allow them to read the question, respond to it, and have other members respond also.
2. After responding to each question, have each participant tell how this now affects them (e.g., liked to play checkers as a child and still likes to play now, returned to favorite vacation spot last year).
3. Vary the cards to meet the needs of the participants and the purpose of the group.

CONTRIBUTORS

Diane Wagner, Gail Alexander, Sue Myers

A BLAST TO THE PAST

Tell about your childhood sweetheart.

Describe your first automobile.

What was your favorite activity as a child?

Tell about your favorite movie or television show.

Name one of your favorite songs.

Tell about your favorite birthday present.

Tell about the first time you got into mischief.

Tell about the chore you disliked most as a child.

Describe what you most wanted as a child.

Tell about the funniest thing you ever did.

Tell about your best friend when you were younger.

Describe your favorite childhood game.

Tell about what you wanted to be when you grew up.

What was your favorite activity as a young adult and why?

Tell about your favorite vacation.

Tell about your most positive memory.

Describe your favorite childhood toy.

Tell about your favorite childhood pet.

Tell about your favorite childhood book.

Describe the types of things you did after school.

LEISURE ACTIVITY CHARADES

SPACE REQUIREMENTS

Classroom or activity room

MATERIALS

3x5 cards, marker

GROUP SIZE

Small or medium group

GOALS

1. To increase participants' awareness of the wide variety of leisure activities.
2. To improve participants' creative expression through play acting.
3. To facilitate social interaction among participants in a cooperative and competitive environment.

PREPARATION

Gather materials
Write letters of a leisure word and numbers on 3x5 cards
Examples:

1	1	1	1	1	1	
H	I	K	I	N	G	

2	2	2	2	2	2	2
G	O	L	F	I	N	G

ACTIVITY DESCRIPTION

Give each group member a card with a letter and a number on it. Members form subgroups by matching their number with others who have the same number.

When each group has found each other, each shows his or her letter to other members of the group. The group unscrambles the leisure activity that the letters on their cards spell out, and then acts out their leisure activity for the other groups. The other groups are to guess the leisure activity similar to regular charades.

Discussion may center on the diversity of leisure activities, how familiar the groups were with the activities acted out, or if there were any activities that members of the group would like to try.

DEBRIEFING QUESTIONS

1. How easy or difficult was it to find the other members of your group?
2. How easy or difficult was it to determine the word given your group?
3. How easy was it for the group to act out the activity?
4. How easy was it for the other group(s) to guess the activity?
5. How many of the activities were already familiar to you?
6. Which activities would you like to try in the future?
7. Which activities are you already good at?
8. Describe the diversity of activities mentioned today.
9. Can you think of something that's not a leisure activity?
10. Why do you suppose leisure activities are so diverse among today's group members?
11. Summarize what you've learned today.

LEADERSHIP CONSIDERATIONS

1. Make sure that there are enough cards to meet the size of the group.
2. If play continues, distribute new cards so that members of the larger group end up in different subgroups.
3. Unless the group is large, keep the activity words short so that several subgroups can be formed.

VARIATIONS

1. Words on the cards can be made according to themes, such as passive activities, low-cost activities, activities that can be done at the local community center or park, or seasonal activities.
2. Teams may be formed and points awarded for creativity, first activity to be guessed, or time limits.

CONTRIBUTOR

Jean Folkerth

SHARING AND LEARNING ABOUT ME

SPACE REQUIREMENTS

Classroom or activity room

MATERIALS

3x5 cards, sharing and learning statements, small bag or bowl

GROUP SIZE

Small to medium group

GOALS

1. To increase participants' awareness of leisure values and interests regarding personal experiences.
2. To improve participants' ability to disclose feelings and values in an appropriate manner.

PREPARATION

Gather materials
Write sharing and learning statements on 3x5 cards and place in bag or bowl

ACTIVITY DESCRIPTION

Ask participants to gather around a table or sit in a circle. Explain that the bag or bowl is going to be passed around the circle, and each participant is to take one card from it. Each participant will then read the sentence aloud and finish it accordingly. Once this is completed, collect the cards, pass the bag or bowl again, and repeat the activity until all the cards have been used.

Discussion may focus on similarities and differences between answers, specific responses of the participants, how these responses have changed over time, and how they relate to the participants' leisure.

DEBRIEFING QUESTIONS

1. What was the common theme of the groups' responses?
2. What leisure interests are shared by the group?
3. Who had interests unique from the rest of the group members?
4. Who in the group places the greatest value of leisure pursuits?
5. Who in the group places the least value on leisure pursuits?
6. What answers surprised you, including your own?
7. What role does leisure play in your life currently?
8. How does this compare with the role it has played in the past?
9. On a scale of 1–10, with 1 being highest, rate the priority you give to leisure activities.
10. What did you learn from this activity today?

LEADERSHIP CONSIDERATIONS

1. Provide each participant with equal time in discussing answers. Redirect the discussion as necessary.
2. Find a subject that less verbal participants can relate to and focus on this issue to maximize participation and positive communication.

VARIATIONS

1. Read the statements aloud, and allow each participant the opportunity to respond.
2. Vary content of the questions/statements depending on the nature of the leisure education session.
3. Have participants' develop sets of questions/statements to put on the index cards.

CONTRIBUTORS

Diane Wagner, Gail Alexander, Sue Myers

SHARING AND LEARNING ABOUT ME

When I'm feeling down I like to...

The thing that I value most is...

The most important person in my life is...

The happiest time in my life was...

My ultimate goal in life is...

My feelings are most hurt when...

My favorite vacation spot is...

In my leisure time I like to...

My favorite pet is...

During the summer I like to...

My favorite hobby is..

The person I most like to spend my time with is...

For fun I...

My favorite food is...

If I won the lottery I would...

The color that describes my feelings right now is...

My favorite holiday is...

My favorite magazine/book is...

My favorite winter activity is...

The one hobby I most want to learn is...

Two barriers in my life are...

I prize leisure because...

My overall attitude toward leisure can be summed up as...

The biggest change I need to make in my leisure is...

Next month I'd like to...

LEISURE MYSTERIES

SPACE REQUIREMENTS

Classroom or activity room

MATERIALS

3x5 cards, pencils

GROUP SIZE

Small group

GOALS

1. To improve participants' ability to identify leisure interests and abilities.
2. To improve participants' ability to share leisure interests with others.
3. To encourage participants to interact with one another based on similar or dissimilar leisure interests.

PREPARATION

Gather materials

ACTIVITY DESCRIPTION

Have the group form a circle and distribute a 3x5 card and pencil to each participant. Introduce the activity by saying that each person will write his or her name and a leisure activity that he or she does and that is unknown to the others in the group on the card. Allow 1–2 minutes.

Collect the cards and shuffle. Read the activity on one of the cards aloud. Group members must guess who the activity belongs to. When the person is guessed correctly, he or she answers the following questions:

1. When did you begin the activity?
2. Who sparked your interest in the activity?
3. How often do you do the activity?
4. How might one become involved in this activity?

After reading each person's card, encourage group members to ask additional questions of each other. Close with drawing some similarities and differences among the group members, using the debriefing questions provided.

DEBRIEFING QUESTIONS

1. Who shared similar leisure activities within the group?
2. Can they participate together?
3. Can someone in the group teach you something new?
4. Does someone have a skill that others would like to learn?
5. Where would they go to learn it?
6. What new leisure activities did you hear about today?
7. How easy or difficult was it to identify people based on their leisure interests?
8. What did you learn from doing this activity today?

LEADERSHIP CONSIDERATION

1. The leader should keep the activity progressing, while allowing participants to share necessary information.

VARIATIONS

1. If the group is too large, break it into two or three smaller groups.
2. Content can be changed according to group needs. For example, what is your favorite place to go? What piece of equipment do you resemble most? What is your favorite leisure memory?

CONTRIBUTORS

Susan D. Schmunk, Jean Folkerth

REINTRODUCING LEISURE INTO YOUR LIFESTYLE

SPACE REQUIREMENTS

Classroom or activity room

MATERIALS

Handout, pencils

GROUP SIZE

Individuals or small group

GOALS

1. To increase participants' awareness of current or future leisure time management.
2. To increase participants' knowledge of importance and benefits of leisure.
3. To provide participants with appropriate structure and guidance to initiate a successful leisure experience.
4. To increase participants' ability to set appropriate goals and divide each goal into separate and consecutive objectives.

PREPARATION

Gather materials
Make one copy of the handout for each participant

ACTIVITY DESCRIPTION

Ask participants to gather around a table or sit in a circle. Give each participant a copy of the handout and a pencil. Introduce the session by explaining the purpose, goals, and expected outcomes.

Read the questions aloud, give participants 2–5 minutes to complete each question on paper, and discuss the answers. (Certain questions may just be discussed verbally, according to the leader's discretion.)

At the end of the session, each participant is given a homework assignment based on the information learned during the group, especially question #11. Each participant sets a goal for participation in one activity during the next week. Each participant then writes objectives or actions it will take to complete this activity.

Discussion may focus on barriers to leisure, the importance of leisure planning, or developing leisure alternatives.

DEBRIEFING QUESTIONS

1. What role does leisure play in your life?
2. How important do you consider your leisure time to be?
3. What benefits do you gain from participating in leisure?
4. What are some of the barriers that prevent you from participating as you would like to?
5. Why is it important to plan for your leisure?
6. What sorts of leisure activities require planning?
7. What are the advantages of having several leisure alternatives in mind?
8. What activity would you like to participate in next week?
9. What goals or objectives do you need to accomplish to participate in this activity?
10. How does setting goals help us make sure we accomplish them?

LEADERSHIP CONSIDERATIONS

1. Be aware of cognitive deficits of the participants and be prepared to provide assistance as necessary.
2. Avoid close-ended questions that require simple yes/no responses.
3. Remain aware of using language that fits the population and using confrontation when necessary.

VARIATIONS

1. Participants may be asked to write their answers on a blackboard, if functioning level is high enough.
2. Questions should be adapted according to the population and type of facility (e.g., inpatient versus outpatient).

CONTRIBUTOR

Diane Wagner

REINTRODUCING LEISURE INTO YOUR LIFESTYLE

1. Introduce yourself and state where you live and with whom.

2. Define leisure/recreation.

3. Why do you participate in leisure/recreation?

4. What benefits do you get from leisure?

5. Name the different categories of recreation.

6. Name 1–3 activities that you enjoy.

7. How do you feel when you participate in each of the above activities?

8. Name something that you have given up doing in the past year or two.

9. Why did you give this up?

10. Discuss two activities that you currently participate in and enjoy.

11. Select one activity to accomplish within the next week.*

* Leader will provide necessary assistance and structure, including homework assignments, to enable participants to complete this activity

WHAT ACTIVITY AM I?

SPACE REQUIREMENTS

Classroom or activity room

MATERIALS

3x5 cards, marker, tape

GROUP SIZE

Small group

GOALS

1. To increase participants' awareness of a variety of leisure activities.
2. To increase participants' knowledge of the characteristics of various leisure activities.
3. To generate social interaction among participants.

PREPARATION

Gather materials
Write leisure activities on the cards (1 for each participant)

ACTIVITY DESCRIPTION

Tape an activity card to each participant's back. The participant should not see his or her card.

Instruct participants to ask other participants questions regarding the leisure activity on his or her back. Only questions that can be answered "yes" or "no" may be asked. For example, "Am I an organized sport?" The participant may only ask one question per person, if the group is large enough.

When the person guesses his or her activity, he or she may sit down or remain in the game to answer questions for other participants. Each participant should confirm his or her guess with the leader.

After participants have guessed their activities, discuss what types of questions got the most informative responses, whether each person considers the activity to be leisure, which activities were the hardest to guess or respond to, and what activities were familiar to the participants.

DEBRIEFING QUESTIONS

1. How easy or difficult was it to guess your activity?
2. What types of questions yielded the most informative responses?
3. Do you think of that activity as a leisure activity?
4. What other leisure activities were mentioned today?
5. Before you guessed your activity correctly, what else did you think it might be?
6. Which activities mentioned today are new to you?
7. Which activities mentioned today are familiar to you?
8. Which activities do you participate in?
9. Which activities would you like to learn?
10. Which activities share common characteristics?
11. Why might it be helpful to know the common characteristics?
12. Summarize what you learned form this activity today.

LEADERSHIP CONSIDERATIONS

1. Encourage people to interact and ask questions of several participants.
2. Give limited clues if some group members have a low frustration tolerance.

VARIATIONS

1. Activity cards can be developed according to themes, such as sports, activities done in the home, activities done alone, or large group activities.
2. Instead of asking questions, have the other participants act out the activity when the person comes near.
3. Have pictures of the activities or the equipment they require instead of the words written out.
4. Limit each participant to 5–7 questions.

CONTRIBUTOR

Jean Folkerth

PAST, CURRENT, AND FUTURE LEISURE

SPACE REQUIREMENTS

Classroom or activity room

MATERIALS

Handout, pencils

GROUP SIZE

Individuals or small group

GOALS

1. To improve participants' ability to identify previous and current leisure interests and skills.

2. To improve participants' ability to clarify goals for leisure participation in the future.

3. To increase participants' awareness of leisure options, resources, and constraints.

PREPARATION

Gather materials
Make one copy of the handout for each participant

ACTIVITY DESCRIPTION

Ask participants to gather around a table or sit in a circle. Discuss how leisure changes across the life span, especially with the occurrence of disability or illness.

Distribute a copy of the handout and a pencil to each person. Participants complete the form and then discuss answers. Each category of leisure should have 1 or 2 activities for the particular heading.

Allow time to discuss answers for future leisure participation and problem solving regarding this issue. Discussion may focus on the differences between past, current and future leisure involvement, what barriers or constraints have changed the participants' activities, and how leisure barriers may be overcome through selection of different activities or adaptation.

DEBRIEFING QUESTIONS

1. Compare your past, present, and predicted future leisure activities. What are the similarities? What are the differences?

2. What patterns do you find in your leisure participation?

3. How important do you consider your leisure time to be?

4. What benefits do you gain from participating in leisure?

5. What are some of the barriers that prevent you from participating as much as you would like to?

6. Why is it important to plan your leisure?

7. What sorts of leisure activities require planning?

8. What are the advantages of having several leisure alternatives in mind?

9. What activity would you like to participate in next week?

10. What goals or objectives do you need to accomplish to participate in this activity?

11. How does setting goals help us make sure we accomplish them?

LEADERSHIP CONSIDERATIONS

1. Explore the issue of why participants "gave up" leisure interests from their past.

2. Focus on future leisure goals.

VARIATIONS

1. Verbally implement the activity if participants have difficulty writing.

2. Modify categories depending on the needs and leisure interests of the participants.

CONTRIBUTOR

Diane Wagner

PAST, CURRENT, AND FUTURE LEISURE

	PAST	PRESENT	FUTURE

Craft

_____

Community Activity

_____

Something you do with your
hands (e.g., woodworking)

_____

Card game

_____

Board game

_____

Social activity

_____

Form of exercise

_____

Passive activity
(e.g., reading, listening to music)

_____

Spectator activity
(e.g., watching sports, movies)

_____

Outdoor activity

_____

LEISURE ACTIVITY MOBILE

SPACE REQUIREMENTS

Classroom or activity room with tables and chairs

MATERIALS

Magazines, construction paper, heavy string, 1/4" dowel rods cut in 4"–6" pieces (or drinking straws), scissors, glue or tape, crayons, paper clips

GROUP SIZE

Small group

GOALS

1. To increase participants' knowledge of a variety of leisure activities.
2. To increase participants' ability to identify and discuss their favorite leisure activities.

PREPARATION

Gather materials
Make sample mobile

ACTIVITY DESCRIPTION

Ask participants to gather around a table. Place materials in the center of the table. Introduce the activity by explaining that each participant will make a leisure activity mobile of their favorite activities. Each person should think about 5–6 of their favorite activities and look for examples in the magazines.

When a picture is found it is cut out and pasted on a piece of construction paper. When 5–6 pictures are found, assemble them into an activity mobile that can hang from the ceiling or light fixture. Pictures may be on one or both sides of the construction paper. (If pictures are not balanced, paper clips can be taped to the back of the paper.)

Encourage discussion throughout concerning how participants' activities are similar or different and how they were chosen. After each person has completed a mobile, facilitate a discussion on what types of activities they enjoy, when they last participated in the activity, and who they typically participate with, depending on the previous leisure education sessions held. Each participant may be asked to describe or explain his or her activity mobile to the group.

DEBRIEFING QUESTIONS

1. What are some of the activities most frequently identified today?
2. What are some unique activities identified today?
3. Explain your favorite leisure activities and why you selected them to the group.
4. How similar are each of the activities you identified?
5. How often do you participate in your identified activities?
6. In one sentence, tell the group what your choice of leisure activities says about you.
7. How would your mobile have been different 5, 10, or 15 years ago?
8. How will it be different 5, 10, or 15 years from now?
9. What are some reasons your leisure interests may have changed or will change?

LEADERSHIP CONSIDERATIONS

1. Help participants become aware of their leisure interests, without stressing making "ideal" or artistic mobiles.
2. Magazines should include a variety of leisure activities pictured.
3. Participants may be encouraged to sketch their activities with crayons or drawing pencils instead.

VARIATIONS

1. Focus the mobile on activities done alone, in the home, or with their family, depending on the purpose of the leisure education session.
2. Mobiles can be made with leisure equipment (e.g., racquets, books, paintbrushes) if strong dowel rods and lightweight rope are used.

CONTRIBUTOR

Norma J. Stumbo, Adapted from: Borba, M. and Borba, C. (1982). *Self-esteem: A classroom affair* (Vol. 2). Minneapolis, MN: Winston Press, Inc.

KITCHEN BINGO

SPACE REQUIREMENTS

Classroom or activity room

MATERIALS

Bingo card, pictures, bingo chips, scissors, glue, caller's list

GROUP SIZE

Small group

GOALS

1. To increase the participants' recognition of commonly used kitchen utensils.

2. To increase participants' ability to relate kitchen utensils to the act of cooking.

PREPARATION

Make one copy of the bingo card and pictures for each participant

ACTIVITY DESCRIPTION

Ask participants to gather around a table or sit in a circle. Kitchen bingo is played the same as standard bingo. Each participant receives a bingo card, a sheet of 16 pictures of kitchen items, and several bingo chips. Participants cut and paste the 16 pictures onto their bingo cards. Call items from the list one at a time and the players find the symbol and cover it on their game boards. A person wins when an entire row (horizontal, vertical, or diagonal) is covered.

Discussion may focus on how each utensil is used in cooking, how many of the participants recognize the utensils as ones in their own kitchens , how often the individuals cook, or the individuals' favorite foods to cook.

DEBRIEFING QUESTIONS

1. How many of the utensils were familiar to you prior to the game?

2. How many of the utensils were new to you prior to the game?

3. How often during the week do you cook in your own home?

4. What is your favorite food to cook?

5. How is each of the utensils used in cooking?

6. Where is a good place to buy kitchen utensils?

7. Can cooking be considered a leisure activity?

8. How many of you enjoy cooking?

9. How many of these utensils are in your kitchen?

LEADERSHIP CONSIDERATIONS

1. Allow ample learning/review time prior to the actual activity.

2. Eliminate or add different utensils that may be used in the current cooking groups.

VARIATIONS

1. Have the actual utensils available so the group can associate them with the drawings. Hold up the utensil and say its name during the game and participants can then find it on their card.

2. For more advanced groups, state the use of the utensil and have the group identify it on the form.

CONTRIBUTOR

Cheryl Gordon

KITCHEN BINGO CALLER'S LIST

Mixer
Measuring spoons
Coffee pot
Metal spatula
Drinking glass
Ladle
Salt and pepper shakers
Place setting
Blender
Paper towels
Tea kettle
Rolling pin
Waffle iron
Microwave
Cookie jar
Toaster

KITCHEN BINGO

KITCHEN BINGO

THREE SIDES OF SELF

SPACE REQUIREMENTS

Classroom or activity room

MATERIALS

Handout, pencils

GROUP SIZE

Small group

GOALS

1. To improve participants' understanding of the negative and positive messages they receive(d) during childhood.

2. To improve participants' understanding of who the strongest messages come/came from.

3. To improve participants' understanding of how these messages affect their physical, thinking, and social self-images.

4. To improve participants' ability to overcome or build on other people's messages to improve their self-identity.

PREPARATION

Gather materials
Make one copy of the handout for each participant

ACTIVITY DESCRIPTION

Ask participants to gather around a table or sit in a circle. Give each participant a copy of the handout and a pencil. Explain that the purpose is to explore messages that we each receive about ourselves from others. The feedback that we get help us to form our identities and self-images. These messages may come in three forms: physical, thinking, and social. All three become integrated into how we view ourselves.

Ask participants to recall childhood messages or images that they have within each of the three areas that are negative (top half of form). In each circle, the participants are to place the types of negative messages that they received from others about this aspect (e.g., physical—being called "fatty" or not being picked for the dodgeball game; thinking—being held back in school or not learning as fast as other students; social—not getting invited to parties or not being asked for a date).

Give participants 5–10 minutes to think about the kinds of negative messages they were given as children and teenagers from parents, teachers, adults, or other children. When the participants are finished, the leader should help process some of these incidences, noting who the strongest messages came from and how they affected the participant.

The second set of circles is for positive messages about the same three areas (physical, thinking, and social). Ask participants to complete these circles (bottom half of form) in the same manner as before, only with positive messages they received.

Again allow 5–10 minutes for completion. Help the group process the positive messages, noting specific incidences and message senders. The final discussion focuses on how we are affected by other people's perceptions of us and how this can be built on or reversed. Encourage awareness of the messages and where they came from. Begin to either strengthen them (for positive ones) or defeat them (for negative ones). Strategies for overcoming the negative messages should be shared with the group.

DEBRIEFING QUESTIONS

1. What are some strong negative messages you received about your physical self?

2. What are some strong negative messages you received about your thinking self?

3. What are some strong negative messages you received about your social self?

4. What are some strong positive messages you received about your physical self?

5. What are some strong positive messages you received about your thinking self?

6. What are some strong positive messages you received about your social self?

7. From whom did the majority of these messages come?

8. How have these messages affected the way you view yourself?

9. What are some strategies for filtering out the helpful messages from the harmful ones?

10. How can you strengthen the helpful messages?

11. How can you weaken or ignore the harmful messages?

12. What can you do to create a more positive self-identity?

LEADERSHIP CONSIDERATIONS

1. Participants should be able to choose not to share information with the group.

2. Know participants well enough so that potentially harmful situations can be controlled.

VARIATIONS

1. Activity may be used with children to determine current messages and how they feel about them.

2. Activity may be used with parents to determine the types of messages they may be giving to their children.

CONTRIBUTOR

Norma J. Stumbo, Adapted from: Borba, M. and Borba, C. (1982). *Self-esteem: A classroom affair* (Vol. 2). Minneapolis, MN: Winston Press, Inc.

THREE SIDES OF SELF

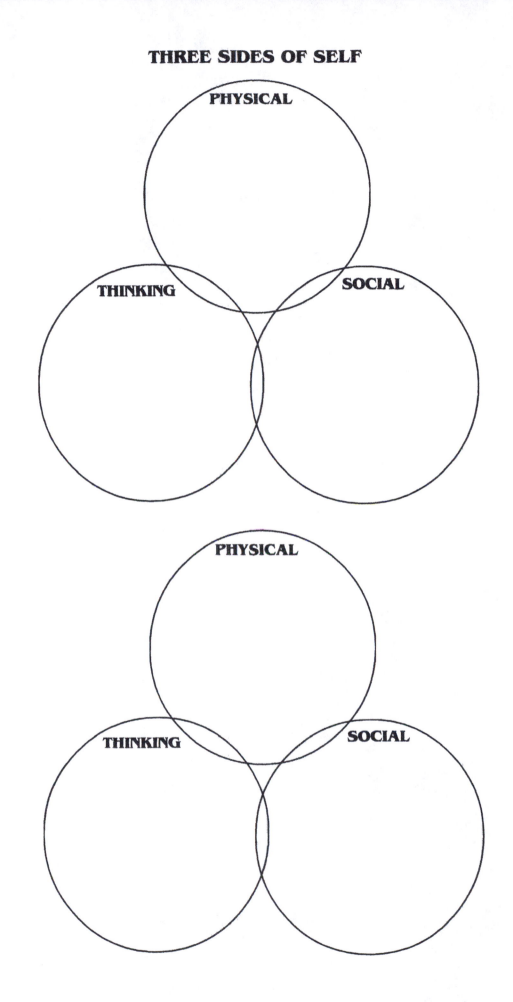

LEISURE ACTIVITY AWARENESS

SPACE REQUIREMENTS

Classroom or activity room

MATERIALS

Handout, answer key, pencils

GROUP SIZE

Small group

GOALS

1. To increase participants' awareness of various types of leisure activities.
2. To increase participants' cognitive and problem-solving skills.

PREPARATION

Gather materials
Make one copy of the handout for each participant

ACTIVITY DESCRIPTION

Have group form circle and distribute handouts and pencils. Introduce the activity's purpose of helping the participants become aware of various types of leisure activities. This will be accomplished through a game format where the participants are given letter and word clues in order to discover the incomplete leisure activity word. The letter clues are the vowels found in each of the words. The word clues are objects related to the activity. Allow 10–15 minutes.

After completion, discussion may focus on how difficult the activity was, how familiar the group's participants are with each of the activities, or how the word clues relate to the activities.

DEBRIEFING QUESTIONS

1. How easy or difficult did you think this activity was?
2. How much did the clues help you name the activity?
3. Were any activities mentioned new to you?
4. Which of the activities are your favorites?
5. Which of the activities would you like to learn?
6. Do all these activities represent leisure to you?
7. Describe the variety of the activities mentioned today.
8. If you could add two of your favorite activities to this game, what would they be?

LEADERSHIP CONSIDERATIONS

1. Encourage the participants to attempt figuring out the word before using the word clue for help.

VARIATIONS

1. Depending on cognitive level of participants, may need to include first letter of activities for an additional clue.
2. Substitute activities or topics that relate to the leisure education session.

CONTRIBUTORS

John Paule, Jean Folkerth

ANSWERS

1. Football
2. Golf
3. Racquetball
4. Lacrosse
5. Tennis
6. Hockey
7. Volleyball
8. Baseball
9. Wallyball
10. Jogging
11. Badminton
12. Soccer
13. Archery
14. Swimming
15. Bowling
16. Fishing
17. Weightlifting
18. Fencing
19. Skiing
20. Aerobics
21. Pet Care
22. Reading
23. Traveling
24. Lounging

LEISURE ACTIVITY AWARENESS

Directions: Complete the leisure activities below by using the letter clues (which are all the vowels of the word) and word clues to the right.

1. _ O O _ _ A _ _   Yardlines

2. _ O _ _   Clubs

3. _ A _ _ U E _ _ A _ _   Court

4. _ A _ _ O _ _ E   Long Handled Stick

5. _ E _ _ I _   Racquet

6. _ O _ _ E _   Goal

7. _ O _ _ E _ _ A _ _   Net

8. _ A _ E _ A _ _   Bat

9. _ A _ _ _ _ A _ _   Walls

10. _ O _ _ I _ _   Sweats

11. _ A _ _ I _ _ O _   Birdie

12. _ O _ _ E _   Kicking

13. A _ _ _ E _ _   Bow

14. _ _ I _ _ I _ _   Water

15. _ O _ _ I _ _   Lanes

16. _ I _ _ I _ _   Pole

17. _ E I _ _ _ _ I _ _ I _ _   Bench

18. _ E _ _ I _ _   Foil or Saber

19. _ _ I I _ _   Snow or Water

20. _ E _ O _ I _ _   High, Low, or Step

21. _ E _   _ A _ E   Arf!

22. _ E A _ I _ _   Novel Experience

23. _ _ A _ E _ I _ _   Abroad

24. _ O U _ _ I _ _   Laid Back

LEISURE PICTOGRAMS

SPACE REQUIREMENTS

Classroom or activity room

MATERIALS

Handout, answer key, pencils

GROUP SIZE

Small group

GOALS

1. To increase participant's knowledge of a variety of leisure activities.
2. To increase participants' problem-solving abilities, with regard to leisure.

PREPARATION

Gather materials
Make one copy of the handout for each participant

ACTIVITY DESCRIPTION

Ask participants to gather around a table or sit in a circle. Introduce the activity by stating that there are a variety of leisure activities available to the participants. It may be necessary to share some examples of these with the participants. Ask some of the participants to name some leisure activities that they participate in. Distribute the handouts and pencils. The purpose of this exercise is to decipher the pictograms into common leisure activities. Generally, the diagrams are phonetic versions of the activities. Allow 5–10 minutes.

After participants have completed all or most of the pictograms, ask them which ones were the hardest, in which of the activities they have participated, and in which they would like to participate.

DEBRIEFING QUESTIONS

1. How easy or difficult was it to decipher the activities?
2. How did you problem-solve to find the answers?
3. In which of these activities have you participated?
4. Which is your favorite activity?
5. Which would you like to participate in?

LEADERSHIP CONSIDERATIONS

1. Some of the pictograms are harder than others. Select the ones that the group will have the least trouble with to start the activity.
2. This activity probably best suited for use as a "warm-up" activity to a longer leisure education program on the diversity of leisure activities.

VARIATIONS

1. Devise original pictograms, depending on the topics or activities to be covered.
2. Ask the participants to develop their own set of pictograms of their favorite leisure activities.

CONTRIBUTOR

Jean Folkerth

ANSWERS

Free time
Bowling
Bridge
Tennis
Archery
Hiking
Bird watching
Photography
Badminton
Wheelchair basketball
Canoeing
Gardening
Movies
Aerobics
Karate
Rugby

LEISURE PICTOGRAMS

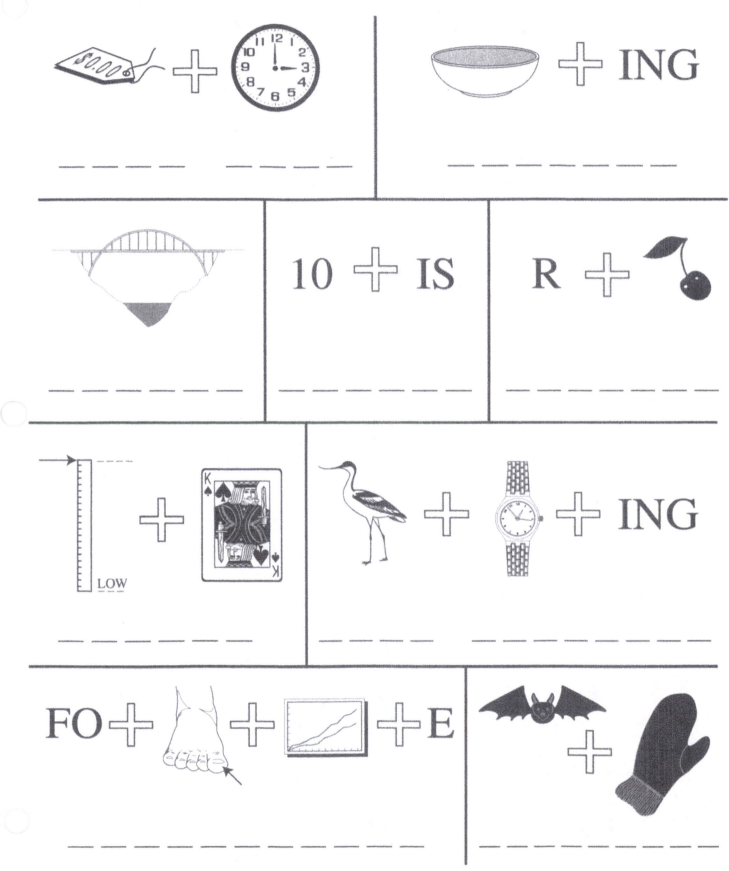

LEISURE PICTOGRAMS

LEISURE SEARCH

SPACE REQUIREMENTS

Classroom or activity room

MATERIALS

Handout, answer key, pencils

GROUP SIZE

Small group

GOALS

1. To improve participants' knowledge of a variety of leisure activities.
2. To increase participants' word recognition and concentration skills.

PREPARATION

Gather materials
Make one copy of the handout for each participant

ACTIVITY DESCRIPTION

Have participants sit around a table or at desks. Distribute copies of handout and pencils. Introduce activity by stating that there are a number of leisure activities and hobbies. The purpose of the activity is to introduce participants to a variety of leisure activities.

If participants are unfamiliar with word-find and fill-in-the-blank types of puzzles, explain that the words may be found going across, down or diagonally within the top portion. When a word is circled, they are then to fill in the blanks below for each of the 25 words found. Words that do not fit on the list below do not count.

Allow 10–15 minutes for completion. After participants are finished, begin discussion on the various activities or hobbies listed by asking questions such as if anyone participates in any of the activities, where they might go to participate, or how one might learn a new skill.

DEBRIEFING QUESTIONS

1. How many of the activities are familiar to you?
2. In which activities have you participated?
3. In which activities would you like to participate?
4. Which of the group members share similar interests?
5. Which of the group members has a unique interest?
6. How diverse are your own leisure interests?
7. Where do you go to participate in your leisure activities?
8. Do any of your leisure interests require equipment?
9. Who do you usually participate with?
10. Where can you go to learn new leisure skills?

LEADERSHIP CONSIDERATIONS

1. Participants must have sufficient cognitive and problem-solving skills to complete the activity. If not, the activity may be completed in pairs or groups.
2. The activity should be used as a discussion starter to begin a leisure awareness session.

VARIATIONS

1. The activity can either be played competitively (e.g., timed, first one done wins) or cooperatively (e.g., partners).
2. Adapt the words so they fit with typical activities of the participants or a theme (e.g., seasonal activities).
3. Replace the activities with leisure resources (e.g., pieces of equipment, places to go in the community).

CONTRIBUTORS

D. Clawson, Jean Folkerth

ANSWERS

1. Cross stitch
2. Reading
3. Bowling
4. Weaving
5. Racing spectator
6. Dancing
7. Marbles
8. Music listening
9. Yoga
10. Golf
11. Driving
12. Badminton
13. Fishing
14. Hockey
15. Swimming
16. Cycling
17. Darts
18. Horseshoes
19. Checkers
20. Painting
21. Pottery
22. Euchre
23. Cooking
24. Photography
25. Singing

LEISURE SEARCH

```
R G U E R H C U E G N I T N I A P P
D A R T S O M D D A D G Y Y Q E M H
A D C H E C K E R S Y M R G Y U S O
N G N I L W O B I G H E E B S Y W T
C A G O N U K N E C T M B I V G B O
I H N W K G G M T T S J C Y N A F G
N O I F F I S I O E B L X I D N L R
G C H E N I T P O W I O L M O S O A
N K S G G S H E S V C I V Y W G P
I E I I S E S A T C Y N P O P I N H
K Y F S L E V E D C T X G B B M I Y
O W O B S I N C N O I A Z Z M M V O
O R R R N I T R N A S T T E R I I M
C A O G N F L E I S U R E O T N R X
M H L G E I S U G N I D A E R G D E
```

FILL IN THE BLANKS AND CIRCLE THE WORD.

Example: L E I S U R E

1. C _ _ _ S S _ _ _ _ H   14. H _ _ _ _ Y

2. R _ _ _ _ _ G   15. S _ _ _ _ _ _ G

3. B _ _ _ _ _ G   16. C _ _ _ _ _ G

4. W _ _ _ _ _ G   17. D _ _ _ S

5. R _ _ _ _ G S _ _ _ _ _ _ _ R   18. H _ _ _ _ _ _ _ _ S

6. D _ _ _ _ _ G   19. C _ _ _ _ _ _ S

7. M _ _ _ _ _ S   20. P _ _ _ _ _ _ G

8. M _ _ _ C L _ _ _ _ _ _ _ G   21. P _ _ _ _ _ Y

9. Y _ _ A   22. E _ _ _ _ E

10. G _ _ F   23. C _ _ _ _ _ G

11. D _ _ _ _ _ G   24. P _ _ _ _ _ _ _ _ _ Y

12. B _ _ _ _ _ _ _ N   25. S _ _ _ _ _ G

13. F _ _ _ _ _ G

LEISURE WORD SCRAMBLE

SPACE REQUIREMENTS

Classroom or activity room

MATERIALS

Handout, answer key, pencils

GROUP SIZE

Small group

GOALS

1. To improve participants' knowledge of a variety of leisure activities.
2. To increase participants' word recognition and concentration skills.

PREPARATION

Gather materials
Make one copy of the handout for each participant

ACTIVITY DESCRIPTION

Have participants sit around a table or at desks. Distribute copies of the handout and pencils. Introduce the activity by stating that there are a number of various leisure activities and hobbies.

If participants are unfamiliar with word scramble puzzles, explain that the letters of each word are mixed up and the object is to unscramble the word to find a leisure activity.

Allow 10–15 minutes for completion. After participants are finished, begin discussion on the various activities or hobbies listed by asking questions such as if anyone participates in any of the activities, where they might go to participate, or how one might learn a new skill.

DEBRIEFING QUESTIONS

1. How many of the activities are familiar to you?
2. In which activities have you participated?
3. In which activities would you like to participate?
4. Which group members share similar interests?
5. Which group members have unique interests?
6. How diverse are your own leisure interests?
7. Where do you go to participate in your leisure activities?
8. Do any of your leisure interests require equipment?
9. Who do you usually participate with?
10. Where can you go to learn new leisure skills?

LEADERSHIP CONSIDERATIONS

1. Activity requires cognitive skills and letter/word recognition. If participants are unable to complete on their own, the activity may be completed in pairs or groups.
2. The activity should be used as a discussion starter to begin a leisure awareness session.

VARIATIONS

1. Scrambled words can be changed to meet the needs of the participants and the topic(s) of discussion.
2. Clues might be given for difficult words.
3. The activity can either be played competitively (e.g. timed, first one done wins) or cooperatively (e.g., partners).

CONTRIBUTOR

Jean Folkerth

ANSWERS

1. Skiing
2. Bowling
3. Basketball
4. Games
5. Baseball
6. Arts and crafts
7. Tennis
8. Badminton
9. Fishing
10. Reading
11. Swimming
12. Painting
13. Hockey
14. Biking
15. Aerobics

LEISURE WORD SCRAMBLE

1. kisign   _____

2. wblnogi   _____

3. sabakletlb   _____

4. msage   _____

5. abseblal   _____

6. rtsa nda fctasr   _____

7. tnines   _____

8. miadnbnto   _____

9. hifisgn   _____

10. irnedga   _____

11. wsimimgn   _____

12. inptnaig   _____

13. ohcyek   _____

14. kibgin   _____

15. srobaeic   _____

FUN AROUND THE CLOCK

SPACE REQUIREMENTS

Classroom or activity room

MATERIALS

Handout, pencils

GROUP SIZE

Small group

GOALS

1. To improve participants' interaction with others in a group setting.
2. To improve participants' awareness of leisure activities.

PREPARATION

Gather materials
Make one copy of the handout for each participant

ACTIVITY DESCRIPTION

Ask participants to gather around a table or sit in a circle. Give each group member a copy of the handout and a pencil. Explain that when a certain time is called out, each participant must find someone who meets that description. The participants should introduce themselves to each other and have them sign his or her name on the line next to it. Allow 30 seconds per time called. Each participant can sign each person's form only once and you should not sign any forms. The one with the largest number of names collected wins (although having a winner is not necessary). This activity could be used as a mixer at the start of a leisure education session.

DEBRIEFING QUESTIONS

1. Introduce yourself to the group and tell about your favorite leisure activities.
2. Describe what you have in common with two members in the group.
3. Who in the group shares a leisure interest with you?

LEADERSHIP CONSIDERATIONS

1. Make sure there is plenty of room to move about.
2. Make sure that people stop long enough to introduce themselves.

VARIATIONS

1. Categories can be changed to meet the needs of the participants and topic(s) of discussion.
2. At the end of the activity, ask participants to introduce each other by what they have in common.

CONTRIBUTOR

Jean Folkerth

FUN AROUND THE CLOCK

1:00   Likes the same music _____

2:00   Has the same kind of pet _____

3:00   Likes the same kind of exercise _____

4:00   Lettered in the same sport in high school or college _____

5:00   Dislikes the same sport _____

6:00   Has the same hobby _____

7:00   Likes to read the same kinds of books _____

8:00   Reads the same newspaper _____

9:00   Collects the same things _____

10:00   Likes the same food _____

11:00   Enjoys the same vacation spot _____

12:00   Likes the same television program _____

FEELINGS CONNECTION

SPACE REQUIREMENTS

Classroom or activity room

MATERIALS

Handout, pencils

GROUP SIZE

Small group

GOALS

1. To increase participants' awareness of different types of feelings associated with leisure activities.

2. To encourage group cooperation through sharing of feelings and personal experiences.

PREPARATION

Gather materials
Make one copy of the handout for each participant

ACTIVITY DESCRIPTION

Have the group form a circle and distribute the handout and pencils. Introduce the activity by saying that each of us has personal feelings or impressions about certain leisure activities. We often participate in activities, not because of the physical requirements of the activity, but for the feelings that they evoke from us. For example, we all have certain feelings about "birthday parties" or "vacations." In this activity, each person will write down activities associated with certain feelings and share their answers with the group. Allow 10 minutes.

Read through the list of feelings, encouraging participants to share and explain their answers with other group members. Draw out similarities and differences among group members.

To close the discussion, focus on selecting activities that encourage or diminish certain feelings. For example, if a person is bored, he/she may want to try _____ but stay away from _____ . This may be one consideration in the leisure planning process.

DEBRIEFING QUESTIONS

1. What feelings do you most associate with leisure in general?

2. What feelings does your favorite activity invoke?

3. What were the similarities among the activities mentioned by group members?

4. What were the differences among the activities mentioned by group members?

5. Are feelings during leisure unique to the person or similar among everyone?

6. When you know what activities evoke certain feelings, how does this help you plan?

7. What did you learn about leisure and feelings today?

8. How can you use this information to plan for your leisure?

LEADERSHIP CONSIDERATION

1. Participants can list more than one activity per feeling if they so choose.

VARIATIONS

1. Have participants exchange completed forms with other group members and try to guess by the responses to whom the paper belongs.

2. The list of feelings can be changed to meet the needs of the group and topic(s) of discussion.

CONTRIBUTORS

Gretchen Nachazel, Jean Folkerth

FEELINGS CONNECTION

WHAT LEISURE ACTIVITY MAKES YOU FEEL . . .

Entertained? _____

Relaxed? _____

Challenged? _____

Excited? _____

Bored? _____

Satisfied? _____

Invigorated? _____

Romantic? _____

Competitive? _____

Frustrated? _____

Cooperative? _____

Creative? _____

Healthy? _____

Anxious? _____

Happy? _____

Satisfied? _____

LEISURE ASSERTIVENESS: REASONS OR EXCUSES?

SPACE REQUIREMENTS

Classroom or activity room

MATERIALS

Handout, pencils

GROUP SIZE

Small group

GOALS

1. To increase participants' awareness of how leisure time is spent.
2. To increase participants' awareness of whether they use reasons or excuses for not participating in leisure activities.
3. To increase participant's awareness of the importance of scheduling time for leisure participation.

PREPARATION

Gather materials
Make one copy of the handout for each participant

ACTIVITY DESCRIPTION

Have the group form a circle and distribute the handouts and pencils. Introduce the purpose of the activity: to examine each person's leisure time, how it is used, and how it might be used better.

Have participants complete the handout in stages. The first stage is to list 10 leisure activities that they enjoy doing. Allow 5 minutes. The second stage is to estimate how much time per week is devoted to the activity. Allow 5 minutes. The third stage is to decide whether they have a valid reason or an excuse for not participating more in activities they enjoy. Allow 5 minutes.

Discussion should focus on their favorite activities, how much time is spent on them each week and the reasons or excuses they have for not participating as much as they like. Focus on making time for leisure participation on a daily or weekly basis. This activity may be used prior to a session on leisure planning and decision-making skills.

DEBRIEFING QUESTIONS

1. How much time do you spend, on average, on leisure per week?
2. Would you like to spend more or less time on your leisure?
3. Why do you not spend the amount of time you want to on your leisure?
4. Would most people see these as reasons or excuses?
5. What kind of priority do you give to your leisure time?
6. What kind of decisions would you need to make to align your current leisure pattern with your ideal leisure pattern?
7. What might be a starting point for moving in that direction?
8. What would you need to plan or do differently than you currently do?
9. What barriers (or excuses) do you need to remove before you start?
10. How motivated are you to make this change?
11. What is your next step?

LEADERSHIP CONSIDERATION

1. Participants should be encouraged to be honest with their answers and to share only the amount of information they feel comfortable with.

VARIATIONS

1. The activity could focus on the reasons/excuses for nonparticipation. For example, are these similar reasons/excuses they use for not doing other things (e.g., related to work or family?). Is there a pattern of reasons/excuses they use?
2. Create another column on the form for listing the exact reasons or excuses used.
3. Time frame may be changed to "time each month" depending on the group.

CONTRIBUTORS

John Paule, Jean Folkerth

LEISURE ASSERTIVENESS

DIRECTIONS

1. List 10 leisure activities that you like to do now or would like to become more involved in.
2. List the approximate amount of time each week that you participate in this activity.
3. Check either the Reason or Excuse column, depending on whether you think you have a valid reason or make excuses for not participating more in the activity.

ACTIVITY	TIME EACH WEEK	REASON?	EXCUSE?
1. _____	_____	_____	_____
2. _____	_____	_____	_____
3. _____	_____	_____	_____
4. _____	_____	_____	_____
5. _____	_____	_____	_____
6. _____	_____	_____	_____
7. _____	_____	_____	_____
8. _____	_____	_____	_____
9. _____	_____	_____	_____
10. _____	_____	_____	_____

EXPOSURE TO LEISURE FEELINGS

SPACE REQUIREMENTS

Classroom or activity room

MATERIALS

Handout, pencils

GROUP SIZE

Small group

GOALS

1. To increase participants' awareness of different leisure activities.
2. To increase participants' awareness of their current leisure participation patterns.
3. To increase participants' awareness of the feelings they get from participating in leisure activities.
4. To improve participants' communication and interaction skills in a small group situation.

PREPARATION

Gather materials
Make one copy of the handout for each participant

ACTIVITY DESCRIPTION

Have the group form a circle and distribute the handout and pencils. Introduce the activity by explaining that we may participate in a variety of leisure activities because of the feelings realized during the activity.

Have participants check their favorite activities from the list. They may add other activities not listed. Allow 5 minutes. From the activities they checked, have participants select their 5 favorite activities, listed in any order. Allow 2–3 minutes. Finally, they are to write in the feeling(s) they get from participating in these 5 favorite activities. Allow 5 minutes.

Discussion should focus on what activities were selected as the top 5. How were they chosen?

Was it difficult to narrow the list to just 5 or did they have a difficult time coming up with 5 activities?

Focus on what types of feelings were listed. What types of feelings do the participants seek in their leisure activities? Do they get these feelings just from leisure or from other areas of life (e.g., work) as well?

Close the discussion with a summary of the needs and feelings that leisure may provide.

DEBRIEFING QUESTIONS

1. Describe your favorite leisure activities.
2. How would you describe the pattern of your activities throughout the year?
3. What feelings do you seek during leisure activities?
4. What feelings do you avoid during your leisure activities?
5. Are the feelings that you seek found for you only in your leisure?
6. How do those feelings compare to other situations (e.g., work)?
7. How are your feelings during leisure different than other experiences?
8. Are feelings in leisure the same for every person?
9. Summarize what you've learned about feelings and leisure today.

LEADERSHIP CONSIDERATION

1. Note that many of the activities on the list are considered nontraditional leisure activities. Encourage participants to think broader than large-group physical skill activities.

VARIATION

1. Modify list depending on leisure activities/interests of the participants.

CONTRIBUTORS

Robert Wolfe, Jean Folkerth

EXPOSURE TO LEISURE FEELINGS

Directions: Check all the activities that you do on a regular basis.

_____ Talk or socialize	_____ Improve job skills	_____ Have fun
_____ Entertain	_____ Creative activities	_____ Escape
_____ Food activities (e.g., picnic, cookout, dining out)	_____ Make things	_____ Hide in house/room
	_____ Play games	_____ Hobbies
_____ Make music	_____ Crafts	_____ Keep mind active
_____ Relaxation	_____ Make transitions	_____ Work for money
_____ Fitness/exercise	_____ Family activities	_____ Travel/vacation
_____ Work for family/home	_____ Personal healthcare	_____ Explore new horizons
_____ Sports	_____ Outdoor recreation	_____ Plan for future
_____ Watch sports	_____ Help others	_____ Dance
_____ Home improvement/ maintenance	_____ Fix things	_____ Competitive activities
	_____ Hunt for food	_____ Buy for others
_____ Community groups	_____ Grow spiritually	_____ Addictions (e. g., smoking, drugs, drinking, eating, gambling)
_____ Listen to music	_____ Maintain plants	
_____ Attend church	_____ Nothing	_____ Self-improvement
_____ Study/learn	_____ Volunteer	_____ Care for pets

From the list above, select your 5 favorite activities and write the feelings associated with them.
Example   Activity *Hobbies*   Feelings *Satisfaction, enjoyment, sense of accomplishment*

| **Activity** | **Feeling(s)** |

1. _____

2. _____

3. _____

4. _____

5. _____

TIME WARP

SPACE REQUIREMENTS

Classroom or activity room

MATERIALS

Handout, pencils

GROUP SIZE

Small group

GOALS

1. To increase participants' understanding of their leisure activity values.
2. To increase participants' ability to use a group planning and decision-making process.
3. To increase participants' ability to compromise within a small group.

PREPARATION

Gather materials
Make one copy of the handout for each participant

ACTIVITY DESCRIPTION

Have the group form a circle and distribute the handout and pencils. Discuss values and how each person has an individually held value system. Most people do not think about their values until they come into conflict within another person's values. The second part of the activity will help participants learn compromise skills and let them see other people's values.

Instruct each person to look over the activities on the list and decide 5 activities that he or she would take with them into the future. Each person is to circle the 5 chosen activities. Individuals may not add activities to the list. Allow 5 minutes.

Form small groups (3–5 people) and have them discuss the chosen activities and come to a group consensus on only 5 activities. Allow 15–20 minutes. Each group then presents their choices to the others, explaining why each activity was chosen to take to the future. Other group members may make comments and note similarities and differences.

The discussion should focus on the values that the selected activities represent, how groups came to consensus, the apparent leaders and followers in each group, how individual values may be compromised temporarily for the group values, etc.

DEBRIEFING QUESTIONS

1. How did you select your own 5 activities?
2. How easy or difficult was this to do?
3. How did the small groups select their 5 activities?
4. How easy or difficult was this to do?
5. Who were the leaders and followers in your group?
6. How did the group incorporate everyone's values into one list?
7. How were disagreements settled?
8. How satisfied are you with the final list of your small group?
9. How similar or dissimilar were the activities mentioned by all the small groups?
10. What did you learn about your own leisure values today?
11. What did you learn about other people's leisure values today?
12. What did you learn about getting to group consensus today?
13. How will you use this information in the future?

LEADERSHIP CONSIDERATIONS

1. Encourage discussion between group members, with each person justifying why he or she selected certain activities.
2. Note how each group uses decision-making and compromise skills.

VARIATIONS

1. Have all groups make 1 list of 5 activities, going through another round of compromise and decision making.
2. Substitute list of activities with pieces of leisure-related equipment (e.g., tennis racquet, art works, golf carts).
3. Substitute list of activities with different places across the state or country (e.g., Sears Tower, Yosemite National Park).

CONTRIBUTORS

J. Kreimer, Jean Folkerth

TIME WARP

Scientists have discovered how to send people into the future. While discovering this, they also found that the people in the future do not know how to use their free time any other way except to watch television. You have been chosen you to come up with five activities to take to the future and teach them how to do leisure activities. Decide from the following list which activities would be the most beneficial to send to the future.

Football	Knitting
Bowling	Baseball
Lacrosse	Roller-skating
Basketball	Bike riding
Soccer	Reading
Coin collecting	Board games
Card games	Kite flying
Weightlifting	Cricket
Drawing	Golfing
Hiking	Ice skating
Jumping rope	Motorcycling
Racquetball	Downhill skiing
Water skiing	Surfing
Singing	Dancing
Puppetry	Running
Arts and crafts	Camping
Horseback riding	Exercising
Fishing	Tennis
Sailing	Ping-Pong
Video games	Polo
Volleyball	Painting
Weaving	Music
Pet shows	Canoeing
Amusement parks	Skateboarding
Hang gliding	Mountain climbing
Cross-country skiing	

LEISURE BRAINSTORMING

SPACE REQUIREMENTS

Classroom or activity room

MATERIALS

Handout, pencils

GROUP SIZE

Small group

GOALS

1. To increase participants' awareness of different types of leisure activities.
2. To increase participants' letter and word recognition skills.

PREPARATION

Gather materials

Make one copy of the handout for each participant

ACTIVITY DESCRIPTION

Have the group form a circle and distribute handouts and pencils. Discuss the wide variety of activities available for leisure participation. Discuss the group's definitions of leisure and what types of activities they consider to be leisure activities.

Instruct participants that they are to think of activities, experiences, or opportunities that begin with each letter of the alphabet and fill in the activity next to the letter on the handout. Encourage participants to be creative and think of nontraditional activities (e.g., plant care, reading the newspaper). Participants should work independently. Allow 5–10 minutes.

When finished, have each participant share his or her responses with the group. Encourage discussion of similarities and differences, whether some activities are seasonal, where the activities can take place, or if they require a partner or special equipment.

DEBRIEFING QUESTIONS

1. What was the most common leisure activity mentioned?
2. Which activities were mentioned once?
3. Which activities can you do in the summer? in the winter?
4. Which activities require a special facility?
5. Which activities require no special facility at all?
6. Which activities can be done alone?
7. Which activities require at least one other person?
8. Which is one of your favorite activities?
9. Which activity was new to you?
10. Does all leisure have to be an activity with a beginning and an end?
11. Summarize what you've learned about leisure activities today.

LEADERSHIP CONSIDERATIONS

1. Encourage creativity by having a few examples of nontraditional activities ready as needed.
2. Allow any activity as long as the participant considers it a leisure activity. If any activities are questioned, ask for group discussion or vote.

VARIATIONS

1. Modify the instructions so that participants come up with leisure resources, activities that require partners, or activities that can be done for less than $10.
2. If competition is warranted, give prizes for the most creative, most complete, or first to finish.

CONTRIBUTOR

Jean Folkerth

LEISURE BRAINSTORMING

A _____

B _____

C _____

D _____

E _____

F _____

G _____

H _____

I _____

J _____

K _____

L _____

M _____

N _____

O _____

P _____

Q _____

R _____

S _____

T _____

U _____

V _____

W _____

X _____

Y _____

Z _____

LEISURE AWARENESS CROSSWORD

SPACE REQUIREMENTS

Classroom or activity room

MATERIALS

Handout, answer key, pencils

GROUP SIZE

Small group

GOALS

1. To increase participants' awareness of leisure activities.
2. To improve participants' problem-solving skills.

PREPARATION

Gather materials
Make one copy of the handout for each participant

ACTIVITY DESCRIPTION

Have the group form a circle and distribute the handout and pencils. Introduce the activity by asking how many participants have done crossword puzzles before. Explain that a crossword puzzle will be used to help them identify leisure activities through the clues given. Allow 10–15 minutes.

Discussion should focus on what activities were hard to figure out, how participation in or knowledge of the activity helped some people figure out the words, or what other clues might have been given.

DEBRIEFING QUESTIONS

1. How many of you had completed crossword puzzles before?
2. How easy or difficult was it for you to complete the crossword?
3. Which types of clues were easiest to answer?
4. Was it easier to think of answers for those activities you've participated in before?
5. Write an alternate for one clue.
6. Which activities do you participate in?
7. Which activities would you like to participate in?
8. What other types of problems can you solve by searching for clues?
9. Summarize what you've learned today in this activity.

LEADERSHIP CONSIDERATIONS

1. If some people finish earlier than the others, have them provide additional clues for the words to the other participants.
2. This could be used as an introductory activity for other leisure education sessions.

VARIATIONS

1. Activity can either be done competitively or cooperatively.
2. Substitute local activities or facilities of interest to the participants.
3. Follow a theme related to a certain activity (e.g., baseball, a certain hobby, things to do at the mall).

CONTRIBUTORS

Mary Miller, Jean Folkerth

ANSWERS

ACROSS	DOWN
1. Table	1. Tennis
3. Swimming	2. Gym
6. VCR	4. Movie
8. Fishing	5. Golf
9. TV	7. Racquet
11. Loom	10. Volleyball
12. Brush	13. Hockey
14. Camera	15. Map
16. Pool	
17. Kite	

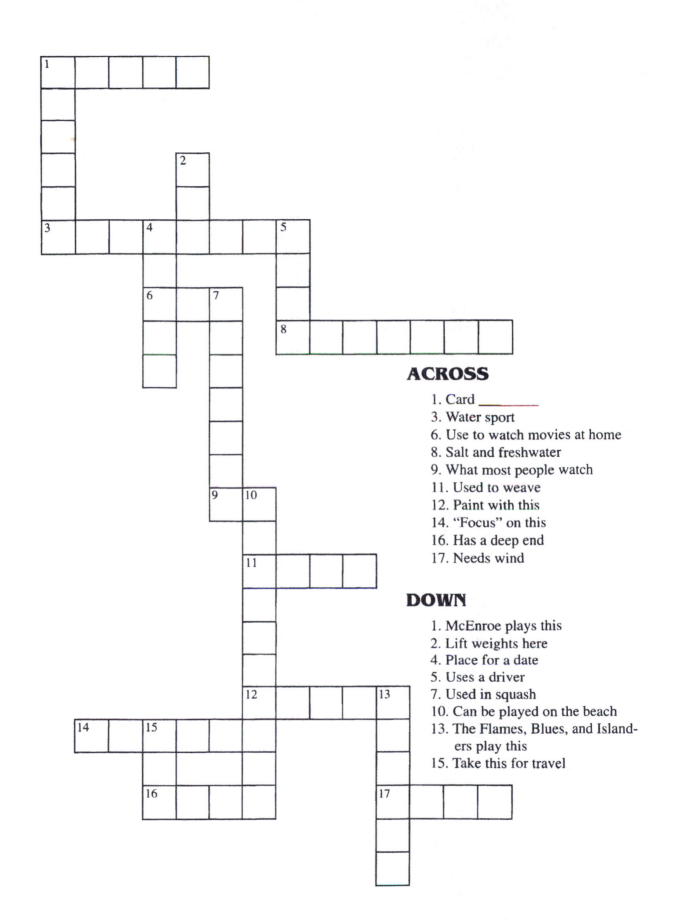

ACROSS

1. Card _____
3. Water sport
6. Use to watch movies at home
8. Salt and freshwater
9. What most people watch
11. Used to weave
12. Paint with this
14. "Focus" on this
16. Has a deep end
17. Needs wind

DOWN

1. McEnroe plays this
2. Lift weights here
4. Place for a date
5. Uses a driver
7. Used in squash
10. Can be played on the beach
13. The Flames, Blues, and Islanders play this
15. Take this for travel

LEISURE COLLAGE

SPACE REQUIREMENTS

Classroom or activity room with tables and chairs

MATERIALS

Magazines, glue, scissors, construction paper

GROUP SIZE

Small group

GOALS

1. To increase participants' awareness of their leisure interests and values.

2. To increase participants' ability to verbalize their leisure interests, values, and motivations in a small group.

3. To increase participants' ability to recognize similarities and differences in terms of leisure interests and values.

PREPARATION

Gather materials

ACTIVITY DESCRIPTION

Have group members sit around a table. Discuss leisure interests and values. For example, a person who enjoys running or jogging may value fitness, or a person who enjoys quilting may enjoy structure and creativity. Ask participants to name a favorite leisure activity and related values.

The purpose of the leisure collage is for participants to create a representation of their favorite leisure activities and the values they represent. Distribute the supply of magazines, construction paper, glue, and scissors. Each person is asked to create a collage that represents themselves and that they will share with the group after completion.

As participants are completing the collages, the leader may ask questions of the group about the particular collages they are working on, such as the last time they participated in certain activities, and if the collages have certain themes unfolding.

When participants are finished, each member shows his or her collage to the group and shares why each picture was selected and what it represents. Draw out similarities and differences and help participants note any particular themes.

DEBRIEFING QUESTIONS

1. Explain your collage to the group.
2. Why did you select each of the pictures to include in your collage?
3. What do each of these activities represent to you?
4. What interests do you share with others in the group?
5. What interests are unique to you?
6. Why are leisure interests so individualized?
7. What is the overall message or theme of your collage?
8. Would your leisure collage be the same a year from now? How might it change?
9. What did you learn about your own leisure interests and values today?
10. Summarize what you learned about the group's leisure interests and values.

LEADERSHIP CONSIDERATIONS

1. Supply a wide variety of magazines to represent a variety of interests.
2. Consider whether participants may use words as well as pictures.
3. Emphasize that neatness does not count as much as representing true interests and values.
4. Be aware that some participants may not be willing to share their collages.

VARIATIONS

1. Have participants make 3 collages representing past, present, and future leisure.
2. Emphasize self-expression by having participants create collages representing their personalities. Different pictures could be used, such as colors, facial expressions, articles of clothing, or weather.
3. Emphasize future leisure by creating collages of "leisure wish lists."

CONTRIBUTOR

Norma J. Stumbo

NAME THAT ACTIVITY

SPACE REQUIREMENTS

Classroom or activity room

MATERIALS

Cards with descriptions of leisure activities

GROUP SIZE

Small group

GOALS

1. To increase participants' awareness of a wide variety of leisure activities.
2. To increase participants' awareness of the characteristics of leisure activities.

PREPARATION

Gather materials
Make 1 copy for every 4 participants and cut into cards

ACTIVITY DESCRIPTION

Have participants sit around a table or in a circle. Ask group members to tell about their favorite activities. The purpose of this activity is to highlight the diversity of leisure activities and their characteristics.

Divide the group into teams of 4 players. Group members take turns reading the cards out loud and then naming a leisure activity that fits the description. Play continues until all cards are finished. There is no "winner" in this activity, although a game board may be created if desired.

During play, facilitate the discussion by clarifying whether the activities named meet the description and if participants have been involved in the activities. At the conclusion focus on how difficult it was for players to think of matching activities, if participating in a variety of leisure activities made answering easier, and the wide variety of activities available.

DEBRIEFING QUESTIONS

1. How easy or difficult was it to think of activities that matched the descriptions?

2. Was it easier if to think of activities if you are familiar with several leisure activities?
3. Which of the activities mentioned have you participated in?
4. Which of these activities would you like to participate in?
5. Give the group a clue for your favorite leisure activity and see if they can guess it.
6. Describe your own leisure activity participation.
7. How does your leisure activity participation compare with others in the group?
8. Summarize what you've learned during this activity today.

LEADERSHIP CONSIDERATION

1. Facilitate discussion among group members by asking open ended questions about the responses they give.

VARIATIONS

1. Instead of only one player responding to each description card, ask each player to name a different activity that matches the description, before proceeding to the next card.
2. Create different playing cards as needed to meet the purpose of the leisure education session.

CONTRIBUTOR

Norma J. Stumbo

SPORT YOU NEED A BALL TO PLAY	TYPE OF PHYSICAL EXERCISE
ARTS AND CRAFTS ACTIVITY	SPORT YOU PLAY WITH A CLUB
ACTIVITY THAT COSTS MONEY	PIECE OF SPORT EQUIPMENT
ACTIVITY YOU DO IN THE MOUNTAINS	SOMETHING CHECKED OUT OF A LIBRARY
SOCIAL GROUP TO JOIN	SOMETHING YOU CAN KNIT
ACTIVITY DONE IN THE COMMUNITY	ACTIVITY DONE ON GRASS
WINTER SPORT	TYPE OF DANCE
SOMETHING YOU CAN SEW	SOMETHING YOU CAN RENT

SPORT THAT REQUIRES ICE SKATES	ACTIVITY YOU CAN DO AT HOME
VOLUNTEER GROUP TO JOIN	INDOOR ACTIVITY
OUTDOOR SPORT	MUSICAL INSTRUMENT
INDIVIDUAL ACTIVITY	WHERE YOU FIND PUZZLES
SPORT YOU NEED TO SIT FOR	RECREATION ACTIVITY THAT COSTS NOTHING
CARD GAME THAT CAN BE PLAYED ALONE	SPORT YOU PLAY WITH A PARTNER
SOMETHING YOU FIND IN A MUSEUM	FAMILY LEISURE ACTIVITY
PIECE OF COMPUTER EQUIPMENT	BOOK TO READ FOR FUN

TYPE OF ART	ACTIVITY YOU CAN WALK TO
TYPE OF FESTIVAL	TEAM SPORT
RACQUET SPORT	BOARD GAME
ACTIVITY TO DO ON VACATION	WATER SPORT
PLACE TO VOLUNTEER	

A MATTER OF VALUES

SPACE REQUIREMENTS

Classroom or activity room

MATERIALS

List of values questions

GROUP SIZE

Small group

GOALS

1. To increase participants' awareness of personal values regarding leisure.
2. To increase participants' ability to empathize with other people's feelings and beliefs.
3. To increase participants' ability to publicly affirm own feelings.

PREPARATION

Gather materials

ACTIVITY DESCRIPTION

Have the group form a circle and introduce the topic of values clarification. The purpose of this activity is to increase awareness of personal values and to be able to justify or discuss them with others in a small group setting.

Read each question and lead a group discussion on the value it represents. Ensure that all answers are accepted by the group, and that each individual has an adequate chance to respond to each question. The debriefing questions below can be used for the closing discussion.

DEBRIEFING QUESTIONS

1. Which question was the easiest for you to answer?
2. Which question was the most difficult for you to answer?
3. What leisure values did your answers represent?
4. Discuss the value you give to leisure within your life.
5. How did others in the group differ from your values?
6. How do people develop their values toward leisure or anything else?
7. In just a few words, describe how much or how little you value your own leisure.
8. What did you learn about your leisure values today?
9. Why is it important to know about your leisure values?
10. Why is it important to know that your leisure values may differ from those of other people?
11. What did you learn today that you can use in the future?

LEADERSHIP CONSIDERATIONS

1. Do not allow participants to criticize others' beliefs or values during the discussion.
2. Encourage the acceptance of varying viewpoints of the participants.

VARIATIONS

1. Modify the questions to reflect the intent of the leisure education session.
2. Have the participants come up with questions they want the group to answer.

CONTRIBUTOR

Norma J. Stumbo
Adapted from: Stock, G. (1987). *The book of questions*. New York, NY: Workman Publishing Company, Inc.

A MATTER OF VALUES

1. Would you be willing to participate in an afternoon of mud volleyball with your best clothes on for $40,000?

2. Would $50,000 be enough money to induce you to put a loyal healthy pet to sleep?

3. If you could prevent either an earthquake in a foreign country that would kill 40,000 people, a plane crash at the local airport that would kill 200 people, or an automobile accident that would kill an acquaintance of yours, which would you choose? What if the person were a close friend?

4. Would you rather be happy but slow to learn and unimaginative or unhappy yet bright and creative?

5. For $1,000,000 would you be willing to never again see or talk to your best friend?

6. If you had to choose between a society without sport or a society without art, which would you choose?

7. If you could hold the title of world champion in any sport, what sport would it be?

8. Would you be willing to give up all television for the next five years if it would induce someone to provide for 1,000 starving children in a foreign country?

9. If you could have a leisurely 4-hour chat with any one in the world, living or dead, who would that be?

10. If you had $500 to either spend on a vacation, clothes, or relatives, which would you choose?

11. If you could only learn one new leisure skill in the next five years, what skill would you like to learn?

12. If you were banished to a remote island with no other people residing there, what three nonliving things would you take for your leisure time?

13. If you were notified that your home was going to burn to the ground tomorrow, what three things would you salvage today for your leisure time?

14. You are responsible for choosing one leisure activity to take into the next hundred years for all humanity. What activity would you choose?

15. You are hired to give a parents' clinic on childrearing. What one leisure value would you choose to tell the parents that they should teach their children?

16. You can receive personal instruction from a world renowned sports figure for a day. What sport would you choose to receive instruction in?

17. You are hired to design a park that encompasses one square city block. What types of things would you include in the park design?

PROBLEM SOLVING

SPACE REQUIREMENTS

Classroom or activity room

MATERIALS

List of possible problems

GROUP SIZE

Small group

GOALS

1. To increase participants' ability to think of alternatives to solve problems.

2. To have participants select the most appropriate or best alternative to solve a problem.

PREPARATION

Gather materials

ACTIVITY DESCRIPTION

Ask participants to gather around a table or sit in a circle. Introduce the activity by discussing problems and how they are solved. Many times people do not look at all the alternatives before they begin to take action to solve problems. The purpose of this activity is look at various problems and have the participants role-play some possible solutions. At the end of every "problem" the group will vote on the most appropriate solution.

Read one of the situations and ask for volunteers to role-play a solution to the problem. Allow 1–2 minutes for the individuals to decide how they want to act out the solution.

When the volunteers have thought of a possible solution, they act it out for the rest of the group. When all individuals have role-played a solution, the group first will clarify if they have any questions on the individual role-plays and then vote on the most appropriate solution.

Throughout the role-plays, note what types of role-plays win the group's votes. For example, the most creative, the simplest, or the one that requires others to help. These observations will be brought to the group's attention when finished.

Discussion may focus on why certain role-plays won votes, why other were rejected, the theme(s) that carried out through the role-plays, how solutions to problems are found, and what actions people take in real life.

DEBRIEFING QUESTIONS

1. How would you describe most of the solutions to these role-plays?
2. What were the common characteristics of the "winning" role-plays?
3. What were the common characteristics of those that did not win?
4. How do you usually come up with solutions to your problems?
5. How successful has this process been for you?
6. What other options are there that you choose not to take?
7. What would be the consequences if you chose these options?
8. How do we know whether we've found a good solution to a problem?
9. What did you learn about solving problems today?

LEADERSHIP CONSIDERATIONS

1. Introduce role-playing if the group is unfamiliar with it.
2. Encourage expressive role-plays so that people can be creative and group members' understanding is enhanced.

VARIATIONS

1. Choose different scenarios to be acted out based on the age, needs, and interests of the clients.
2. Eliminate the voting and just have the group discuss options that were acted out, plus any others they can think of.
3. Have the group come up with leisure scenarios that have given them problems.

CONTRIBUTOR

Norma J. Stumbo
Adapted from: Borba, M. and Borba, C. (1982). *Self-esteem: A classroom affair* (Vol. 2). Minneapolis, MN: Winston Press, Inc.

POSSIBLE PROBLEMS

1. You are fishing and your line is stuck to a rock.

2. Your bike has a flat tire. You're at school or at the mall.

3. You are swinging a bat at a ball and the bat breaks.

4. You are trying to read the newspaper outside on a windy day.

5. You have waited in line for an hour to see a movie and when you get to the ticket window, you realize you left your wallet at home.

6. Someone has taken your seat at a concert.

7. You are short and standing at the back of a crowd and can't see the main stage.

8. You are about to sneeze in the middle of a lecture on medieval art.

9. You can't get your motorcycle started.

10. Someone has taken your favorite toy.

11. You're the last person to be chosen for the team.

12. A bully at the park wants to take away your snacks.

13. You get to the swimming pool 5 minutes before it closes.

ARE YOU MORE LIKE . . .

SPACE REQUIREMENTS

Classroom or activity room with enough space for people to move about freely

MATERIALS

List of questions

GROUP SIZE

Small to large group

GOALS

1. To increase participants' ability to make decisions.
2. To increase participants' self-aware-ness of personal values and traits.
3. To increase participants' awareness of other people's personal values and traits; to examine differences and similarities among people.
4. To increase participants' ability to publicly affirm personal values.

PREPARATION

Gather materials

ACTIVITY DESCRIPTION

Ask participants to gather around a table or sit in a circle. Discuss differences and similarities among people's values. The purpose of this activity is for the participants to decide, when given two options, which of the options they are more like.

Have participants come to the center of the room. Read each pair of options and have group members individually decide which of the options they are most like. Designate to which side of the room they are to move. For example, if you are more like a teacher move to the right, if you are more like a student, move to the left.

Instruct participants to note who stands on their side of the room for each set of options. At the end of the activity, each individual will have to tell one person who is most like him or her, and one person who is most different from him or her.

Closing discussion should focus on similarities and differences, what people have learned about each other, and the importance of values.

DEBRIEFING QUESTIONS

1. Who was most like you? most unlike you?
2. Why are values important to have?
3. How do your values affect your thoughts and behaviors?
4. From what sources do you get your values system?
5. What types of events may change your value system?
6. Describe your values or attitudes to-ward leisure.
7. How did you develop these values or attitudes?
8. How do these values relate to other values or attitudes that you hold?
9. From where did you receive the stron-gest messages about leisure?
10. How have your values and attitudes affect your participation in leisure?
11. How might you want to change your values or attitudes toward leisure?
12. How do you think they might change in the future?
13. Describe what you've learned about your leisure values and attitudes today.

LEADERSHIP CONSIDERATIONS

1. Remind participants to observe other people's values so they can state simi-larities and differences at the end.
2. Group participants must choose 1 of the 2 options. Do not allow people to stand in the middle.
3. Allow enough time between options for people to make choices and con-verse with people within their group.

VARIATION

1. Modify the forced-choice options to meet the intent of the leisure education session and the needs of the group.

CONTRIBUTOR

Norma J. Stumbo

ARE YOU MORE LIKE. . .

1. A leader or a follower?

2. More physical or mental?

3. A paddle or a Ping-Pong ball?

4. A roller skate or a pogo stick?

5. A unicycle or a bicycle built for two?

6. A neighborhood park or an amusement park?

7. Work or leisure?

8. A romance novel or a comic book?

9. An acquaintance or a close friend?

10. *The Wall Street Journal* or *The National Enquirer*?

11. Christmas or the Fourth of July?

12. A hang glider or a gardener?

13. The present or the future?

14. A relaxing day in the country or a hustling day in the city?

15. A hot tomato or a couch potato?

16. A mirror or a window?

17. Tennis or badminton?

18. A snowflake or a raindrop?

19. Someone who sits on the outside looking in or someone who sits on the inside looking out?

20. An old movie classic or a short cartoon?

21. Swimming in deep waters or wading at shore?

22. A two-week vacation or a weekend jaunt?

23. A flannel shirt or a silk blouse?

24. An organized activity or a spontaneous play time?

25. A black and white photograph or a colorful collage?

CLARIFYING VALUES AND ACTIONS

SPACE REQUIREMENTS

Classroom or activity room

MATERIALS

Handout, pencils

GROUP SIZE

Small group

GOALS

1. To increase participants' awareness of personal values in relation to leisure.

2. To increase participants' understanding of how values are expressed through actions.

3. To increase participants' understanding of how values are reflected throughout life.

ACTIVITY DESCRIPTION

Have the group form a circle and distribute the handout and pencils. Discuss the definition of values and how they affect actions taken. Include the differences in people's values and actions, why these values are different, and how values relate to leisure.

Instruct participants to complete the handout by first listing their 5 most cherished values in the first column. Be prepared to give personal examples of his/her own leisure values. Allow 5 minutes.

Next, ask participants to think of actions that they take that express each of the values (second column) and actions that they take that oppose each of the values (third column). Allow 10 minutes.

Facilitate a discussion on each group member's values and how each person felt he or she expresses the value or opposed it. Allow other participants to provide feedback and alter-native ways of expressing values. The discussion may focus on what feelings occur when a strong value is repeatedly opposed and how to overcome that.

DEBRIEFING QUESTIONS

1. Describe your top 5 values to the group.

2. How similar or different are these from other members in the group?

3. Select 1 value. What actions do you take to reinforce that value? What actions detract from that value?

4. How are values related to actions?

5. How do you feel when your actions are in alignment with your values?

6. How do you feel when you actions are not in alignment with your values?

7. What can you do to ensure that your values and actions match?

8. Summarize what you learned about your leisure values today.

LEADERSHIP CONSIDERATIONS

1. Be aware that some participants may not be willing to share their values.

2. Participants must be aware of the concept of values prior to the start of the activity.

3. Have participants focus on values made prevalent by their leisure participation.

VARIATION

1. Time limits may be imposed on the actions expressing or opposing the values. For example, the participants are restricted to naming actions they have taken within the last week or month.

CONTRIBUTOR

Norma J. Stumbo

CLARIFYING VALUES AND ACTIONS

I VALUE	I EXPRESS THIS BY	I OPPOSE THIS BY
Example: Creativity	Making quilts Gardening	Watching too much TV Spending time on the phone

1.

2.

3.

4.

5.

VALUES AUCTION

SPACE REQUIREMENTS

Classroom or activity room

EQUIPMENT

Values auction forms A and B, play money in denominations of $5, $10, $20, $50, and $100

GROUP SIZE

Small group

GOALS

1. To improve participants' ability to clarify their values and attitudes.

2. To improve participants' ability to prioritize their values and attitudes.

3. To improve participants' ability to publicly affirm their values and attitudes.

PREPARATION

Gather materials
Make one copy of the forms for each participant
Organize $2000 in play money in varying denominations for each participant

ACTIVITY DESCRIPTION

Ask participants to gather around a table or sit in a circle. Introduce the topic of values, how they guide everyday life, and how we come to have certain values. Ask participants to share some of their values with the group. Be prepared to share some of your values as well.

Distribute the values auction form (Form A) and pencils to group members. Instruct participants to read over the list and hand out $2000 to each person.

Each person is to consider their values and place a dollar amount that they are willing to bid for lifetime possession of that value. The total should not be more than $2000. The rules of the auction are as follows:

- Smallest bid is $5

- No borrowing or credit

- Pay immediately on winning the bid

- No returns or refunds

- Money not used on a losing bid cannot be placed on another value

- When a player's money runs out; he or she cannot bid anymore

Begin the auction with the first value, starting the bidding at $5. If possible "sound" like an auctioneer, move at a brisk pace, and close each round of bidding with "going once...going twice...sold!" Each player should keep track of how much they bid and what the top bid was for that value.

Give participants a copy of Form B. Close with the following debriefing questions.

DEBRIEFING QUESTIONS

1. How many items that you bid on were you able to buy?

2. How did you decide on the amount you were going to bid?

3. Have you ever done or been any of the things that you bid on? If so, which ones? If not, why not?

4. Are you satisfied with your purchases? What items would you be willing to drop from your list? What items do you definitely want to keep?

5. Did you run out of money? What item did you want most when you ran out of money?

6. What values are represented?

7. How well do the items you bought reflect your values?

8. In looking at the Form B, what would you change about your bidding?

9. What did you learn about your leisure values today?

LEADERSHIP CONSIDERATION

1. Know basics of auction rules and etiquette.

VARIATIONS

1. Ask participants to come up with their own lists of values and create one master list for the auction.

2. Allow people who lose a bid to use that money on another item.

3. Modify the items on the list to represent other topics for discussion.

CONTRIBUTOR

Norma J. Stumbo

VALUES AUCTION: FORM A

	AMOUNT BUDGETED	HIGHEST AMOUNT I BID	TOP BID
Satisfying and fulfilling marriage	_____	_____	_____
Freedom to do what you want	_____	_____	_____
Being a leader	_____	_____	_____
Love and admiration of friends	_____	_____	_____
Travel and tickets to any cultural or athletic event as often as you wish	_____	_____	_____
Complete self-confidence with a positive outlook on life	_____	_____	_____
Happy family relationship	_____	_____	_____
Recognition as the most attractive person in the world	_____	_____	_____
Long life free of illness	_____	_____	_____
Complete library for your private use	_____	_____	_____
Satisfying religious faith	_____	_____	_____
Month's vacation with nothing to do but enjoy yourself	_____	_____	_____
Outstanding athletic ability	_____	_____	_____
World without prejudice	_____	_____	_____
Chance to eliminate poverty	_____	_____	_____
International fame and popularity	_____	_____	_____
Understanding of the meaning of life	_____	_____	_____
World without corruption or cheating	_____	_____	_____
Freedom within your work setting	_____	_____	_____
Really good love relationship	_____	_____	_____
Success in your chosen profession or vocation	_____	_____	_____

VALUES AUCTION: FORM B

AUCTION ITEM	VALUES REPRESENTED
Satisfying and fulfilling marriage	love, companionship
Freedom to do what you want	personal autonomy
Being a leader	admiration, recognition of abilities
Love and admiration of friends	love, friendship, approval
Travel and tickets to any cultural or athletic event as often as you wish	travel, pleasure, athletics, aesthetics
Complete self-confidence with a positive outlook on life	emotional well-being
Happy family relationship	close family ties
Recognition as the most attractive person in the world	appearance
Long life free of illness	health
Complete library for your private use	knowledge
Satisfying religious faith	religion
Month's vacation with nothing to do but enjoy yourself	pleasure
Outstanding athletic ability	recognition
World without prejudice	justice
Chance to eliminate poverty	altruism
International fame and popularity	recognition, approval
Understanding of the meaning of life	wisdom
World without corruption or cheating	honesty
Freedom within your work setting	work autonomy
Really good love relationship	love, closeness, intimacy
Success in your chosen profession or vocation	professional achievement

VALUES DISCUSSION

SPACE REQUIREMENTS

Classroom or activity room

MATERIALS

List of values discussion topics

GROUP SIZE

Small group

GOALS

1. To increase participants' awareness of personal values and attitudes.
2. To increase participants' awareness of the values and attitudes of others.
3. To improve participants' ability to publicly affirm their values and attitudes.
4. To increase participants' discussion and listening skills

PREPARATION

Gather materials
Make one copy of the discussion topics for each group

ACTIVITY DESCRIPTION

Ask participants to gather around a table or sit in a circle. Introduce the topic of values to the group. Discuss the concept of values, how they impact on daily behavior, how values are chosen, and how values may be publicly affirmed.

Divide into subgroups of 3–4. Instruct the groups to review the handout and choose a topic that they would like to discuss. Allow 5 minutes.

Each group will discuss the selected topic for 5–10 minutes. The rules of the discussion are:

- Only one person may talk at a time
- Listeners try to determine what values the person talking has about the topic
- Each person gets a chance to talk on the topic

Select 1 person from each subgroup to start the discussion. The listeners determine the speaker's values, jotting notes and asking clarification questions as needed. Allow enough time for 3–4 topics to be discussed, 10 to 15 minutes per topic.

At the end have each person present (either to the subgroup or to the larger group) the values that they have listed for each person. The person then can either agree or disagree with the values that people have stated for them.

The closing discussion should center on what people learned about their value system, how differently others perceived them from how they perceive themselves, if their values have changed, and how their values impact their lives.

DEBRIEFING QUESTIONS

1. Which values were the easiest to detect?
2. How often were you correct about someone's values?
3. How often were group members correct about your values?
4. At what times do we think about our values?
5. How have your values changed over time? Why?
6. How do your values impact your life?
7. Why is it important to understand your values?
8. How does it feel to publicly affirm your values?
9. What did you learn about your own value system today?
10. What did you learn about others' value systems today?

LEADERSHIP CONSIDERATIONS

1. It is helpful if everyone knows each other, so values can be more quickly determined.
2. Be prepared to give an example by talking about a subject for 1–2 minutes and asking what values are represented.

VARIATION

1. Change the topics to meet the goals of the leisure education session and the needs of the participants.

CONTRIBUTOR

Norma J. Stumbo

VALUES DISCUSSION

1. What is your favorite food?
2. What would you like to do to become famous?
3. What would you do if you found $1,000 on a vacant lot?
4. Say something about war.
5. How do you feel about growing old?
6. Say something about police officers.
7. What brings you joy?
8. How do you look when you get angry?
9. What do poor people need most?
10. Describe the ideal mother.
11. How do you feel when someone laughs at you?
12. Finish the sentence: "The best thing about today is . . ."
13. What does America mean to you?
14. What kind of people are the luckiest people in the world?
15. What is something that bothers you?
16. What do you think it's like after you die?
17. What would you do if you wanted to be a friend to someone who could not speak English?
18. What TV or movie star would you like to invite to your birthday party?
19. What is the worst thing parents can do to children?
20. What is your best friend like?
21. Say something about cigarettes.
22. Describe a good neighbor.
23. Say something about school.
24. If you could change your age, what age would you rather be?
25. What kind of store would you like to own and operate?
26. What kind of TV commercial would you like to make?
27. If you became President of the United States, what two things would you do?
28. Name two famous people you'd like to have for parents.
29. What color do you think of when you think of happiness?
30. If you could become invisible, where would you like to go?
31. What kind of job do you want to have in 20 years?
32. What do you like to daydream about?
33. What would you like to invent to make life better?
34. What is your favorite sport and why?
35. What would you do if you had a magic wand?
36. How would you describe yourself to someone who does not know you?
37. Tell about a time when you felt proud of yourself.
38. What would you like to say to the person you see when you look in the mirror?
39. If you could have only one pen pal, who would you want that to be?
40. Tell about your favorite leisure activity and why you chose it.

ALLIGATOR RIVER EPISODE

SPACE REQUIREMENTS

Classroom or activity room

MATERIALS

Story, paper and pencils or flip chart and markers

GROUP SIZE

Small group

GOALS

1. To increase participants' awareness of personal values and attitudes.
2. To increase participants' awareness of other's values and attitudes.
3. To improve participants' ability to publicly affirm their values and attitudes.
4. To increase participants' self-awareness.

PREPARATION

Gather materials
Make one copy of the story for each participant

ACTIVITY DESCRIPTION

Ask participants to gather around a table or sit in a circle. Discuss the concept of values, the process of valuing, how values are acquired throughout life, and the importance of clarifying and publicly affirming values. Distribute a copy of the story to participants.

Read the story to group members. After reading the story, have group members rank the characters in the story with regard to desirability as friends or close associates. This can either be done individually (give participants paper and pencil) or in a group and written on the flip chart.

After participants have ranked the characters, discuss how each participant ranked his or her list. Ask other members to comment and justify their answers. What values are represented by the characters? Are these the values participants think they hold? Is the order appropriate to the values? How do these values affect their lives? Ask participants to give examples of behaviors that exemplify these values. Close discussion by summarizing how values, attitudes, and behaviors relate.

DEBRIEFING QUESTIONS

1. What values do each of the four characters represent?
2. Which of the story's characters are you most like?
3. How closely do your values match that of the story character you chose?
4. Would you do anything differently than that character?
5. How many in the group selected the same character?
6. Why is it important to recognize your value system?
7. Why is it important to recognize the value system of others?
8. What did you learn about your values today?
9. What did you learn about the values of others today?

LEADERSHIP CONSIDERATION

1. Some groups, especially those with cognitive difficulties, may need clues to remember the characters.

VARIATIONS

1. After each person has ranked the characters, have the group discuss what values each represents. Then allow participants to reorder their lists (if necessary) to reflect what they believe their values to be.
2. Add other characteristics to the characters as necessary.
3. Increase or decrease the number of characters as necessary.
4. Do not give an ending to the story and have participants complete the ending as if they were Angie.

CONTRIBUTOR

Norma J. Stumbo

ALLIGATOR RIVER EPISODE

Once there was a river called Alligator River because it was full of alligators. No one could swim it. As the years passed, the alligators died off, but the river kept its name. It wasn't good for swimming because of pollution caused by dumping from various factories, including the Alligator Leather Goods Company.

On one side of the polluted river lived Angie. She was an attractive 15-year-old who was sweet and kind to everyone and made no trouble for her parents. She was going steady with Gary, who lived on the other side of the river. He liked going steady with Angie because she was so popular and pretty and never did anything to get into trouble. Angie was happy that she and Gary were going together, although they went to rival schools.

Angie and Gary used to meet every afternoon after school on the old bridge over Alligator River. Both of them were oblivious to the hundreds of cars that whizzed past them every day. They thought about the bridge only as a beautiful spot to meet.

One day Gary wasn't there and Angie could not imagine what had happened. She went home feeling low. She was wondering what to do, when the phone rang. It was Gary. He sounded far away and not at all like himself. He told Angie he was feeling awful and was really, really sick. He was alone and pleaded with her to come over to his house to help him.

Angie immediately ran out of the house to go to help Gary. Just as she reached the bridge, she saw that it had finally collapsed from age and the weight of too much traffic. Angie wished she could swim across, but she knew that no one would dare to do that because the water was so polluted. What could she do? Gary needed her, and he might die without her help.

Then she remembered Sam, a boy from school who had his own boat. Maybe he would take her across in his boat. Angie dashed over to Sam's house. She told him about Gary's illness and explained that the bridge had collapsed.

Sam was willing to help Angie, but for a price. He told her he would take her across if she stole a camera for him from one of the stores down the street. Angie was horrified and pleaded with Sam to take her across without that condition. Sam would not change his mind.

What could Angie do? She went over to Bob's house to ask him for help. Bob was a good friend who always listened well. She told Bob why she had to go across Alligator River and asked him to talk Sam into taking her without the condition. Bob liked Angie and would have liked to help her, but he did not want to get involved. He did not believe in violence and knew that, if he interfered, Sam might get violent. He felt this wasn't any of his business, so he apologized to Angie for not helping.

Angie thought for a while, then, seeing no other alternative, agreed to steal for Sam. She managed to shoplift the camera Sam wanted and took it to him. Sam then took her across the river.

On arriving at Gary's home, she found Gary very ill, so she got medical help. At first Gary did not know what was going on around him, but later, when he recognized Angie, he was very glad she had come when he needed her.

THE PREDICAMENT

SPACE REQUIREMENTS

Classroom or activity room

MATERIALS

Story

GROUP SIZE

Small group

GOALS

1. To improve participants' awareness of their values and attitudes.
2. To improve participants' awareness of the impact of their values on their behavior.
3. To improve participants' ability to examine options and resulting consequences.
4. To increase participants' self-awareness.

PREPARATION

Make one copy of the story for each participant

ACTIVITY DESCRIPTION

Ask participants to gather around a table or sit in a circle. Discuss the topics of values, how each person has a unique set of values, how these values influence the person's behaviors and actions, and how some actions are socially acceptable and some are not. Distribute a copy of the story to each participant.

Read the story to the group participants. After completing the story, ask each participant how he or she would behave in this situation. What would he or she do next? Then, ask each individual what types of values this shows. Respect for others? fairness? truthfulness? besting the other person? revenge?

Have participants discuss how this story and summary reflect the larger picture of their values. Discuss differences and similarities, how this impacts the aspects of their lives, and how they could be changed.

DEBRIEFING QUESTIONS

1. How closely do your values and behavior reflect either of the two main characters?
2. What values are represented by each of the characters?
3. If you could rewrite the story to reflect your own values, what would you change?
4. Who in the group rewrote the story similar to you?
5. How are our values reflected in our behavior?
6. How do we become aware of our values?
7. How do our values reflect the options we choose to situations we encounter?
8. What did you learn about your values today?
9. What did you learn about others' values today?

LEADERSHIP CONSIDERATION

1. Remain as nonjudgmental as possible.

VARIATIONS

1. Have participants think of common sayings that match their proposed actions (e.g., "an eye for an eye," "all is fair in love and war," "do unto others as you would have them do unto you").
2. End the story where the woman leaves the package and ask participants to make up their own endings from this point.
3. Modify the story to match the intent of the leisure education session and the needs of the participants.
4. Ask individuals to respond to the story in writing and then compare their answers within small groups. Have subgroups vote on the most appropriate response and present it to the larger group.

CONTRIBUTOR

Norma J. Stumbo

THE PREDICAMENT

My girlfriend Katie and I went skiing one weekend and stopped for lunch. We went through the
line and I took the money out of my wallet to pay.
We then walked to our table.

When we arrived at our table, Katie said,
"Dan, you dropped a $5 bill near the cash regis-
ter." I got up and walked toward the $5 bill that
was lying on the floor. As I walked over there, I
saw a little boy pick up the $5 bill and give it to
his mother.

I approached his mother and said, "Excuse me,
ma'am, but I lost $5 back here and I just saw your
boy give it to you." She replied, "I do not know
what you're talking about." Again I said, "Ma'am,
I saw your kid pick it up and give it to you. My
girlfriend also saw it, and I would kindly like my
$5 back, please." Well, all she said was that she
did not know what I was talking about. I became
upset and walked back to my table. All through
lunch I kept glaring at the lady and giving her dirty
looks.

After a while, the lady and her little boy got up
and left the restaurant. After they left I glanced
over to the table where they were sitting and noticed a package underneath one of the chairs.

Suddenly, I got an idea. I walked over to the
table, picked up the package, and brought it back
to my table with the thought in mind that she'd return in search of the package. Sure enough, 5 minutes later she returned. Upon noticing that her
package was not at her table, she glanced at me
and knew from my smile that I had taken it.

She walked up to me and asked me for the
package. I replied, "What package?" And she
said, "I know you have it—now give it back to
me!" Again, I replied, "What package? Lady, I do
not know what you are talking about." She then
turned and rushed out.

LEISURE SENTENCE COMPLETION

SPACE REQUIREMENTS

Classroom or activity room

MATERIALS

Handout, pencils

GROUP SIZE

Small group

GOALS

1. To increase participants' self-awareness of personal goals, beliefs, values, and attitudes.

2. To increase participants' ability to express personal opinions and feelings within a small group setting.

3. To increase participants' ability to empathize with other people's beliefs and values.

PREPARATION

Gather materials
Make one copy of the handout for each participant

ACTIVITY DESCRIPTION

Have the group form a circle and distribute the attached form and pencils. Introduce the activity by discussing how each individual has a set of values and attitudes, including those toward leisure. Have the group share some of their individual beliefs and values about leisure.

Have group participants complete the handout individually. Allow 5–10 minutes. After each person has completed the form, ask individuals to share their responses and compare them with other people in the group. Encourage insights into their own and others' values and attitudes (e.g., similarities, differences, inconsistencies).

Discuss how values affect the behaviors, how value systems are derived (e.g., from parental and family messages, from society at large), and how values change. At the end, the participants should have a clear idea of what their value systems are, especially in relation to their leisure behavior.

DEBRIEFING QUESTIONS

1. How do your values affect your thoughts and behaviors?

2. From what sources do you get your values system?

3. What types of events may change your value system?

4. In 1 or 2 sentences, describe your values or attitudes toward leisure.

5. How did you develop these values or attitudes?

6. How do these values relate to your other values or attitudes?

7. From where did you receive the strongest messages about leisure?

8. How have your values and attitudes affected your participation in leisure?

9. How might you want to change your values or attitudes toward leisure?

10. How do you think your values might change in the future?

11. In 1 or 2 sentences describe what you've learned about your leisure values and attitudes today.

LEADERSHIP CONSIDERATIONS

1. Be aware that some individuals may not be willing to share their responses.

2. Do not allow participants to criticize each other for their statements. Explain that everyone should try to appreciate the different perspectives of the group members.

VARIATIONS

1. Modify the sentence completion statements to reflect the content of the leisure education session.

2. Ask group participants to come up with 3–5 statements to add to the list for everybody to complete.

CONTRIBUTOR

Norma J. Stumbo

LEISURE SENTENCE COMPLETION

Directions: Complete each of the following statements with regard to your leisure.

1. On vacation, I like to _____

2. If I had $100 I would _____

3. The happiest day in my life was when _____

4. My favorite leisure activity is _____

5. I am really good at making _____

6. The type of conversation I like best is _____

7. I laugh when _____

8. I like to spend my time _____

9. If I could create a park, I would _____

10. When I want to be alone I _____

11. When I am bored I _____

12. I want to learn how to _____

13. I could teach someone to _____

14. My favorite night out on the town includes _____

15. If I could do anything for a day I would _____

16. I enjoy _____

17. I spend most of my time _____

18. I would like to be known most for my _____

19. If I had 1 free hour tomorrow I would _____

20. I need to be more patient when _____

21. When I am alone at home I _____

22. My favorite vacation place is _____

23. I need to make better decisions about _____

24. My favorite person to spend time with is _____

25. If I were on a deserted island I would _____

26. I am better than other people at _____

27. I wish I had more time for _____

28. I get sad when _____

29. When I enter a new group I feel _____

30. I do not like activities that _____

31. The best things in life are _____

32. I am most optimistic about _____

33. I always find time for _____

LIFE VALUES

SPACE REQUIREMENTS

Classroom or activity room

MATERIALS

Handout, pencils

GROUP SIZE

Small group

GOALS

1. To increase participants' understanding of values and the valuing process.

2. To increase participants' mutual understanding of each other's values and unique identities.

3. To increase participants' awareness of their own personal values and how they affect their leisure.

PREPARATION

Gather materials
Make one copy of the handout for each participant

ACTIVITY DESCRIPTION

Have the group form a circle and distribute the attached form and pencils. Discuss the nature of values and how they guide what people do every day. Ask participants to share some of their most important values with the group. Have individuals complete the handout. Allow 10–15 minutes.

After completion, ask participants to form subgroups of 2–3 and compare their answers with each other. Have them determine commonalties and differences among values of group members.

Bring small groups back together and compare small groups' answers with each other. Discussion may focus on why the lists are different, factors that influence the order (e.g., age, marital status, political involvement), how values change over time, or what values they see changing in the next 5–10 years.

Close discussion with how these values affect their leisure. Discussion may focus on how values penetrate all aspects of life, how values may often conflict, or how values affect behavior.

DEBRIEFING QUESTIONS

1. How similar or different were the lists of the small groups?

2. How were the rankings determined?

3. How close are your own personal values to the list created by the group?

4. How do your values affect your thoughts and behaviors?

5. From what sources do you get your values system?

6. What types of events may change your value system?

7. In one or two sentences, describe your values or attitudes toward leisure.

8. How did you develop these values or attitudes?

9. How does this relate to other values or attitudes that you hold?

10. From where did you receive the strongest messages about leisure?

11. How has your values and attitudes affect your participation in leisure?

12. How might you want to change your values or attitudes toward leisure?

13. How do you think they might change in the future?

14. In one or two sentences, describe what you've learned about your leisure values and attitudes today.

LEADERSHIP CONSIDERATIONS

1. Allow enough time for group participants to be able to complete the rankings and how values influence leisure behavior.

2. Encourage group participants to accept other people's answers and not criticize each other based on differences.

3. Be prepared to give a personal example of how the your personal values affect your leisure decisions and behaviors.

VARIATIONS

1. Categories to be ranked may be changed to reflect the intent of the leisure education session.

2. Appoint one person in each small group to be the recorder to determine difference and similarities between group members.

3. Have each person display his or her top 3 choices on large pieces of paper attached to the walls. This visual display helps people remember what each individual's values are.

4. Display each person's rankings on large pieces of paper (similar to #3) without the individual's name on it. Have group participants guess whose values are listed and discuss why they think so.

CONTRIBUTOR

Norma J. Stumbo

LIFE VALUES

Directions: Below is a list of 18 values arranged in alphabetical order. Your task is to arrange them in order of their importance to YOU as guiding principles in YOUR life. Study the list carefully, then place a 1 next to the value which is MOST important to you, place a 2 next to the value which is second most important to you, etc. Work slowly and think carefully. If you change your mind, feel free to change your answers.

_____ An exciting life (a stimulating, active life)

_____ A prosperous life (money and material possessions)

_____ Career

_____ Family security (close relationships and frequent involvement)

_____ Freedom (independence, free choice)

_____ Health

_____ Inner harmony (freedom from inner conflict)

_____ Mature love (sexual and spiritual intimacy with another person)

_____ Nature (concern for the environment)

_____ Peace (resolution by nonviolent means)

_____ Pleasure (recreation, relaxation)

_____ Religion

_____ Salvation (deliverance from sin, eternal life)

_____ Security (protection from foreign enemies, criminals)

_____ Self-respect (self-esteem)

_____ Sobriety

_____ Social approval (adapting self for approval of others)

_____ Wisdom

How do your values affect your leisure. For example, if you value pleasure do you spend a lot of time at leisure? If you value prosperity do you own a lot of leisure equipment or take expensive vacations?

GROUP BRAINSTORMING

SPACE REQUIREMENTS

Classroom or activity room

MATERIALS

3x5 cards

GROUP SIZE

Small group

GOALS

1. To increase participants' ability to generate ideas or solutions to a problem.
2. To increase participants' ability to review alternatives and make decisions.
3. To increase participants' ability to express opinions and share feelings with others.
4. To encourage participants to be creative in coming up with alternatives.

PREPARATIONS

Gather materials
Write the scenarios on 3x5 cards (one for each team)

ACTIVITY DESCRIPTION

Ask participants to gather around a table or sit in a circle. Discuss consideration of alternatives and making decisions. Decisions are made on a daily (if not hourly) basis and affect how we lead our lives. Most people develop patterns (sometimes uncreative and stagnant ones) for looking at alternatives and making decisions. The purpose of this activity is to use brainstorming as a method to examine alternatives for decision-making.

Divide the group into teams of 4–5. Distribute the scenario cards and review the rules for brainstorming. Give participants 5–10 minutes to come up with a list of solutions to the problems using the brainstorming method. After all ideas have been exhausted, ask participants to look at each idea and analyze whether or not it is a feasible solution to the problem. Then participants are to decide on the best solution to the problem. Each group presents their solutions to the other groups.

The discussion may focus on the appropriateness of the solutions, how each group came to a consensus and determined what was appropriate, how the use of brainstorming helped to come up with new ideas, how brainstorming can be used in their future lives, and how evaluating alternatives helps to make better decisions.

DEBRIEFING QUESTIONS

1. How many ideas were generated for each problem?
2. How did the group come up with ideas?
3. How appropriate were the solutions developed by the group?
4. How did the process of brainstorming help come up with solutions?
5. How did the group decide on the best solutions?
6. How can this process be used in your own life?
7. How do you usually come up with solutions to your problems?
8. How successful are you in generating ideas to solve your problems?
9. How do you decide which alternative to select to solve your problem?
10. What did you learn about solving problems today?

LEADERSHIP CONSIDERATION

1. Model appropriate brainstorming rules during the activity (be aware of verbal and nonverbal feedback).

VARIATIONS

1. Modify the scenarios to meet the intent of the leisure education session and the needs of the participants.
2. Put the group's ideas on large pieces of paper on the wall so they can all see the new ideas as they go.

CONTRIBUTOR

Norma J. Stumbo

RULES FOR BRAINSTORMING

1. No evaluation: During the first part, no criticism of any kind is allowed. Both positive and negative feedback are forbidden. Analysis at this point stifles creativity.

2. Think up wild ideas: It is easier to tame down a wild idea than to pep up a bland idea. If wild ideas do not come up, it is evidence that the participants are screening their ideas before saying them out of fear that they may sound foolish.

3. Quantity breeds quality: Quantity should be encourage. The more choices there are to choose from, the more likely some will be good ideas.

4. Combine and modify: Encourage everyone to build on or modify ideas of others, which leads to new ideas. Use this for the last stage.

POSSIBLE SCENARIOS FOR BRAINSTORMING

1. How many ways can you think of to deal with stress?

2. You have $75 and an entire Saturday free to spend it in any way you choose.

3. Take an object (e.g., chair, pencil, cup, pillow) and determine different ways you could use it in leisure.

4. You have $25 to spend at the grocery store to buy food to prepare dinner for two of your friends. What would you buy and what would you make?

5. You have a paper bag, a piece of cardboard, poker chips, dice, colored markers, and play money. What type of game would you devise?

6. You mistakenly made a lunch date on the same day with two of your friends who don't like each other. What do you do?

7. What are the 3 best ways to improve your health?

IS IT WORTH THE RISK?

SPACE REQUIREMENTS

Classroom or activity room

MATERIALS

Handout, pencils

GROUP SIZE

Small group

GOALS

1. To increase participants' ability to examine the advantages and disadvantages of asserting oneself.

2. To increase participants' ability to express personal opinions and feelings with others.

3. To improve participants' ability to realistically examine the benefits and disadvantages to risk taking.

PREPARATION

Gather materials
Make one copy of the handout for each participant

ACTIVITY DESCRIPTION

Ask participants to gather around a table or sit in a circle. Discuss how difficult it is to be assertive in tough situations and how sometimes publicly affirming wishes may do more harm than good. Not getting wants and desires filled, however, leaves one with a sense of loss and sometimes anger.

Provide a few examples of public affirmations that may be hard to confront:

1. A coworker invites you to a party but you really do not want to go. You want to tell her but you're not willing to be assertive. Is it worth the risk?

2. You have had an alcohol problem in the past and an old friend keeps inviting you to events where alcohol consumption is expected. You do not want to hurt his feelings but you are afraid that if you go, you will start drinking again. Is it worth the risk?

3. You would like to attend classes at a local community college to learn a new skill but you feel like you are too old. Is it worth the risk?

4. Your boss invites you to play golf but every time you go, she cheats on her score. You would like to tell her that she either has to keep the correct score or you are not willing to play golf with her again. Is it worth the risk?

Give each participant a copy of the handout and a pencil. Ask participants to think of a time they have had difficulty with their leisure—for example, meeting new people, not taking enough time to relax, or not knowing what to do.

Next, each participant should list the advantages and disadvantages of being assertive. After the two lists are complete, the participants are to write whether he/she feels the risk of being assertive is worth it.

Discussion should focus on each person's situation, the pros and cons of being assertive, and whether they decided it was worth it. Discussion should also focus on using the method of this activity for future decision making.

DEBRIEFING QUESTIONS

1. Describe your difficult situation.

2. Which did you list more of: advantages or disadvantages?

3. What was your conclusion about whether the risk was worth it?

4. How similar is your situation to others in the group?

5. How similar were your advantages and disadvantages to others in the group?

6. What are the overall advantages of being assertive?

7. What are the overall disadvantages of being assertive?

8. How can you use this process to assess risk in other situations?

9. What are the long-term benefits of being assertive?

10. What did you learn about assertion and risk taking today?

LEADERSHIP CONSIDERATIONS

1. Suggest ideas for comparing advantages and disadvantages. For example, look at both lists and find things with equal value that cancel each other out, or assign each item a point value (1–10) and derive a ratio of advantages to disadvantages.

VARIATIONS

1. Modify the situation to a statement that they would like to make to another person about their own leisure. For example, someone might want to say to his or her employer "When you make me work overtime, I feel like I miss out on my family's activities."

CONTRIBUTOR

Norma J. Stumbo

IS IT WORTH THE RISK?

DIFFICULT SITUATION

_____

_____

_____

_____

ADVANTAGES

_____

_____

_____

_____

_____

DISADVANTAGES

_____

_____

_____

_____

_____

IS IT WORTH THE RISK?

_____

_____

_____

_____

GOAL SETTING

SPACE REQUIREMENTS

Classroom or activity room

MATERIALS

Handout, pencils

GROUP SIZE

Small group

GOALS

1. To increase participants' awareness of the importance of goal setting in leisure.
2. To increase participants' ability to set goals for leisure participation.
3. To improve participants' understanding of the steps to take toward achieving their goals.

PREPARATION

Gather materials
Make one copy of the handout for each participant

ACTIVITY DESCRIPTION

Ask participants to gather around a table or sit in a circle. Discuss goal setting and its importance to leisure as well as other aspects of life. Ask participants if they set goals for their own leisure participation. In this activity, participants will be asked to examine different areas of leisure that they may want to set goals in, to establish those goals, and then to determine what actions are needed to meet those goals.

Distribute the handouts and pencils to participants. In the first column participants write anything they would like to learn to do (or learn to do better) in this leisure category. In the second column participants list the actions it will take to accomplish these goals. These should be small, concrete, and manageable steps. In the third column, participants assign realistic dates to accomplish these goals. Allow 10–15 minutes. (Each participant should complete a minimum of 3 categories.)

After the participants have completed their forms, ask them to read them aloud to the other group members. The other members are to provide constructive feedback as to whether these actions and dates are realistic.

Closing discussion should focus on the importance of goal setting in leisure and follow-up.

DEBRIEFING QUESTIONS

1. Before today, have you thought about setting goals for your leisure?
2. If so, what kind of goals have you set? Were they accomplished?
3. Why is it important to set goals for your leisure, as well as other areas of your life?
4. What kinds of goals did you set today?
5. Does anyone in the group share similar goals?
6. What steps or actions need to be taken to attain those goals?
7. What resources do you need to help you attain those goals?
8. What follow-up is needed to help make sure you attain those goals?
9. How will you feel once you attain your goals?
10. Summarize what you've learned about setting goals for leisure today.

LEADERSHIP CONSIDERATION

1. May want to hand out this sheet ahead of time so participants arrive with completed forms.

VARIATIONS

1. The categories can be changed to suit the intent of the leisure education session and the needs of the participants.
2. Have participants determine their own categories, based on their leisure interests or activities.
3. Form groups to conduct a follow-up.

CONTRIBUTOR

Norma J. Stumbo

GOAL SETTING

WHAT I'D LIKE TO LEARN TO DO OR BECOME BETTER AT...	**ACTION STEPS**	**DATES**
...in music		
...in art		
...in sports		
...in crafts		
...in the outdoors		
...in leisure		
...in relating to others		
...in my home		
...with friends		
...socially		
...with my family		

PRIORITIZING VALUES

SPACE REQUIREMENTS

Classroom or activity room

MATERIALS

Prioritizing values game board and playing pieces

GROUP SIZE

Small group

GOALS

1. To improve participants' ability to clarify their values in relation to leisure, work and relationships.
2. To increase participants' problem-solving abilities and decision-making skills.
3. To improve participants' ability to clarify their priorities in relation to attaining leisure satisfaction.

PREPARATION

Gather materials
Make one copy of the game board and pieces for each participant

ACTIVITY DESCRIPTION

Ask participants to gather around a table or sit in a circle. Discuss values and the importance they have in relation to the decisions we make and the actions we take. Often it may be difficult to make decisions because we may have conflicting values. The purpose of this activity is to help participants understand their values and how they make decisions based on these values.

Distribute a game board and 3 sets of playing pieces (leisure, work, relationships) to each participant. The participants are to arrange the playing pieces from 1–12 (with 1 being the most important) in order of importance. Allow 5–10 minutes per area. Participants are free to arrange and rearrange the playing pieces as many times as they like. This can be done for all or just one of the areas during a particular session.

Once everyone has finalized a game board for one area, discuss the priorities of each individual. Discussion may center around what makes each item a priority for each individual and the differences between boards of participants.

DEBRIEFING QUESTIONS

1. What were your priorities in each of the three areas?
2. Who in the group had very similar answers? Who had very different answers?
3. How easy or difficult was it to prioritize the cards?
4. What does the order you put them in tell you about your values?
5. With which cards was the order difficult to decide?
6. With which cards was the order easy to decide?
7. In 1 or 2 sentences, describe to the group your priorities in each of the 3 areas.
8. How often do you think about your priorities or values?
9. Summarize what you've learned from this activity today.

LEADERSHIP CONSIDERATION

1. Allow enough time for participants to think about and be satisfied with their selections of priorities.

VARIATIONS

1. Modify the categories within each area to meet the intent of the leisure education session and the needs of the participants.
2. Give the boards and playing pieces to each of the participants to keep for when they have decisions to make or need to clarify what they want from a given situation.
3. Limit the number of cards to 5–6 if prioritizing 12 is too many.
4. Have participants complete the leisure game board once for how they spend the majority of their time currently and once for how they would like to spend their time.

CONTRIBUTOR

Norma J. Stumbo

PRIORITIZING VALUES GAME BOARD

1	7
2	8
3	9
4	10
5	11
6	12

PRIORITIZING VALUES LEISURE PLAYING PIECES

LEARNING Learning new skills, taking classes, reading about hobbies, perfecting skills	**SOCIALIZING** Being with others, sharing companionship, talking with close friends and relatives
STAYING AT HOME Being comfortable in my home, lounging around my home, fixing and repairing things	**GOING SOMEWHERE** Being on the go, seeing new places, returning to visit familiar places, traveling
PHYSICAL CHALLENGE Being put to the test, using my muscles, overcoming physical obstacles	**EXCITEMENT** Seeking new adventures, meeting new people, doing things I have not done before, trying something different
PLANNING IN ADVANCE Planning and organizing the details ahead of time, examining alternatives and making decisions, making reservations	**SPONTANEOUS** Living for the moment, doing things that strike me at the last minute, picking up and going somewhere today
PLAYING CATCH UP Starting or finishing chores that have not been done throughout the week, completing unfinished projects	**FULFILL COMMITMENTS** Visiting relatives, baby-sitting, taking people where they need to go, volunteering
BEING ALONE Having time to myself, being able to spend time thinking, doing what I want to do	**KEEPING MY MIND OFF WORK** Doing anything that keeps my mind off work, doing the opposite of what my work requires

PRIORITIZING VALUES WORK PLAYING PIECES

GOOD PAY Pay makes the job worth doing well, adequate pay for the job requirements	**GOOD HOURS** Decent and flexible hours, hours of work meet other personal obligations
BEING CHALLENGED Job allows me to use my special skills and talents, always something new to strive for	**BEING STIMULATED** Enough variety to keep from getting bored, makes me think and be creative
BEING ABLE TO GIVE INPUT My opinions are respected, I am asked often to help other people make decisions	**HAVING PEOPLE'S RESPECT** Having the respect of my employers and coworkers, people look up to me, people often compliment me
HAVING INDEPENDENCE Having expectations to get the job done by myself, being able to carry a task to completion, making my own decisions	**JOB SECURITY** Job will be there as long as I want it, there is no or little threat of layoffs or firings
OPPORTUNITY FOR ADVANCEMENT There is room for advancement, able to "work up the ladder," positions above me that I am qualified for	**EQUAL OPPORTUNITY** Every person is treated equally, no one gets special treatment from the employers
COWORKER RELATIONSHIPS Coworkers get along well, everyone is friendly and cooperative, competition is minimized	**PRIDE IN WORK** Take pride in quality workmanship and a job well-done, efforts in quality pay off, reward system for quality work

PRIORITIZING VALUES RELATIONSHIPS PLAYING PIECES

LAUGHTER A partner with a good sense of humor and there is lots of laughter in the relationship	**COMMON INTERESTS** Sharing common interests (including leisure interests), sharing mutual friends and experiences
INDEPENDENT INTERESTS Having different interests from each other, having separate friends, being able to go places without the partner	**PHYSICALLY ATTRACTIVE** Partner who is handsome or good-looking, physically fit, well-shaped, well-groomed
OPEN COMMUNICATION Ongoing communication, ability to listen and talk to each other openly about problems, concerns or experiences	**TRUST** Partner that is trustworthy with my feelings and emotions, would not do anything to purposefully hurt me or the relationship
HONESTY Honest about feelings and actions, no worry about the partner lying or not telling me something important	**OPEN ABOUT FEELINGS** Willing to talk about feelings, willing to listen to me about my feelings, helps to comfort me
NOT CLINGING Not overly dependent on me, gives me room to breathe and lets me do the things that I want to do, is not demanding	**PUTS ME FIRST** Partner puts me ahead of other people and interests, lets me now that I am important
ROMANCE Shares romantic moments, makes me feel special, accepts and encourages intimacy in the relationship	**INTELLIGENCE** Partner is bright, able to think things through, does well in school or on the job, likes to be mentally challenged

ALTERNATIVES AND CONSEQUENCES

SPACE REQUIREMENTS

Classroom or activity room

MATERIALS

List of possible scenarios

GROUP SIZE

Small group

GOALS

1. To increase participants' ability to consider alternative actions in response to situations.
2. To increase participants' ability to solve problems and make decisions.
3. To increase participants' ability to take actions that correspond with their values.
4. To increase participants' knowledge of the consequences stemming from decisions.

PREPARATION

Gather materials

ACTIVITY DESCRIPTION

Ask participants to gather around a table or sit in a circle. Discuss values and how they relate to actions and behaviors. Sometimes values are situational—they depend on the circumstances surrounding the situation. Other times values are concrete and transferable across situations. Each person has his or her own values and makes decisions based on those values. Problems arise, however, when our behaviors to do not match our values.

Read each scenario. Ask each participant how he or she would respond in the situation and to explain his or her answer. Each participant will also be asked to consider the value that underlies the action proposed as well as the consequences. The evaluation of consequences is as important as the search for alternatives. If alternatives are chosen without thought to the consequences, the risks of making a poor choice increase.

After the scenarios have been reviewed, close by discussing the actions and values presented by the group participants. What similarities and differences surfaced? What actions conflicted with their values? What actions would be more appropriate to match their values? How did they make decisions about the actions they would take? What effect did the consequences have on their decisions? How will their values affect them in the future?

DEBRIEFING QUESTIONS

1. What values were represented by the group when they considered alternatives?
2. How thoroughly did the group search for alternative solutions to the problems?
3. How thoroughly did the group consider consequences to each of the alternatives?
4. How often did suggested actions conflict with values within the group?
5. How were group members' decisions similar to or different from one another?
6. What are some good ways to think of lots of alternatives?
7. What can you do to make sure your actions match your values?
8. In 1 or 2 sentences, tell the group about your priorities in leisure.

LEADERSHIP CONSIDERATION

1. Start with an example of a situation and possible actions to acquaint the group with this type of activity.

VARIATIONS

1. Write the scenarios on cards and give them to the participants to read.
2. Divide the group into subgroups to discuss the scenarios before coming into the larger group for discussion.
3. Add scenarios depending on the purpose of the leisure education session and the needs of the participants.
4. Present scenarios and then ask participants to role-play what they would do in that situation. After the role play, the actions are debriefed concerning choices, values, and consequences.

5. Have participants brainstorm as many alternative actions as possible and then choose the 3 most favorable alternatives and their respective consequences. Have the group vote on the most favorable choice.

CONTRIBUTOR

Norma J. Stumbo

POSSIBLE SCENARIOS

1. You are on 2-week vacation in another state. On the third day of trip you discover that your wallet has been stolen. You and your family only have $20 total. What do you do?

2. Your family pays $80 for a summer swimming pass to the community pools. You know of a family down the street that lets neighbor kids get in on their pass for free. What would you do?

3. You are rappeling with a group of friends when you notice that the rope of the person below you is ready to break. No one is close enough to help and the person is a novice. What would you do?

4. You raised your children not to watch television more than 2 hours per day. You know that when they go to the baby-sitters, they watch television constantly. You have employed this baby-sitter for just under a year and she has reasonable rates. What do you do?

5. Your spouse has been complaining that you spend too much time watching sports on television. You come home one day and find that the television set is not working. Your suspect that your spouse has done something to the set. What would you do?

6. You take pride in a beautiful flower and vegetable garden in your backyard. One day you see that several flowers and vegetables have been picked. You suspect that your neighbor across the fence picked them. What would you do?

I LEARNED THAT...

SPACE REQUIREMENTS

Classroom or activity room

MATERIALS

Handout, pencils

GROUP SIZE

Small group

GOALS

1. To increase participants' awareness of personal values.
2. To reinforce the content participants learned in other leisure education activities.

PREPARATION

Gather materials
Make one copy of the handout for each participant
Note: this activity is used as a follow-up to another activity

ACTIVITY DESCRIPTION

Ask participants to gather around a table or sit in a circle. This activity ideally follows another leisure education activity. It can contribute to the discussion and can reinforce the benefits of the activity.

Immediately following a leisure education activity have participants complete the handout. Provide examples such as "I realized that...I was not clear about my own religious beliefs, " or "I was surprised that...I felt disappointed when someone gave an opinion about an issue that was different than mine."

Instruct participants to pay careful attention to their own feelings and emotions that arose when other people made statements throughout the activity. Allow 5–10 minutes.

Ask participants to share their finished statements with others in the group. To what degree are their answers similar or different? What is the most important thing that came out of this activity? What can they use in the future?

DEBRIEFING QUESTIONS

1. What answer surprised you the most?
2. Who gave similar answers within the group?
3. Who gave different answers within the group?
4. The most important thing I learned from this activity was...
5. The one thing I most want to remember from this activity is...
6. The one thing I can use in the future is...

LEADERSHIP CONSIDERATIONS

1. Be careful that discussion does not interrupt the flow of the participants completing the statements.
2. Participants' finished statements should be short and clear.
3. Participants may discuss, but not necessarily defend, their answers. Do not allow criticism from other participants.

VARIATIONS

1. The beginning statements can be changed to better evaluate particular activities.
2. If this is done repeatedly after several sessions, ask participants to save these forms and bring them to a final session for summary observations about themselves and what they have learned.

CONTRIBUTOR

Norma J. Stumbo

I LEARNED THAT...

1. I learned that _____

2. I realized that _____

3. I relearned that _____

4. I noticed that _____

5. I discovered that _____

6. I was surprised that _____

7. I was pleased that _____

8. I was unhappy that _____

9. I have a unique perspective on _____

10. I could not believe that _____

11. I would like to remember that _____

12. I want to tell somebody about _____

13. I found out that I could be better at _____

14. I really do not like to _____

15. The best thing that happened was _____

16. I would never have known that I _____

17. The thing I treasure most is _____

18. I am really good at _____

19. If I had to do it over again I would _____

20. I am special because _____

PIONEER LIVING

SPACE REQUIREMENTS

Log cabin or nature center

MATERIALS

Any artifact or equipment used in the 1800s (for discussion purposes); tablecloth, butter churn, butter bowl, wooden spoon, pitcher of cold water, wooden bowls, tin bucket, butter molds, cups, cloths, 3 whipping cream containers

GROUP SIZE

Small to medium group

GOALS

1. To understand how pioneer living differed from modern living (e.g., survival versus leisure time).

2. To introduce participants to their local heritage and to teach them about early settlers.

3. To build a sense of appreciation for pioneers who contributed to the development of the community, state, and country.

4. To increase participants' understanding of the chore of food preparation, using the process of churning butter.

PREPARATION

Gather materials
Make arrangements for location to conduct activity

ACTIVITY DESCRIPTION

Have everyone step inside the cabin and look around to stir their curiosity for the lifestyle and equipment. Once everyone is seated explain that this is the accommodations the pioneers had and ask how it differs from their homes. Discuss issues such as having only one room versus several, using a wood stove for cooking and heat, chores such as chopping wood, and the missing conveniences (e.g., electricity, phone, television). Allow them each to notice something different from their home. Demonstrate and explain the use of any equipment available. Discuss how little leisure time was available because of all the chores necessary just to get through an average day.

Invite everyone to help with a chore (butter churning). Have materials set up. Explain what is happening and give background information while the participants take turns churning the butter.

DEBRIEFING QUESTIONS

(Will depend on the topics covered)

LEADERSHIP CONSIDERATION

1. Allow as much discussion and stories from others as possible. Provide work demonstrations and pass around equipment throughout the discussion, to keep the participants interested.

VARIATIONS

1. This program can be adapted easily to older adults for a reminiscence program.

2. As an intergenerational program, the seniors can show children how it was when they grew up.

CONTRIBUTORS

Gary Koenig and Steve Swanson

BACKGROUND INFORMATION

The pioneer family was close-knit and supplied its own basic needs such as food, clothing, shelter, and tools. Early settlers had to know how to do everything for themselves—from candle making to quilting, rail-splitting to well-digging, delivering babies to setting bones. Animals were raised not only for meat, but also for eggs, milk, wool, fat, and leather. Plants were valued as food, for their fibers, and for their use in preparing medicines. Wood for building materials and fuel played a vital role in the life of the pioneers. They ate an abundance when there was food and when there wasn't food they went hungry. Families had children because they needed workers. Children worked all day and went to school at night in the home with everyone else. They only studied when there was no other work to be done and enjoyed school more than work.

In its natural state milk spoils very rapidly, but processing it in foods such as butter, cheese, and yogurt, preserves it and will last for a longer time without losing its nutritive value. Many areas of the world have developed individual ways of handling milk which date back for centuries. During pioneer times, churning butter was accomplished by first collecting the cream or top fat that rises to the top of the milking pail. This fat would be saved in a container which was placed by the fireside to slowly warm. Often this took 2 to 3 days before the cream was ready or "clabbered." The best butter was made from clabbered cream which was slightly thickened and soured, but not curdled and separated.

Churns were usually small homemade wooden barrels with a cover and dasher—a stick like a broom handle fastened to two x-shaped slats on the bottom that agitated up and down. After the buttermilk was poured off, the butter was washed by pouring cold water over the solid mass and working it by hand or with a wooden paddle. The butter was then chilled and shaped into designs. Some settlers measured their butter into round wooden molds. These molds pressed a design onto the butter which became a trademark of the person making that butter. Anyone who bought their butter knew who had made it.

Churning was time-consuming, usually taking 30–40 minutes per batch. To make the time go faster, the children often said this traditional chant in rhythm to their churning:

> Come, butter, come,
>
> Come, butter, come,
>
> Peter standing before the gate,
>
> Waiting for the butter cake,
>
> Come, butter, come.

BUTTER CHURNING INSTRUCTIONS

SET-UP

On the table place tablecloth, butter churn, butter bowl, wooden paddle, pitcher of cold water, wooden bowls, tin bucket, and butter molds. Under the table place cups for sampling buttermilk, cloth for wiping any spills and whipping cream containers (3). If cream is cold, place it in a sunny window. Watch that it does not get too warm.

DIRECTIONS

Empty one container of cream into churn. Explain that the cream we use today is different, because we heat it to kill the bacteria. Teach the children the chant, "Come, butter, come." Have the children say the chant together and ask each one to hold the bottom of the churn while the next child is churning to help keep the cream warm. Check the churn for the whipped cream stage. When the whipped cream turns to butter, you cannot change it back.

Continue churning until finished. Show the children that the fat has separated from the whey. Pour off the buttermilk and give samples to those who would like to taste it. Place butter in butter bowl and begin washing with cold water. Let the children take turns doing this. Place finished butter into small wooden bowl and shape into a design.

LEISURE EDUCATION AWARENESS PROGRAM (LEAP)

SPACE REQUIREMENTS

Classroom or activity room, community facilities

MATERIALS

Telephone books, telephones, newspapers, chalk-board and chalk or whiteboard and markers, paper, pencils, handouts

GROUP SIZE

Small group

GOALS

1. To improve participants' ability to develop positive leisure attitudes, recreational skills, and an awareness of recreation facilities and opportunities within the community.

2. To improve participants' ability to independently express leisure choices while in a group setting and to display carry-over skills within the classroom setting.

3. To improve participants' ability to locate community resources, select the proper equipment/supplies needed for an activity, and use public transportation (when appropriate).

PREPARATION

Gather materials
Make one copy of each handout for each participant
Note: This is a 5-week program, which includes 3 planning weeks (2 hrs. each) and 2 activity weeks (2.5 hrs. each).

ACTIVITY DESCRIPTION

WEEK 1: ACTIVITY DISCUSSION

Week 1 introduces participants to the topics and schedule for the 5-week program. Start the session with a discussion of leisure. Ask participants to complete the Leisure Assessment Questionnaire and discuss the results as a group. Ask them to talk about their favorite activities and the role that leisure plays in their lives. Discuss new activities they would like to try.

Have the group complete the pyramid of leisure. Encourage them to be creative and to use the activity ideas from the previous discussion. Discuss the results as a group.

Have participants review current local newspapers and select several activities they might like to participate in during weeks 3 and 5. Use the Leisure Resource Sheet to help generate ideas. Briefly discuss the decision making that goes into leisure planning, including timing, transportation, and budgeting, and inform participants that these topics will be discussed next week.

WEEK 2: ACTIVITY PLANNING

Start the discussion with a review of week 1. Have participants research facilities using the Community Activity Resources sheet. Discuss appropriate equipment, hours, location, and cost. Use the Public Transportation Resource sheet to discuss transportation options, including availability, cost, and how to use it.

WEEK 3: ACTIVITY

Participate in planned activity.

WEEK 4: ACTIVITY PLANNING

Review activity choice from week 3. What went well? What did not go well? What was learned about planning for activities?

Have participants use the same process as week 2 to determine an activity for week 5. Use the Community Activity Resource sheet and the Public Transportation Resource sheet to guide planning. Continue as in week 2.

WEEK 5: ACTIVITY

Participate in planned activity. Complete evaluation of the 5-week program using the Reaction Survey. Discuss what they learned throughout the program and how they would evaluate the program.

LEADERSHIP CONSIDERATIONS

1. Have each participant give an idea of an activity so that all participants will be involved.

2. Always start with a review of information from the previous week.

VARIATIONS

1. Continue the activity for more than 5 weeks to include additional activities.

2. Have pictures of specific activities for lower functioning groups.

CONTRIBUTOR

Bobbie Jean Leonard

LEISURE ASSESSMENT QUESTIONNAIRE

1. Currently what do you do during your leisure time?

2. With whom do you usually participate in leisure experiences?
   _____ Alone
   _____ Friend(s)
   _____ Family member(s)

3. With how many people do you usually engage in leisure experiences?
   _____ Alone
   _____ Small group (3–5)
   _____ Medium size group (6–12)
   _____ Large group (13 or more)

4. With what age group do you usually engage in leisure?
   _____ Same age
   _____ Younger than myself
   _____ Older than myself

5. During what time of day do you usually participate in leisure experiences?
   _____ Morning
   _____ Afternoon
   _____ Evening

6. What places do you generally utilize during leisure?
   _____ Commercial/business
   _____ Public
   _____ Private

7. How often do you experience leisure?
   _____ Almost daily
   _____ Weekly
   _____ Monthly
   _____ Seasonally

8. What types of transportation do you use to get to activities?
   _____ Walk
   _____ Public transportation
   _____ Family or friends drive me
   _____ Drive myself
   _____ Other

9. How much money do you have to spend on leisure activities per week?
   _____ None
   _____ $1.00 to $5.00
   _____ $5.00 to $10.00
   _____ $10.00 to $15.00
   _____ More than $15.00 per week

LEISURE PYRAMID

Example:

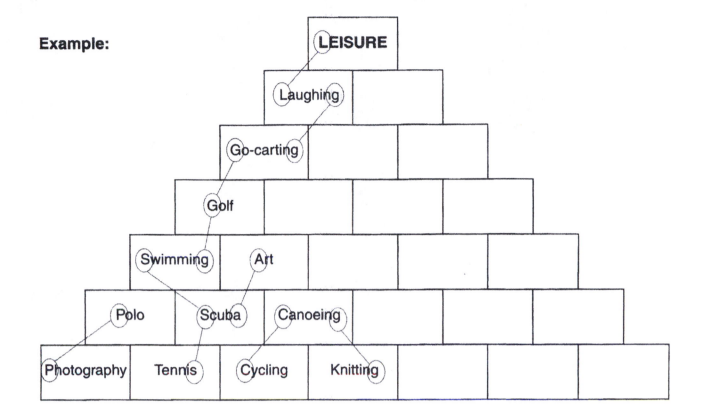

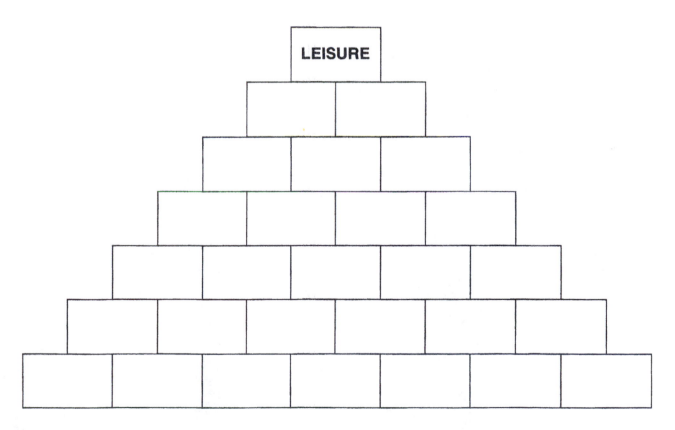

LEISURE RESOURCE SHEET

The Leisure Resource Sheet assists in preparation for or when participants are completing the Leisure Assessment Questionnaire.

Crafts
Ceramics
Cooking
Needlework
Painting
Sewing
Silk Screening
Woodworking

Hobbies
Auto mechanics
Cake decorating
Collecting
Home repair
Photography

Dance/Drama/Music Arts
Dancing
Acting in a play
Going to an art museum
Going to concerts
Playing a musical instrument
Singing in a choir

Educational
Discussion of religion
First aid
Going on cultural trips
Going to museums
Reading
Self-improvement class
Writing

Games
Computer games
Horseshoes
Ping-Pong
Pool
Puzzles
Shuffleboard
Board games
Word games

Sports and Physical Activities
Archery
Basketball
Bowling
Cross-country skiing
Downhill skiing
Football
Ice skating
Physical fitness (exercise, jogging, walking)
Racquetball
In-line skating
Softball
Swimming
Volleyball

Nature/outdoors
Animal care
Boating
Camping
Fishing
Gardening
Hiking
Horseback riding
Snowmobiling
Visiting nature centers

Service to Others
Being a member of a service club
Being a member of a social group
Volunteer as a recreation leader
Volunteer time helping a group that needs it
Volunteering with a community organization

Social Activities
Attending sporting events
Going to amusement parks
Going to carnivals/fairs
Going to other states/locations on vacation
Talking to others

COMMUNITY ACTIVITY RESOURCE SHEET

Name of Activity: _____

Where will it be done: _____

     Name: _____

     Address: _____

     Phone: _____

     Contact: _____

     When does the building open: _____

     When does the building close: _____

     How much does it cost: _____

     What time do we want to be at the building: _____

     Does the facility require a reservation? Yes_____ No _____

     Total number of people: Adults _____ Children: _____

Use the telephone directory and other resources to complete this list of recreation facilities available to you. Consider your means of transportation and the distance you would need to travel when listing facilities.

Recreation Centers

Address: _____   Phone: _____

What programs are offered that interest you? Cost? Distance?

_____

_____

Address: _____   Phone: _____

What programs are offered that interest you? Cost? Distance?

_____

_____

Address: _____   Phone: _____

What programs are offered that interest you? Cost? Distance?

_____

_____

Swimming Pools

Schools: _____   Day/Hours: _____   Cost: _____

_____   Day/Hours: _____   Cost: _____

Community: _____   Day/Hours: _____   Cost: _____

_____   Day/Hours: _____   Cost: _____

Private: _____   Day/Hours: _____   Cost: _____

_____   Day/Hours: _____   Cost: _____

Parks

Location: _____   Facilities: _____

_____

Location: _____   Facilities: _____

_____

Location: _____   Facilities: _____

_____

Fishing

Lakes and Streams: _____

_____

How to obtain a license: _____

Theaters

Movies:	_____	Times:	_____	Cost:	_____
	_____	Times:	_____	Cost:	_____
	_____	Times:	_____	Cost:	_____
Plays:	_____	Times:	_____	Cost:	_____
	_____	Times:	_____	Cost:	_____
Ballet/Dance:	_____	Times:	_____	Cost:	_____
	_____	Times:	_____	Cost:	_____
Musical:	_____	Times:	_____	Cost:	_____
	_____	Times:	_____	Cost:	_____

Bowling Alleys

Location:	_____	Day/Hours:	_____	Cost:	_____
Location:	_____	Day/Hours:	_____	Cost:	_____
Location:	_____	Day/Hours:	_____	Cost:	_____

Leagues to Join? _____

Roller-Skating

Location:	_____	Day/Hours:	_____	Cost:	_____
Location:	_____	Day/Hours:	_____	Cost:	_____
Location:	_____	Day/Hours:	_____	Cost:	_____

Ice Skating

Location:	_____	Day/Hours:	_____	Cost:	_____
Location:	_____	Day/Hours:	_____	Cost:	_____
Location:	_____	Day/Hours:	_____	Cost:	_____

Miniature Golf

Location:	_____	Day/Hours:	_____	Cost:	_____
Location:	_____	Day/Hours:	_____	Cost:	_____
Location:	_____	Day/Hours:	_____	Cost:	_____

Rent Bicycles/In-line Skates

Location:	_____	Day/Hours:	_____	Cost:	_____
Location:	_____	Day/Hours:	_____	Cost:	_____
Location:	_____	Day/Hours:	_____	Cost:	_____

Sailing

Location:	_____	Day/Hours:	_____	Cost:	_____
Location:	_____	Day/Hours:	_____	Cost:	_____
Location:	_____	Day/Hours:	_____	Cost:	_____

Horseback Riding

Location: _____ Day/Hours: _____ Cost: _____

Location: _____ Day/Hours: _____ Cost: _____

Location: _____ Day/Hours: _____ Cost: _____

Team Sports (e.g., Softball, Soccer, Volleyball)

Location: _____ Day/Hours: _____ Cost: _____

Location: _____ Day/Hours: _____ Cost: _____

Location: _____ Day/Hours: _____ Cost: _____

Tennis

Location: _____ Day/Hours: _____ Cost: _____

Location: _____ Day/Hours: _____ Cost: _____

Location: _____ Day/Hours: _____ Cost: _____

Adult Education Classes (e.g., aerobics, self-defense, art)

Location: _____ Day/Hours: _____ Cost: _____

Location: _____ Day/Hours: _____ Cost: _____

Location: _____ Day/Hours: _____ Cost: _____

Dancing (e.g., square dancing, ballroom dancing)

Location: _____ Day/Hours: _____ Cost: _____

Location: _____ Day/Hours: _____ Cost: _____

Location: _____ Day/Hours: _____ Cost: _____

Libraries

Location: _____ Day/Hours: _____ Cost: _____

Location: _____ Day/Hours: _____ Cost: _____

Location: _____ Day/Hours: _____ Cost: _____

Arts and Crafts Supplies

Location: _____ Day/Hours: _____ Cost: _____

Location: _____ Day/Hours: _____ Cost: _____

Location: _____ Day/Hours: _____ Cost: _____

REACTION SURVEY

1. Name 2 things you have learned throughout the 5 weeks of LEAP.

1. _____

2. _____

2. What is leisure/free time?

_____

_____

_____

3. What other skills would you like to learn?

_____

_____

_____

Additional comments:

_____

_____

_____

_____

_____

_____

_____

SOCIAL INTERACTION SKILLS ACTIVITIES

MUSICAL COMPLIMENTS

SPACE REQUIREMENTS

Classroom or activity room

MATERIALS

CD or tape player and soothing music, yarn, large button

GROUP SIZE

Small or large group

GOALS

1. To increase participants' comfort level with verbalizing self-compliments.

2. To increase participant's ability to appropriately give compliments to other group members.

PREPARATION

Gather materials

Thread a long piece of yarn through a large button (length depends on the size of the group) and tie the ends together to form a circle.

ACTIVITY DESCRIPTION

Have the group sit around a table or in a circle. Discuss compliments—what they are and how we feel when we give and receive them. Everyone holds on to the yarn.

Sit outside of the circle and begin playing the music. Have group members slide the button to the next person, and then that person continues by passing it along, and so forth. Stop the music and whomever has the button will have to give himself or herself a compliment. Continue this until everyone in the group has a chance to give himself or herself a compliment. For the next round, the button holder will give another group member of his or her choosing a compliment.

DEBRIEFING QUESTIONS

1. Is it easier to give a compliment to others or to yourself? Why?

2. How would your compliment be different if the person you were giving it

to was an acquaintance versus a close friend?

3. Did anyone dispute a compliment given to him or her (or feel like doing this)? Why?

4. What do you say if someone gives you a compliment?

5. What is something you often get compliments for?

6. Who is someone you often give compliments to?

7. Why is it important to give compliments?

8. Why is it important to be able to receive compliments?

9. Why is giving compliments a good social skill to have?

10. Challenge yourself daily to give three individuals you meet a compliment.

LEADERSHIP CONSIDERATIONS

1. Often group participants will negate compliments given to them (e.g., "This dress isn't nice, it is an old rag."). If this occurs, stop the group and discuss.

2. If group participants have trouble giving compliments to themselves, switch the order and have them start by first giving compliments to each other. Discuss difficulties incurred if there is a need to switch.

VARIATION

1. Have the group members take turns playing the music.

CONTRIBUTOR

Lois Witt Nilson

ASKING FOR HELP

SPACE REQUIREMENTS

Classroom or activity room

MATERIALS

Handout, pencils

GROUP SIZE

Small group

GOALS

1. To improve participants' awareness of the need to ask for help.

2. To improve participants' ability to ask for help appropriately.

ACTIVITY DESCRIPTION

Have the group gather around a table or sit in a circle. Ask participants to describe a few situations in which they have asked for help or that someone else has asked them for help. Discuss the need to ask for help appropriately—for example, locate the best person to ask, know when to interrupt someone else, ask in a calm and polite voice, tell the person the kind of help you need, and thank the person.

   Hand each participant a copy of the handout and a pencil. Ask each individual to fill in one response to each situation. Allow 5–10 minutes. Ask each individual to explain his or her response to the first situation. Compare answers and look for similarities and differences. Ask the participants to comment on each of the answers. Continue this process for each situation. Close with a discussion about asking for help appropriately, using the debriefing questions provided.

DEBRIEFING QUESTIONS

1. What types of responses are the most appropriate?

2. What are some general "rules" for asking for help?

3. Describe a time when you needed help and how you handled it.

4. Describe the same situation using the rules discussed today.

5. Why is it important to ask for help appropriately?

6. How do you tell when you need help and when you need to do something yourself?

7. What did you learn about asking for help today?

8. How will you use this information this week? next month? next year?

LEADERSHIP CONSIDERATIONS

1. Encourage participants to develop their own set of rules for asking for help.

VARIATIONS

1. Role-play both negative and positive behaviors.

2. Change situations to meet the needs, interests, and ages of the participants.

CONTRIBUTOR

Norma J. Stumbo

ASKING FOR HELP

Directions: For each of the scenarios write down at least one response.

1. Alfred needs help up the stairs. He sees Mary walking by and says, "Hey, you! I need help! Right now." What is a better way to ask Mary for help?

_____

_____

2. Stacey and Harold want to play a board game. Stacey says, "I don't understand these stupid directions. You figure out how to play the game!" What is a better way for Stacey to ask for help?

_____

_____

3. The curbcut is blocked and Jose can't get up to the sidewalk. He yells at the closest person, "Get over here and help me up this curb!" What is a better way for Jose to ask for help?

_____

_____

4. Charlotte can't quite reach the tennis racquet on the top shelf of the equipment closet. She says to the leader, "Get this racquet for me!" What is a better way to ask for help?

_____

_____

5. Jack can't find a seat in the dark movie theatre. He says loudly, "Does anyone know where there's an open seat?" What is a better way for Jack to find a seat?

_____

_____

6. Nancy doesn't know what a certain food is on the menu. She says to the server, "What's that stuff?!" What is a better way for Nancy to ask for information?

_____

_____

"YOU SAID WHAT?!"

SPACE REQUIREMENTS

Classroom or activity room

MATERIALS

Flip chart and markers, dictionary

GROUP SIZE

Small group

GOALS

1. To increase participants' self-awareness with regard to their behavior.
2. To increase participants' awareness of impulsive behavior and methods to manage this behavior.
3. To increase participants' awareness of impulsive behavior as a frequent sequelae of traumatic brain injury.

PREPARATION

Gather materials

ACTIVITY DESCRIPTION

Have the group sit around a table or in a circle. Ask participants to describe what impulsiveness means. Emphasize that impulsiveness is a frequent sequelae of traumatic brain injury. Encourage each participant to contribute to the definition and write these contributions on the flip chart. The group then reviews its definition and compares it to the dictionary definition.

Ask for examples of impulsiveness and write them on the flip chart. Ask the group why it is helpful to be aware of impulsive behavior and to do something to change it. Record ideas on the flip chart.

Divide the group into subgroups of 3–4. Give each subgroup a hypothetical situation to role-play. The subgroups meet for 20 minutes to rehearse a skit based on the situation. Each subgroup then performs its role-play for the entire group. Ask other group members to identify impulsive behavior, and how the individual could change this behavior. Record ideas on the flip chart.

DEBRIEFING QUESTIONS

1. What is impulsive behavior?
2. What are some examples of impulsive behavior?
3. What are some examples of your impulsive behavior within the last day or week?
4. What are the consequences of impulsive behavior?
5. What are ways to reduce impulsive behavior?
6. What are the consequences of reducing impulsive behavior?
7. What is one thing you can do to reduce your impulsive behavior?
8. How will you remember to reduce your impulsive behavior?

LEADERSHIP CONSIDERATIONS

1. This is an activity for clients who have some level of abstract reasoning. Clients with more concrete thought processing will require more assistance but can potentially benefit from the activity.
2. Family members may benefit from inclusion; however, as the topic may be sensitive for the clients, the clients should be included in the decision making.

VARIATION

1. The skits may be videotaped, which could provide valuable feedback to the client regarding posture, mannerisms, and voice intonation.

CONTRIBUTOR

Tami Pringnitz Guerrier

"YOU SAID WHAT?!"

HYPOTHETICAL SITUATIONS

The following situations involve several people, one of whom is exhibiting impulsive behavior.

1. While on lunch break, several coworkers are socializing by the coffee table. Another coworker, who is obviously pregnant, joins them. One individual immediately puts his or her hand on the pregnant woman's stomach. The coworker, clearly offended, steps back and then leaves the group.

2. While shopping with a friend, an individual decides he or she must purchase a stereo. The friend attempts to point out the benefits of shopping around and shopping at stores specializing in stereos. The individual decides he or she must have the stereo this weekend, so he or she purchases it from a department store. Once home, the individual realizes the controls are very difficult for him or her to read and use.

3. As a group of coworkers are socializing, the topic of the upcoming football game is brought up. One coworker states, "I'll bet anyone $50 my team will win." Not thinking that the $50 is half of his paycheck, an individual takes the bet. Later, after losing the bet, the coworker pressures the individual to pay up. The individual also learns later that gambling is against his or her company policy.

4. While visiting the state fair, an individual crosses paths with someone he or she feels is particularly good looking. Immediately, the individual approaches this person and says, "You're cute. Would you like to go out with me?"

REFERENCES

Kneipp, S. (1985). *Group activities for head injured persons: A handbook*. Philadelphia, PA: Community Skills Program.

Kneipp, S. (1986). *Group activities for head injured persons: Handbook II*. Philadelphia, PA: Community Skills Program.

Kneipp, S. (1988). *Therapeutic fun for head injured persons and their families*. Philadelphia, PA: Community Skills Program.

PICK ME UP BOUQUET

SPACE REQUIREMENTS

Classroom or activity room

MATERIALS

Handout, pencils

GROUP SIZE

Small group

GOALS

1. To improve the participant's ability to give and receive positive feedback.
2. To have participants gain an understanding of how others perceive them.

PREPARATION

Gather materials

ACTIVITY DESCRIPTION

Have the group sit around a table or in a circle and give each participant a copy of the handout and a pencil. Each participant puts his or her name on the form. Everyone passes their form to the person to the right. Each participant writes something positive about this person in one of the petals or leaves of the flower. The papers continue to rotate around the table so that each person writes about every other person in the group. The papers should end up with the originator. Each participant reads aloud all of the positive comments written on his or her flower.

Discussion should focus on the importance of positive feedback, if participants were surprised by anything written on their forms, and the difficulties of giving positive feedback.

DEBRIEFING QUESTIONS

1. What are 2 of the items on your flower that you are surprised by?
2. Summarize in 1 sentence what the compliments say about you.
3. How easy or difficult was it to give someone a compliment?
4. How easy or difficult was it to receive compliments?
5. How would your compliment be different if the person you were giving it to was an acquaintance versus a close friend?
6. Did anyone dispute a compliment given to him or her (or feel like doing this)? Why?
7. What do you say if someone gives you a compliment?
8. What is something you often get compliments for?
9. Who is someone you often give compliments to?
10. Why is it important to give compliments?
11. Why is it important to be able to receive compliments?
12. Why is giving compliments a good social skill to have?
13. Challenge yourself daily to give 3 individuals you meet a compliment.

LEADERSHIP CONSIDERATIONS

1. Participants must be able to read and write.
2. Participants must be familiar with one another.

VARIATION

1. At the end of the activity, have each individual write in the middle of the flower what they like best about themselves. Discussion should include whether that was difficult, and whether it matched what anyone else wrote about them.

CONTRIBUTORS

Cynthia Rodgers, Marilyn Tense, Christine Lundin

LEISURE UNO

SPACE REQUIREMENTS

Classroom or activity room

MATERIALS

Poster board, glue sticks, scissors, colored dots (blue, red, green, and yellow), pictures cut from magazines

GROUP SIZE

Small group

GOALS

1. To increase participant's ability to share materials and communicate positively.
2. To increase participants' awareness of colors and activities.

PREPARATION

Gather materials

Cut out pictures from magazines depicting 4 different leisure activities (e.g., listening to music, reading, playing sports, doing arts and crafts)

ACTIVITY DESCRIPTION

Have the group sit around a table or in a circle. Explain to participants that they will be making and playing a card game involving matching colors and pictures. Review the colors and pictures with participants. Explain that the pictures are of activities that people might do in their free time (e.g., listening to music, reading, playing sports, doing arts and crafts).

MAKING LEISURE UNO

1. Give participants previously cut leisure pictures (4 music, 4 sports, 4 arts and crafts, 4 reading) and poster board.
2. Have participants mark each card at the top with one of the four colored dots (blue, red, green, and yellow). There will be 16 cards: 4 blue, 4 red, 4 green, and 4 yellow.
3. Participants will glue each set of pictures on each of the four colors (e.g., blue sports card, red sports card, yellow sports card, and green sports card).
4. Allow the cards to dry.
5. Combine the cards from participants to make a deck.

PLAYING LEISURE UNO

1. Divide participants into pairs or small groups.
2. Deal 5 cards to each player and place the rest of the deck face down between the players (draw pile).
3. Turn over one card and leave face up to start. Participants take turns matching pictures or colors of the last card facing up.
4. A player who matches the color or the picture should place his or her card face up on the top of the pile.
5. If a player cannot make a match he or she must pick one card from the draw pile. If this card matches the card on the discard pile, it may be played. If not, the participant continues to draw cards until a match is found.
6. When a player is down to one card, he or she must say "Uno."
7. Failure to say "Uno" and being caught results in the player having to pick 2 cards from the draw pile.
8. The game is over when 1 player runs out of cards.

DEBRIEFING QUESTIONS

1. Would you consider this a competitive game or a cooperative game?
2. Were group members able to share materials well?
3. What did you learn today from doing this activity?

LEADERSHIP CONSIDERATIONS

1. Participants may need assistance cutting, or may choose to cut independently as much as possible.
2. Participants may need encouragement to wait their turns.

3. Younger participants may need assistance and reminders when matching colors.

VARIATIONS

1. If matching colors is difficult, only two colors can be used.

2. Different themes or activity areas may be used for the pictures (e.g., numbers, animals, letters, places, countries).

CONTRIBUTOR

Jennifer Church
Adapted from the game "Uno" produced by International Games

WHEEL OF LEISURE CHARADES

SPACE REQUIREMENTS

Classroom or activity room with tables or desks

MATERIALS

Markers, chalkboard and chalk, tape, spinner, list of suggested words and phrases

GROUP SIZE

Small group

GOALS

1. To increase participants' positive communication with one another (verbal and nonverbal) in small groups.
2. To increase participants' knowledge of leisure activities.

PREPARATION

Gather materials

ACTIVITY DESCRIPTION

Divide the group into 3 teams. Give each team a pack of markers, tape, and a piece of paper for each team member. Instruct participants to write their first names on the paper and tape it to the front of their desks or table. Have the group determine a group name and write this on the chalkboard.

RULES OF THE GAME

1. Pick a leisure word or phrase and draw the correct number of blanks on the board.
2. Each team will get a turn to spin the spinner. If they land on 1, 2, or 3, the team guesses a letter. If that letter is in the word, the team receives that number of points. If the letter is not in the word, no points are received.
3. After guessing a letter correctly, the team can guess the word or phrase. To guess, the entire team must "act out" the leisure word or phrase.
4. The other 2 teams may guess the charade by raising their hands and being called upon. If the acting team is correct, they will receive 5 points, if incorrect, they will deduct 2 points.
5. If another team correctly guesses what the acting team is doing, they will receive 1 point.
6. After each word is guessed, a new word or phrase will be selected, and play continues with a different team going first.

DEBRIEFING QUESTIONS

1. How many new leisure activities did you hear about today?
2. How many of these activities have you participated in?
3. Which are your favorite leisure activities?
4. How well did the group members cooperate with one another?
5. Was this a competitive game, a cooperative game, or both?
6. How did cooperative skills help the activity move along?
7. Which of the leisure activities mentioned also require cooperative skills? competitive skills?
8. Which set of skills are you best at?
9. Summarize what you've learned through this activity today.

LEADERSHIP CONSIDERATION

1. If participants have difficulty writing or spelling, the participants can draw their names as well as themselves for the team names.

VARIATIONS

1. Assign a leader or volunteer to assist each team if necessary.
2. Prior to playing the game, have the participants think of leisure phrases or words as a group.

CONTRIBUTOR

Marian Harrs
Adapted from the TV game show Wheel of Fortune

SUGGESTIONS FOR LEISURE WORDS AND PHRASES

Bowling

Downhill skiing

Nintendo

Roller-skating

Swimming

Singing

Basketball

Frisbee golf

Reading a book

Volleyball

Bike riding

Walking

Ice skating

Playing cards

Camping

Gardening

Going to a play

Hiking

Football

Baseball

GROUP YAHTZEE

SPACE REQUIREMENTS

Classroom or activity room

MATERIALS

Yahtzee game (including five dice and 1 score sheet)

GROUP SIZE

Small group

GOALS

1. To increase participants' attention span.
2. To increase participants' decision-making skills.
3. To increase participants' social interaction skills.

PREPARATION

Gather materials

ACTIVITY DESCRIPTION

Have group members sit around a table, determine who will start, and choose a scorekeeper. One individual will throw the dice 3 times (in accordance with Yahtzee rules) and announce the results to the group. The group will determine by consensus which category to apply the results to and the scorekeeper will mark the total in the appropriate place on the scoresheet. The next individual will throw the dice, announce the results, and again the group will determine by consensus where to apply the results. Game goes around the table until all spaces on the scoresheet are filled. The group then adds up their total score. Additional rounds may be played to improve upon earlier team scores. Complete the activity by using the following debriefing questions.

DEBRIEFING QUESTIONS

1. Is this mostly a cooperative or competitive game?
2. Which type of game are you most comfortable with? Why?
3. Is this mostly a game of chance or a game of skill?
4. Which type of game are you most comfortable with? Why?
5. How well were you able to stay focused on the activity?
6. What helped you stay or become more focused on the game?
7. How satisfied were you with the decisions you made about where to place your numbers?
8. Summarize what you've learned from this activity today.

LEADERSHIP CONSIDERATIONS

1. Be familiar with regular Yahtzee game.
2. Each game takes 10–15 minutes. (Good for patients with a short attention span.)
3. Keep competition to a minimum and emphasize cooperative effort.

VARIATIONS

1. Have participants work in 2 teams.
2. Have individuals complete separate scores sheets.

CONTRIBUTOR

Barb Sauer

WHAT SHALL I WEAR?

SPACE REQUIREMENTS

Classroom or activity room

MATERIALS

Pictures of men and women cut out of catalogs with different types of clothing (e.g., dress, informal, lounging, sportswear), poster board, 3x5 cards

GROUP SIZE

Small group

GOALS

1. To improve participants' ability to determine appropriate attire for various leisure activities.
2. To improve participants' ability to modify leisure activities based on clothes they have and budget allowance for new clothes.

PREPARATION

Gather materials
Cut out pictures and paste them to posterboard
Write leisure situations on 3x5 cards

ACTIVITY DESCRIPTION

Have the group sit around a table or in a circle. Have each group member come up and read a situation card and then pick an outfit from the pictures that would be appropriate for that situation. Other group members discuss the choice and decide whether it is appropriate for that situation.

Discussion questions could center around what they can do if they enjoy a particular leisure activity (e.g., going to the symphony) and don't have the clothes for such an occasion. Alternatives could also be discussed (e.g., concerts in the park, getting together with friends who like the same music).

DEBRIEFING QUESTIONS

1. Give an example of activity that requires special clothing.

2. What clothing do you own that is for a specific leisure activity?
3. What alternatives might there be if you want to do a leisure activity and don't have the right clothing?
4. How do you determine if a leisure activity requires a certain kind of clothes?
5. Why might it be important to wear the right clothing for certain activities (e.g., playing tennis) or events (e.g., dinner in a nice restaurant)?
6. Besides department stores and discount stores, what other places sell clothing?
7. Summarize what you've learned about leisure activities and clothing today.

LEADERSHIP CONSIDERATIONS

1. Stress that there may not be a right or wrong answer but look for obviously inappropriate choices.
2. Be sensitive to cultural issues regarding appropriate dress. Be sure that the pictures chosen reflect the cultural diversity of the group.
3. Include leisure activities specific to the local geographical area.

VARIATION

1. Have the group members work in pairs.

CONTRIBUTORS

Kathy Nesheim Larson, Lois Witt Nilson

SAMPLE SITUATIONS

1. First date
2. Movie at a theater
3. Swimming or going to a water park
4. Hiking
5. In-line skating
6. Shopping
7. Fishing
8. Dining at a fine restaurant
9. Jogging
10. Going to the library

SOCIAL SITUATIONS

SPACE REQUIREMENTS

Classroom or activity room

MATERIALS

List of hypothetical situations

GROUP SIZE

Small group (in physical rehabilitation)

GOALS

1. To improve participants' ability to handle social situations that may occur upon discharge.

2. To improve participants' ability to anticipate their individual reactions to social conversations and situations

3. To encourage group members to give each other feedback on the appropriateness of their anticipated reactions and responses.

PREPARATION

Gather materials

ACTIVITY DESCRIPTION

Have the group sit around a table or in a circle. Discuss situations that participants may be confronted with once released from the rehabilitation facility. The purpose of the activity is to help them mentally prepare for socially awkward or embarrassing situations and to discuss ways to handle them.

Select one group participant to read one of the hypothetical situations aloud and give his or her response. The group should give feedback, perhaps stating what their own responses would be. Continue the discussion as each group member reads and responds to a hypothetical situation. Direct participants to be constructive, socially appropriate, and honest in their feedback.

Discussion may include whether these situations or similar ones have already been encountered by the participants, how the situation may dictate the type of response given, and the concepts of passive, assertive, and aggressive behavior.

DEBRIEFING QUESTIONS

1. Have you encountered any of these situations?

2. What are some rules of thumb for handling awkward situations?

3. What factors need to be considered before you respond to someone's comments or actions?

4. What are the differences between passive, assertive, and aggressive responses?

5. What are the advantages and disadvantages of each?

6. What are the advantages of practicing your response ahead of time?

7. Which types of responses given today would be the most appropriate?

8. What did you learn today that you can use in the future?

LEADERSHIP CONSIDERATIONS

1. Do not let one or more members control the group by always giving the "right" answers. Stress that no answer is perfect or right and everyone deals with these types of situations in their own ways.

VARIATIONS

1. Change the hypothetical situations to fit characteristics of the community or the participants.

2. Change the hypothetical situations to "themes" such as family and friends, dating, or strangers.

3. Change the hypothetical situations for individuals at other types of facilities.

4. Have the participants role-play the situations, taking turns playing both parts.

CONTRIBUTOR

Norma J. Stumbo

HYPOTHETICAL SITUATIONS

1. You and a close friend are going out to eat. Your friend selects a new restaurant that just opened. The restaurant has 12 steps to get to the front door. What would you do? What actions would you take?

2. You and several friends have arranged to have a drink after work at a neighborhood bar. After being there for about two hours, you try to enter the rest room and find that you cannot make it through the doorway. What would you do? What actions would you take?

3. While in the local shopping mall, a child about 6 years old walks up to you and says "Hey, what happened to you?" What is your response?

4. While at a local festival, a child about 6 years old walks up to you and says "Hey, what's wrong with you?" Before you get the chance to say or do anything, the child's parents pull her away and say "Don't you ever do that again! That's rude!" What is your response? What actions do you take?

5. An older man approaches you in the store and starts to tell you about his friend that is "crippled" from the war. His description of the friend's disability and situation is quite lengthy. His last comment is "I know what you're going through." What is your response? What actions do you take?

6. You have just been out of the rehabilitation center for 2 weeks and your friends ask you to go out Saturday night to the local hot spot—a place for singles to meet. You have made plans for Saturday during the day and think you might be tired. What is your response? Will you go?

7. You want to purchase tickets for a concert that you've been wanting to see for a long time. When you call for tickets, the person taking ticket orders says that the wheelchair seating section is sold out and that you cannot sit anywhere else in the concert hall. What is your response? What actions do you take?

8. When getting out of your car, a stranger comes over and starts handling your wheelchair before saying anything to you. You are independent and need no assistance. What is your response?

9. You are independent in getting out of your car. Today you have a friend with you as you drive to the art museum. As you're getting out of your car and your friend stands there talking to you, a stranger yells at your friend for not helping you. What do you tell this person?

10. You've just gotten home from the rehabilitation center and an old friend stops by. Before long, the friend is crying and saying he wished the accident had happened to him instead of you—saying that life just isn't fair. What do you tell your friend?

11. Your old friends seem to feel really uncomfortable around you and eventually they stop calling and asking you to do things with them. It's been over 2 months since you've seen any of them. How would you handle this? What do you do?

LEISURE OBSERVATION

SPACE REQUIREMENTS

Classroom or activity room

MATERIALS

Paper, pencils

GROUP SIZE

Small group

GOALS

1. To increase participants' awareness of how others perceive them.

2. To increase participants' awareness of different characteristics associated with leisure activities.

3. To improve participants' ability to give and receive constructive feedback within a group setting.

ACTIVITY DESCRIPTION

Have the group form a circle and distribute paper and pencils. Discuss the importance of other's perceptions and how they affect social situations. Have participants recall a social situation when someone else's perception affected how they felt about a leisure experience or other social situation.

Instruct each participant to write his or her name on the paper. Each person should then pass his or her paper to the right. That person will then write down a leisure activity that best describes a personality characteristic of the member whose name is on the paper and explain why that activity was chosen. This continues until each group member has written one activity and explanation for each group member.

Collect the papers and read the activities and why they were chosen. The group members are to guess who the activities are describing. After each person is identified, ask if he or she agrees with the selections and if not which activities are better descriptors. Discuss people's perceptions, how important they are, what people may do to change people's perceptions, and the relationship of perceptions to social situations.

DEBRIEFING QUESTIONS

1. Summarize what the group said about you.

2. How well does this match with your own self-perception?

3. Why are people's perceptions important?

4. How can other people's perceptions be changed (for better or worse)?

5. How do people's perceptions affect social leisure situations?

6. Describe a time where an individual's perceptions affected your leisure and the impact that it had.

LEADERSHIP CONSIDERATIONS

1. Review a number of leisure activities available if the participants do not have extensive prior knowledge.

2. The activity works best with people who are familiar with each other.

3. Provide a starting example—perhaps have the participants start with selecting activities and reasons for the leader.

4. Emphasize that it is not the member's favorite activity, but rather one that best describes a personality characteristic.

VARIATION

1. Have each participant complete a similar exercise on himself or herself, and compare with the group's responses.

CONTRIBUTOR

Jean Folkerth

I GIVE . . .

SPACE REQUIREMENTS

Classroom or activity room

MATERIALS

Paper, envelopes, pencils

GROUP SIZE

Small group

GOALS

1. To increase participants' awareness of personal strengths and weaknesses.

2. To increase participants' awareness of other people's perceptions of them.

3. To increase participants' ability to give and receive constructive feedback and criticism in a small group setting.

PREPARATION

Gather materials

ACTIVITY DESCRIPTION

Have the group form a circle and distribute paper, envelopes, and pencils. Discuss the importance of becoming aware of personal strengths and weaknesses through feedback from others. Include how to give and receive constructive feedback, what social boundaries exist for doing so, and how helpful feedback may be in making self-improvements.

Each participant will give one "present" to every other member in the group. Have participants write statements that reflect some attribute, skill, or value that the individual would want the other person to have. For example, "I give Harvey the ability to make friends more easily," "I give Cherise the ability to laugh at herself when things go wrong," "I give Chris the ability to stop criticizing herself in public." Allow 10–15 minutes.

Each participant then puts the statements in envelopes with the receiver's name on the outside and hands it to the individual. After all envelopes have been distributed, each person may open his/her envelopes and read the statements. Each individual may share with the group the enclosed statements or may summarize the statements, if uncomfortable with sharing all statements.

As each person discloses the contents of the envelope, facilitate the discussion by asking what the participant learned about himself or herself, how others people's perceptions differ from their own, and what changes might be made. Focus on helping people find out what others think about them through constructive feedback.

DEBRIEFING QUESTIONS

1. Summarize the overall message you received from the group today.

2. How closely does that match with your self-perceptions?

3. What new insights did you gain from the others' feedback?

4. Why do other people's perceptions of you differ from your self-perceptions?

5. What have you heard today that may prompt changes in your actions or behaviors?

6. How easy or difficult is it to give constructive feedback to others?

7. How easy or difficult is it to receive constructive feedback from others?

8. Why is it important to periodically hear other's perceptions of you?

9. What did you learn about other's perceptions of you today?

10. What did you learn about yourself today?

LEADERSHIP CONSIDERATIONS

1. This can be a threatening activity for those who do not take criticism well. Encourage participants to be constructive and allow individuals to disclose the contents of the statements to whatever level they choose.

VARIATION

1. At the end of the sharing part of the activity, have each person write an "I give" statement to himself or herself.

DISCOVERING YOUR LEISURE PARTNERS

SPACE REQUIREMENTS

Classroom or activity room

MATERIALS

Handout, pencils

GROUP SIZE

Small group

GOALS

1. To increase participants' awareness of patterns and preferences in choosing leisure partners.

2. To increase participants' ability to identify past, present, and future leisure partners.

3. To encourage group participants to make conscious decisions regarding future leisure partners.

PREPARATION

Gather materials
Make one copy of the handout for each participant

ACTIVITY DESCRIPTION

Have the group form a circle and distribute the handouts and pencils. Discuss how most leisure occurs in social situations, requiring the presence of other people. The purpose of the activity is to discover what types of people the participants usually select to participate in leisure with.

Give an example of the characteristics of someone you choose to participate with in your leisure. Have group participants complete the handout. Allow 10–15 minutes.

Ask participants to look for trends in their choices. What patterns have they discovered among their leisure partners? What categories were checked most frequently? Do they enjoy people close to their own age? Does the other person always make decisions about what to do? What does this say about what the individual values in another person? What does this say about

the individual's values? Discuss the similarities and differences among group participants. Discuss how these factors influence the types of people selected for leisure partners, whether they are satisfied with the types of people on their lists, and how new leisure partners may be found.

DEBRIEFING QUESTIONS

1. Summarize the characteristics of your leisure partners.

2. What are the 3 most common characteristics of these leisure partners?

3. How do these individuals differ?

4. How do your leisure partners influence the leisure activities or experiences you participate in?

5. How satisfied are you with your choice of leisure partners?

6. What (if any) changes would you like to make in your choice of leisure partners?

7. What are some of the steps needed to make these changes?

8. Where might you find desired leisure partners?

9. What differences in your leisure participation might occur if you changed leisure partners?

10. What insights did you gain today about your past, present, and future leisure partners?

LEADERSHIP CONSIDERATIONS

1. Encourage group participants to be honest to hightlight true patterns.

2. Encourage group participants to list at least 5 people to uncover patterns.

VARIATIONS

1. Modify the categories to respond to depending on the intent of the leisure education session.

2. This activity may be appropriate for people with substance abuse problems—with a slight modification of categories, it could determine appropriateness of future leisure partners.

3. Complete only one column on the form.

DISCOVERING YOUR LEISURE PARTNERS

Directions: In the columns labeled "initials," write the initials of several people who you often invite to do something and 10 people who often invite you to do something. Then place a check mark in the categories that apply to those people:

R = if the person is a relative
X = if you probably won't do anything with this person again
A = if the person is within 3 years of your age
* = if the person is someone who you really enjoy doing things with
F = if you generally have fun and enjoy yourself with this person
W = if you wish you could do more things with this person
M = if the person has annoying behaviors or you usually argue when you're together
B = if this person is a bad influence on you
L = if you wish you could be more like this person
C = if you feel comfortable with this person
D = if this person usually decides what you will do together

YOU HAVE INVITED THEM   **THEY HAVE INVITED YOU**

INITIALS	R	X	A	*	F	W	M	B	L	C	D	INITIALS	R	X	A	*	F	W	M	B	L	C	D

ARE YOU LISTENING?

SPACE REQUIREMENTS

Classroom or activity room

MATERIALS

List of sample discussion topics

GROUP SIZE

Small group

GOALS

1. To increase participants' ability to self-disclose to another person.
2. To increase participants' ability to build trust with a partner.
3. To increase participants' ability to take social risks with a partner.
4. To increase participants' communication and listening skills.

PREPARATION

Gather materials

ACTIVITY DESCRIPTION

Have the group sit around a table or in a circle. Discuss communication and social skills, such as building trust, self-disclosure, taking risks, and listening. Ask group participants to list important communication skills (e.g., asking questions, listening, giving appropriate responses, taking turns). Explain that the activity will help improve these skills.

Ask each participant to choose a partner he or she doesn't know very well. Each pair is then given one topic to discuss for 5 minutes. After 5 minutes, each participant is instructed to find another partner who they also do not know very well. The new pair is given a new topic to discuss for 5 minutes.

After the discussions are completed, hold a group discussion on the exercise. Reiterate some of the communication and social skills noted previously, and ask the following questions to encourage the group to share their thoughts on the activity.

DEBRIEFING QUESTIONS

1. How well did you feel your partner listened to you? What behaviors indicated whether or not he or she was listening? How do you show an interest in what someone is saying?
2. How easily were you able to share your thoughts or feelings? How much did you screen your comments before saying them?
3. In your usual conversation style, do you usually think you talk too much or too little?
4. If there were more time, would you have continued the conversations?
5. In what ways was your partner like you or quite different from you? Do you like having a partner who is like you or different from you?
6. Would you like your partner to have some of the same experiences? Would you like to have some of his or her experiences?
7. How easy or difficult was it to build trust and self-disclose with another person?
8. How easy or difficult was it to take social risks with another person? What risks did you take?
9. Summarize what you learned in this activity today.

LEADERSHIP CONSIDERATIONS

1. Make sure that paired participants do not know each other well.
2. If a participant feels uncomfortable with the assigned topic, he or she may choose an alternative topic.
3. The activity is especially good when working with a new group because it builds rapport.

VARIATIONS

1. The topics for discussion could be changed to meet the intent of the leisure education session and the needs of the participants.

2. Designate a third person to observe certain communication and/or social skills (e.g., how many times the "listener" asked questions, how many times the "talker" was interrupted).

SAMPLE DISCUSSION TOPICS

1. Tell about the person who has had the most impact on your life.

2. Tell which is more important to you—work or leisure—and why.

3. What are some things you do which you think are unconventional?

4. Tell about a turning point in your life.

5. Describe a time of your greatest despair.

6. Tell some things you would put in your will.

7. Describe the worst hypothetical social evening for you and tell what you would do about it.

8. Share some of your feelings or experiences about death.

WHAT I SEE IN YOU

SPACE REQUIREMENTS

Classroom or activity room

MATERIALS

Handout, pencils

GROUP SIZE

Small group (divisible by 4)

GOALS

1. To increase participants' awareness of how other people view them.
2. To increase participants' awareness of their own self-perceptions.
3. To improve participants' ability to appreciate differences among people.

PREPARATION

Make one copy of the handout for each participant

ACTIVITY DESCRIPTION

Have the group sit around a table or in a circle. Discuss the different traits found in individuals. Everybody possesses traits that make up their personalities and make them special. Individuals can be unaware of how others perceive them or how they perceive themselves.

Divide into groups of 4 and distribute the handout and pencils. Participants are to label each of the 4 boxes with the names of individuals within their groups, including themselves. From the list of traits, participants select the appropriate traits and write them in the boxes with the individual names. They are to include themselves, writing down traits they believe they possess. Allow 5–10 minutes. Encourage everybody to be honest and truthful throughout the activity.

After completion, ask the groups to share what they have written for each person. Discussion may focus on the differences between what the other members saw and what the individual saw in himself or herself. Are there things that other members saw in people that they themselves did not? Are there traits that the individual saw and no one else

did? What are traits you desire to have? Did more than one person see these traits in them? How do the individuals portray these traits to other people? How did you determine if someone possessed a trait or not? How could positive traits be brought out more strongly and the more negative ones diminished? What goals could each individual set to possess more positive traits?

The summary discussion should refocus on the beginning discussion of individual traits and differences among people. Depending on the nature of the leisure education session, individuals might be asked to write down daily and weekly goals to improve their own traits and how they are portrayed.

DEBRIEFING QUESTIONS

1. Describe how other individuals see you. What traits did they list under your name?
2. Describe how you see yourself. What traits did you list under your name?
3. How closely do others' and your own self-perceptions match?
4. What were some of the similarities and differences among members of the group?
5. How can we emphasize our positive traits and downplay our negative traits?
6. What effect do these traits have on our social life and relationships?
7. What effect do these traits have on our leisure participation and leisure partners?
8. How would you like to change your personal traits?
9. What did you learn about yourself today through this activity?

LEADERSHIP CONSIDERATIONS

1. Members of the groups must know each other reasonably well to complete this activity.
2. Be aware that some individuals will be threatened by receiving direct feedback from other individuals in the group.

3. Stress that this is an opportunity to learn how others perceive the group members. While members should be honest, they should also be considerate and give constructive feedback.

VARIATIONS

1. Modify the list of traits to meet the intent of the leisure education session and the needs of the individual clients.

2. It may be less threatening if pairs, instead of groups of four, complete the activity together.

WHAT I SEE IN YOU

1	2
3	4

Friendly	Well-dressed	Pretty
Good looking	Outgoing	Shy
Adventurous	Sensitive	Studious
Cautious	Creative	Talented
Compassionate	Kind	Loving
Caring	Self-confident	Gracious
Intelligent	Family oriented	Athletic
Happy	Smiling	Cheerful
Talkative	Organized	Considerate
Helpful	Professional	Romantic
Fun loving	Willing to take risks	Good listener
Bossy	Pessimistic	Optimistic
Able to make decisions	Humorous	Withdrawn
Sarcastic	Efficient	Physically fit

COMMUNICATION BLOCKS

SPACE REQUIREMENTS

Classroom or activity room

MATERIALS

Handout, list of sample discussion topics, pencils

GROUP SIZE

Small group

GOALS

1. To improve participants' ability to identify blocks to effective communication.
2. To improve participants' ability to reduce their blocks to effective communication.

PREPARATION

Gather materials
Make one copy of the handout for each participant

ACTIVITY DESCRIPTION

Have the group sit around a table or in a circle. Discuss communication skills, emphasizing that communication is important to all interactions between people. Sometimes these communications are blocked by the way we make statements. Not only does that stop us from really listening to the other person, but it minimizes their chances for getting their real message to us. The purpose of this activity is to examine some blocks to effective communication and to discover which blocks participants use most often.

Give each participant a copy of the handout and a pencil. Divide participants into groups of 3. Two people will discuss a topic and a third will observe.

Instruct participants that they are to choose a topic and discuss it for 5–8 minutes. During these conversations, the observer is to mark on the handout each time either person uses a block to communication. If possible, he or she should jot down the statement.

The purpose of using an observer is to have a record for each person to examine after the dia-

logues have been completed. After 5–8 minutes, the roles are changed. Rotate until all 3 have had the chance to be the observer.

Ask each person to look over the forms. Discuss what they may be surprised at, whether they think the blocks reflect their typical language, and where they learned to use these blocks. Review the blocks with the participants and ask them to be aware of when these blocks are used.

DEBRIEFING QUESTIONS

1. What blocks to effective communication did you use today?
2. How typical are these blocks to your everyday communication style?
3. What about your communication blocks surprised you?
4. What purpose have your communication blocks served in the past?
5. What happens to effective communication when people place roadblocks in their path?
6. What are some steps to remove communication blocks?
7. How does being aware of the blocks help in removing them?
8. How will communication improve without blocks or with fewer blocks?
9. What is one change you'll make in removing blocks to effective communication?
10. Summarize what you learned about communication blocks today in this activity.

LEADERSHIP CONSIDERATION

1. Decide whether the participants should view the list of communication blocks before the dialogues.

VARIATIONS

1. Ask the participants to record, during a conversation outside the activity, how many times they use these blocks. If a pattern develops for the individual, he or she is to make note of it and actions that might be taken to diminish it.

2. Write out conversational scenarios for participants to read. After each scenario is read aloud, ask participants to indicate which communication block(s) were present. Ask them to then rewrite the scripts to allow communication to be more effective.

3. Ask the participants to share a recent conversation that they were dissatisfied with. Ask the other participants to analyze what block(s) to communication were present. Ask them to suggest ways to eliminate the block(s) to encourage more effective communication.

SAMPLE DISCUSSION TOPICS

What you would do with more free time?
What you would like to do on vacation?
Which activities would you like to learn but haven't taken the time?
What will your leisure time be like when you become older?

COMMUNICATION BLOCKS	PERSON 1	PERSON 2
1. Persuading with logic, arguing, teaching *Do you realize that... Here is why you are wrong...* *That is not right...The facts are... Yes, but...*		
2. Judging, blaming, criticizing, evaluating *You are bad...You're not thinking straight...* *Your hair is too long...You're a good boy...* *You've done a good job... That's a very good drawing...*		
3. Interpreting, analyzing, diagnosing, offering insight *What you need is...What's wrong with you is...* *You're just trying to get attention...* *You really don't mean that...Your problem is...*		
4. Reassuring, consoling, supporting, excusing *It's not so bad...Don't worry...You'll feel better...* *That's too bad*		
5. Ordering, warning, threatening *You had better...If you don't then...*		
6. Moralizing, preaching, advising, providing answers or solutions *You should...You ought to...It is your duty...What I would do is...* *Why don't you...It would be best for you...*		
7. Questioning, probing, cross-examining, prying, interrogation *Why...Who...Where...What...How...When...*		
8. Diverting, avoiding, bypassing, digressing, shifting *Let's not talk about it now...Not at the dinner table...* *Forget it...That reminds me...We can discuss it later...*		
9. Kidding, teasing, making light of, joking, using sarcasm *Why don't you burn the school down? When did you read* *a newspaper last? Get up on the wrong side of the bed* *this morning?*		

NEGOTIATING CONFLICTS

SPACE REQUIREMENTS

Classroom or activity room

MATERIALS

Handout, pencils

GROUP SIZE

Small group

GOALS

1. To increase participants' understanding of conflict resolution.
2. To increase participants' ability to think through and negotiate conflicts in an appropriate manner.
3. To increase participants' ability to see negative and positive aspects in their own conflict resolution behavior.

PREPARATION

Gather materials
Make one copy of the handout for each participant

ACTIVITY DESCRIPTION

Have the group sit around a table or in a circle. Introduce the topic of conflicts and problems. Being a part of everyday life, problems in relationships are unavoidable. To maintain mental and social health, each individual must learn skills in negotiating and resolving conflicts. Individuals may be asked to share some current or past conflicts within relationships.

Have each individual select one conflict or problem that has been or is currently troublesome. Distribute the handout and ask each person to write his or her conflict at the top. Each individual is to examine each of the principles and write down a negative and positive response that they had or could have had. For example, consider the principle "be open to various solutions." Negative responses could be, "I see everything as black or white," or "I always think I'm right." Positive responses could be, "I listened to my spouse's suggestion that later worked," or "I asked a coworker for help with solutions."

When each person has completed the form, ask whether their actual responses were more often in the negative column or positive column. Ask what steps could be taken to resolve conflicts and problems in a more positive, healthy manner. How do they feel when they exhibit negative behaviors? How does it help to solve the problem? How do (or would) they feel when they exhibit positive behaviors? How do these help solve the problem? Discuss how healthy resolutions leave all parties feeling intact and not threatened. Ask individuals to reexamine the positive solutions and write goals to follow these as suggestions for the future.

DEBRIEFING QUESTIONS

1. Were your responses more often in the positive column or negative column?
2. What are steps you might take to resolve conflicts in a healthier manner?
3. How does it feel to resolve a conflict in a positive, healthy manner?
4. How does it feel to have conflicts that result in negative thoughts or behaviors?
5. What 2 things can you do to resolve conflicts more positively?
6. What would be the benefits of doing so?
7. What did you learn about conflict resolution today?

LEADERSHIP CONSIDERATIONS

1. Become familiar with the concept of codependency (see reference below).
2. Be prepared to give examples for both positive and negative responses.

VARIATION

1. Participants may be asked to complete the activity before they come to the session. This would require a presession discussion on conflict resolution so they understand the principles and negative and positive behaviors.

CONTRIBUTOR

Norma J. Stumbo
Adapted from: Beattie, M. (1989). *Beyond codependency and getting better all the time* (pp. 194-205). San Francisco, CA: Harper/Hazelden Book.

NEGOTIATING CONFLICTS

CONFLICT:		
PRINCIPLES	*NEGATIVE*	*POSITIVE*
Identify and accept the problem. Reduce the problem to its simplest form and begin to write small goals toward its solution.		
Look for solutions that are in the best interest of the relationship. Take care of your best interests and also those of the other person.		
Be open to various solutions. Eliminate black and white thinking—brainstorm new ideas and alternatives.		
Learn to combine emotion with reason. Balancing emotions with reason—dealing with anger but reacting with a certain amount of reason.		
Don't take problems and differences personally. Separate the person from the behavior.		
Don't deny an adverse reaction if it's present, but don't assume one either. Create a neutral situation instead of a negative or hostile one.		
Learn to combine detachment with appropriate action steps. Strive for balance between control and denial or avoidance.		
Practice deliberate, time-limited patience. Allow time to pass before acting on hasty solutions—take time to reflect and think about consequences.		
Be clear about what you want and need. Understand your needs and wants—stop arguing for argument's sake.		
Consider the wants and needs of yourself and others as important. Define what you and the other person want from this situation.		

PRINCIPLES	NEGATIVE	POSITIVE
Separate issues from people. Accept, love, and respect the other person but confront the problem or difference.		
Communicate. Try to get your message through to the other person and listen intently to what they have to say.		
Healthy boundaries are crucial to conflict negotiation. Know what issues you can yield on and those that you can't.		
Consistently foregoing what you want and need isn't conflict negotiation. Do not take care of other people while neglecting yourself.		
Avoid power plays. Avoid the oneupmanship that typically escalates conflicts.		
Learn to recognize when you're negotiating with yourself. When you ask for resolution to a problem and it repeatedly doesn't happen, you are negotiating with yourself.		
Forego naiveté and cynicism. Learn to trust yourself and selected others.		
Save ultimatums for absolute nonnegotiables or late stage negotiation. Ultimatums are only good when they are fair, have an appropriate time frame, and have commitment to follow through.		
Don't waste time negotiating nonnegotiables. Recognize that some boundaries or limitations cannot be moved.		
Let each person keep his or her respect and dignity. Avoid the use of humiliation and be able to shake hands at the end of a conflict.		
Take full responsibility for your behavior. The only behavior that you have control over is your own.		
Look for the gift or the lesson. Be able to recognize what you learned or gained from the resolution.		

PLAY IT AGAIN SAM

SPACE REQUIREMENTS

Classroom or activity room

MATERIALS

Movie that portrays character(s) with disabilities, television, VCR

GROUP SIZE

Small group (in physical rehabilitation)

GOALS

1. To improve participants' ability to handle social situations that may occur upon discharge.

2. To improve participants' ability to anticipate their individual reactions to social conversations and situations.

3. To encourage group members to give each other feedback on the appropriateness of their anticipated reactions and responses.

PREPARATION

Choose movie scenes and prepare tape (set up at start of first scene)
Note: Select 3 to 5 scenes that show social situations. This activity works best when the disabilities portrayed in the movie are similar to ones of the participants.

ACTIVITY DESCRIPTION

Have the group sit around a table or in a circle. Discuss social situations and they way they are handled (appropriately or inappropriately) by different people. Each person has his or her own way of responding to certain situations. Explain that the purpose of this activity is to view certain scenes and then discuss how the participants' actions may differ from the actors.

Play the first scene, long enough for the antecedent, behavior, and consequence to occur (about 2–3 minutes). Stop the tape and ask the participants how they would have handled the situation differently than the characters in the movie. Could they have anticipated the situation and made

changes before it occurred? Since the situation occurred, how could they minimize the embarrassment, risk or consequences that happened? What are the options for responses or behaviors? Continue this for the other preselected scenes.

Discussion should focus on different participants' reactions, if there is ever a "right" or "wrong" reaction, and how to plan ahead.

DEBRIEFING QUESTIONS

1. How would you handle the situation seen in the movie?

2. What can you do to anticipate what may happen in social situations?

3. What changes might you have made prior to the scene shown in the clip?

4. What actions can you take to minimize risk or embarrassment to yourself or others?

5. Create as many different reactions to each of the situations as possible.

6. Why are some reactions better than others?

7. How can you plan ahead for some of these situations?

8. Describe a situation you've been in recently, your reaction, and how you'd like to change your reaction.

9. What did you learn about handling social situations appropriately today?

LEADERSHIP CONSIDERATIONS

1. Be familiar with the movie and select scenes that the participants might be likely to encounter. Contemporary movies work best.

2. Do not let one or more members control the group by giving the "right" answers. Stress that no answer is perfect or right, and everyone deals with these types of situations in their own ways.

VARIATIONS

1. The discussions or topics can change depending on the type of movie selected.

2. This activity may be appropriate for other populations, with a change in the types of movies selected.

3. Have the participants role-play the situations, taking turns playing both parts.

4. If participants' goals warrant it, have family members present and ask for their responses and reactions also.

CONTRIBUTOR

Norma J. Stumbo

SUGGESTED MOVIES

Coming Home
The Other Side of the Mountain
Whose Life Is It Anyway?
A Step toward Tomorrow
Forrest Gump
Born on the Fourth of July
My Left Foot
My Life

HOLIDAY RECOLLECTIONS

SPACE REQUIREMENTS

Classroom or activity room

MATERIALS

Posterboard and markers or chalkboard or chalk, pencils, paper, dice, spinning wheel

GROUP SIZE

Small or large group

GOALS

1. To improve participants' ability to socially interact with others through reminiscing.
2. To improve participants' ability to use long-term memory.

PREPARATION

Gather materials

ACTIVITY DESCRIPTION

Have the group sit around a table or in a circle. Discuss the upcoming holiday, including the history of the holiday, and encourage reminiscence from each participant as to how he or she celebrated that specific holiday. Questions to promote participation could include:

- What traditions did you have to celebrate the holiday as a child? As an adult?
- Who did you celebrate the holiday with?
- Does one particular year celebrating this holiday stand out from the others?
- What particular food items relate to this holiday?

Separate participants into teams of 3–4 and have each team choose an appropriate seasonal name. Participants will then take turns spinning the wheel for points and then try to unscramble seasonal words.

For every word unscrambled, that team gets the number of points on the wheel. Participants take turns trying to unscramble the word and after 3 attempts, if they don't get the answer, it goes to the other team for an opportunity to pick up the points.

DEBRIEFING QUESTIONS

1. How similar or different were your recollections of this holiday with others in the group?
2. Turn to the person on your left and describe to him or her your favorite memory of this holiday in the past.
3. Why are holidays important to most individuals' social lives?
4. How easy or difficult was it to unscramble the words related to this holiday?
5. How well did the team work together to solve the unscrambled words?

LEADERSHIP CONSIDERATIONS

1. Leaders may use visual or verbal cues to promote correct responses from participants.
2. Allow time for participants to attempt all answers.

VARIATIONS

1. Discussions may be used at all the holidays for reminiscing as well as different poems to promote further discussion and creativity.
2. Depending on the skill level of the group, attempt a "Hangman" or "Wheel of Fortune" type of activity where participants have to guess appropriate letters for points as they attempt to identify the words.
3. Prizes can coincide with the holiday.

CONTRIBUTOR

Kelly O'Neil

SPECIFIC HOLIDAY EXAMPLES

VALENTINE'S DAY

E R A H T
Heart

P D I U S C   R W R O A
Cupid's Arrow

G A E G M E N E N T   N G R I
Engagement Ring

E D R   O S R E S
Red Roses

CHRISTMAS

H S I C S T M A R   E R E T
Christmas Tree

G O C R L A N I
Caroling

S S T C R I M A H   V E E
Christmas Eve

Y V T I T I A N   E N C S E
Nativity Scene

SPORTS CARD COLLECTING

SPACE REQUIREMENTS

Classroom or activity room, community facilities

MATERIALS

Baseball, basketball, football, and/or hockey card collecting price guides (e.g., *Beckett Monthly*), sports cards, and sports card collecting supplies.

GROUP SIZE

Small group

GOALS

1. To improve participants' knowledge of sports card collecting as a hobby.
2. To promote an appropriate leisure lifestyle through participation in an integrative hobby interest.
3. To enhance social skills, such as cooperation, finesse, assertion, self-initiation, communication, and compromise.

PREPARATION

Gather materials
Note: This is a multiple-week activity.

ACTIVITY DESCRIPTION

The purpose of this activity is to organize youth into a sports card collector's club to meet weekly or biweekly to trade cards. Trading requires a balance of assertion, cooperation, and decision making.

The club members may choose to share and discuss topics of interest to most card collectors (e.g., which teams will make the playoffs, who will be the rookie of the year or most valuable player). The club could also focus on a cooperative task of putting together a set of sports cards for the current year. The set could then be traded or sold at a sports card show or at a sports card store. The group could divide the proceeds or save the money toward a professional or minor league baseball game field trip.

To enhance appropriate social interaction skills in a larger group environment, the sports club members could earn the privilege of attending a regional sports card collectors show, which usually attracts 85–125 vendors. In this setting, individuals will need to be assertive enough to talk to card dealers to buy, sell, or trade their cards. The youth will be required to initiate and take responsibility for their choices and decisions. The interaction of selling and trading requires cooperation, finesse, decision making, assertion, and control.

DEBRIEFING QUESTIONS

1. What have you learned about sports card collecting?
2. What social skills do you need to collect and trade sports cards?
3. How can knowledge of sports card collecting be used in conversations with others?
4. How can knowledge of sports card collecting be used to meet new people?
5. How can hobbies in general be used in conversations with others?
6. How can hobbies in general be used to meet new people?
7. What other hobbies might you be interested in learning?

LEADERSHIP CONSIDERATIONS

1. Chances are 1 or 2 youth in the agency will already have an interest in sports card collecting. This can help in organizing and structuring the leisure education activity.
2. While you might initiate interest by focusing on the "economics" of sports card collecting, card collecting can provide an opportunity to teach math, language arts, and geography, as well as appropriate communication with peers and adults.
3. Sequence this leisure education activity by starting with the club format and progressing to integrative community activities such as going to sports card stores, sports card shows, and sporting events.
4. Utilize books and videos on the lives of sport stars. Opportunities to discuss

and read about the lives of players (e.g., Jackie Robinson, who not only broke the color barrier in professional baseball, but endured a year of name calling), will provide leaders with opportunities to focus the group on the price of success that many stars had to pay.

VARIATION

1. Invite an adolescent from the community to share his or her hobby of sports collecting. This presentation might be part of a leisure awareness class on developing hobby interests.

CONTRIBUTOR

Anita Magafas

RECIPE FOR FRIENDSHIP

SPACE REQUIREMENTS

Classroom or activity room

MATERIALS

Handout, pencils

GROUP SIZE

Small group

GOALS

1. To increase participants' awareness of the characteristics and values that they treasure in a friend.

2. To increase participants' self-assessment of whether they have the characteristics and values necessary to be considered a friend.

3. To increase participants' awareness of what others value in close friends.

ACTIVITY DESCRIPTION

Participants should be seated in a circle. Give each participant a copy of the handout and a pencil. Discuss the importance of friends and friendships to the quality of life. Ask participants how friends make a difference in their lives, what some characteristics of a good friend are, and how many people would call them a friend. The purpose of the activity is to determine what each person believes to be important characteristics of a friend.

Each person is to complete the "recipe card" for creating an ideal friend. What ingredients make a good friend? In what proportions? What is essential? What adds "flavor" or "spice" to a relationship? Allow 10–15 minutes.

When each participant is finished with their recipe cards, discuss the characteristics each person considered essential to a friendship. Emphasize that social relationships and friends are an important part of developing a leisure lifestyle. Discussion may focus on similarities and differences between participants, as well as how each person thinks he or she matches up to their own expectations of a friend. Realistic expectations and self-assessment are important considerations for this activity.

DEBRIEFING QUESTIONS

1. What ingredients does it take to make a good friend?

2. What ingredients are essential and which are optional?

3. How similar or different was each person's recipe for friendship?

4. How well do you match your recipe for being a friend?

5. What do you need to change to become closer to the recipe you've created?

6. What steps can you take to move closer to your ideal recipe?

7. How realistic are our expectations of ourselves and others?

8. How do we go about finding and making friends?

9. Describe what you learned about friendship today.

LEADERSHIP CONSIDERATIONS

1. Emphasize that people's expectations and definitions of a friend differ.

2. Consider what each person might change in themselves to be considered a better friend to others.

VARIATION

1. Activity may be changed to create recipes for "the perfect leisure day" (including resources and people) or "the perfect leisure partner" (to describe who they would find compatible in leisure participation).

CONTRIBUTOR

Norma J. Stumbo
Adapted from: Borba, M. and Borba, C. (1982). *Self-esteem: A classroom affair* (Vol. 2). Minneapolis, MN: Winston Press, Inc.

RECIPE FOR FRIENDSHIP

FROM THE FILE OF

_____

INGREDIENTS

_____

_____

_____

_____

_____

_____

DIRECTIONS

_____

_____

_____

_____

_____

_____

_____

_____

_____

_____

_____

_____

FRIENDSHIP POEM

SPACE REQUIREMENTS

Classroom or activity room

MATERIALS

Handout, pencils, newsprint, markers

GROUP SIZE

Small group

GOALS

1. To increase participants' awareness of characteristics of being a good friend.
2. To assist participants in determining what qualities they possess that are characteristic of a good friend.
3. To increase participants' awareness of the characteristics that other people value in friends.

PREPARATION

Gather materials
Make one copy of the handout for each participant

ACTIVITY DESCRIPTION

Have the group sit around a table or in a circle. Discuss the topic of friendship. Ask what qualities are valued in friends, and ask participants to describe one of their best friends. The purpose of this activity is to assist them in determining what qualities or characteristics they value most in their friends as well as to determine if they possess these characteristics.

Distribute handouts and pencils and ask participants to think of words beginning with each letter in the word "Friendship" that say something about friendship (e.g., *F*un, *R*eliable, *I*ntriguing). Have participants work on their lists individually or in pairs. Allow 5–10 minutes.

After the participants have completed the words, have the participants tell the words they had for each letter and write these on the newsprint. Then, have the participants discuss each quality and choose the best word for each letter. Write the final words on newsprint next to the letters.

Follow up with discussion on whether any one person possesses all of these traits, which ones the participants feel they possess, and what areas they would like to improve.

DEBRIEFING QUESTIONS

1. What characteristics make a good friend?
2. What qualities are essential and which are optional?
3. How similar or different was each friendship poem?
4. How many of the characteristics that you listed for being a friend do you possess?
5. What do you need to change to have more of the qualities in the poem you've created?
6. What steps can you take to move closer to your ideal of friendship?
7. How realistic are our expectations of ourselves and others?
8. How do we go about finding and making friends?
9. Describe what you learned about friendship today.

LEADERSHIP CONSIDERATION

1. Have some examples ready for "e" and "i" words, as these are usually the hardest ones.

VARIATION

1. The poem can be changed to meet the topic of the session (e.g., social skills, communication, helpfulness, relationships).

CONTRIBUTOR

Norma J. Stumbo.
Adapted from: Borba, M. and Borba, C. (1982). *Self-esteem: A classroom affair* (Vol. 2). Minneapolis, MN: Winston Press, Inc.

FRIENDSHIP POEM

F   _____

R   _____

I   _____

E   _____

N   _____

D   _____

S   _____

H   _____

I   _____

P   _____

LEISURE RESOURCES ACTIVITIES

THE PLACE WHERE I PLAY

SPACE REQUIREMENTS

Classroom or activity room with tables

MATERIALS

Construction paper, white paper, glue, scissors, stapler, crayons or markers

GROUP SIZE

Small group

GOALS

1. To increase participants' awareness of leisure activities and experiences that can be done in the home.

2. To increase participants' awareness of nontraditional leisure activities.

3. To increase participants' awareness of leisure activities that can be done with their families.

PREPARATION

Gather materials

ACTIVITY DESCRIPTION

Have participants gather around a table or sit in a circle. Discuss different types of leisure, recreation, and play activities. Note that some are organized and some are not; some require other people and some can be done alone. Ask what types of leisure the participants have in their neighborhoods or homes.

The purpose of this activity is to find out what kinds of leisure activities can be done in the participants' homes. The finished product will be a book with each sheet representing a room in their home or apartment. They will draw in pictures of things they can do in each room.

Instruct participants to make the booklet. The front and back cover sheets represent the outside of the house or apartment building. The plain white sheets are stapled into the two outside cover sheets. The front and back can be decorated to resemble their house or building. Construction paper can be used to show the roof, chimney, doors, or windows. Each room inside the booklet can also be deco-

rated. On the back of each page, have participants list the types of leisure or play activities that they can do in that room. Allow 30–40 minutes.

Close the activity with a discussion about some of the activities listed in each room. Participants may be asked to share their ideas with the other group members. The participants now have a resource to go to when they feel bored or don't know what to do with their free time.

DEBRIEFING QUESTIONS

1. Describe the rooms in your home.

2. Choose your favorite room. What about this room makes it special for you?

3. What leisure activities can be done in this room?

4. What is your favorite activity that can be done in this room?

5. What other people in your household like doing the same activity?

6. Would you consider most of the leisure in your home to be traditional or nontraditional?

7. If you could change something about your room to make it even better for leisure, what would that be?

8. How can you use this booklet in the future?

9. How might others in your family use it?

10. What did you learn about leisure resources in your home today?

LEADERSHIP CONSIDERATIONS

1. Be aware of family situations with participants, as this activity may cause undue stress for some.

2. Remind participants of ways to be creative (e.g., don't forget pets, plants, books, music, hobbies, telephone).

VARIATION

1. If time is limited, 1 room can be done at each session.

CONTRIBUTOR

Norma J. Stumbo
Adapted from: Borba, M. and Borba, C. (1982). *Self-esteem: A classroom affair* (Vol. 2). Minneapolis, MN: Winston Press, Inc.

LEISURE RESOURCES SCAVENGER HUNT

SPACE REQUIREMENTS

Classroom or activity room

MATERIALS

Handout, pencils, 5 telephone books, 5 local sports schedules, 5 local train schedules, 5 local newspapers, 5 local YMCA/park district brochures.

PREPARATION

Gather materials
Fill in the blanks of the handout for train schedule, newspaper, and YMCA/park department
Make one copy of the handout for each group

GROUP SIZE

Small group

GOALS

1. To increase participants' awareness of available resources that can facilitate participation in leisure activities in the community.
2. To improve participants' ability to use resources to find specific information related to leisure activities.

ACTIVITY DESCRIPTION

Have participants gather around a table or sit in a circle. Asks the group for some examples of resources that give information related to leisure participation.

Introduce the resources the group will be using (telephone book, sports schedule, train schedule, newspaper and YMCA/park district brochure) and how and when they may be used. Divide participants into groups of 2–3. Give each group a copy of the handout, a pencil and 1 of each of the 5 resources.

Each group works together to find the requested information. As groups complete the form, check for accuracy. Provide assistance as needed

until resources have been utilized correctly. Close by using the debriefing questions below.

DEBRIEFING QUESTIONS

1. Name 3 resources you can use to find information about leisure activities.
2. How easy or difficult was it to use some of the resources to locate information?
3. Have you used any of these resources before today?
4. Where can you get resources like the ones we used today?
5. What are some reasons for using the resources to locate information?
6. Where do you get information if you want to go somewhere you haven't been before?
7. Where do you get information about new activities?
8. What did you learn about locating and using leisure resources today?

LEADERSHIP CONSIDERATIONS

1. Prior to the session, fill in blanks of the form to use as an answer key.
2. A coleader may help to provide individual attention to groups as they are working.

VARIATION

1. Substitute other leisure resources (e.g., bus schedule, concert schedule) for the ones listed above.

CONTRIBUTOR

Lisa Noble

LEISURE RESOURCES SCAVENGER HUNT

PHONE BOOK

    1. List the names and the telephone numbers of 3 restaurants in the area.

        1.

        2.

        3.

    2. List the names and telephone numbers of 3 bowling alleys in the area.

        1.

        2.

        3.

SPORTS SCHEDULE

    1. How many home games are there this month?

    2. List the dates and game times of the home games this month.

TRAIN SCHEDULE

    1. If you want to arrive in _____ (town) by _____am/pm on a Saturday, what time would you have to be at the train station?

    2. What time would you arrive in _____ (town)?

NEWSPAPER

    1. What is playing at the _____ Theatre?

    2. What are the show times?

    3. What is the theatre's telephone number?

YMCA/PARK DEPARTMENT BROCHURE

    1. How much is the _____ class?

    2. What day and time do they meet?

    3. For how many weeks does it meet?

WHERE'S THAT LEISURE?

SPACE REQUIREMENTS

Classroom or activity room

MATERIALS

List of leisure environments, stopwatch or timer, paper, pencils

GROUP SIZE

Small group

GOALS

1. To improve participants' knowledge of leisure activities that occur in specific environments.
2. To improve participants' knowledge of nontraditional leisure activities that may fit into their lifestyle.

PREPARATION

Gather materials

ACTIVITY DESCRIPTION

Have participants gather around a table or sit in a circle. Divide the group into two equal teams. Each team is to have 1 person as recorder. Discuss the variety of environments in which leisure may occur. The purpose of the activity is to explore as many of these possibilities as the group can.

The purpose of the game is to generate as many leisure activities within each environment as possible. The leader will call out one environment at a time and the team members must generate as many activities as possible within a 1-minute time limit. Choose 5 of the example environments from the list provided. The team with the most activities at the end of 5 rounds wins.

Specific environments or facilities within the local community may be targeted. The summary discussion should focus on the variety of activities that may occur within one environment. Discussion may also include how to find out what activities are available, how to make choices and decisions for participation, etc.

DEBRIEFING QUESTIONS

1. How many different environments did we name today?
2. On average, how many leisure activities were named for each environment?
3. Were the activities named active? passive? group activities? solitary activities?
4. How can we find out which activities are available in a specific environment? Where can we go for information?
5. If there are several activities that you are interested in, how do you decide which to participate in?
6. What are the advantages of going to environments that can host several activities?
7. What is your favorite place that can offer several activities? What do you like to do there?

LEADERSHIP CONSIDERATIONS

1. Judge whether activities can be done or are available within each of the environments.
2. Give an example before starting (e.g., home environment) and provide a broad interpretation of leisure experiences to encourage creativity.
3. Between each round, you may want to stop the activity and discuss some of the activities mentioned within a certain environment so that immediate attention is paid to each locale.

VARIATIONS

1. Have one team respond to one round, and the second team respond to the next round. The "silent" team may not give clues to the "responding" team. Score in the same manner as above.
2. Reverse the content of the activity. The leader gives an activity and the teams come up with different places in which to participate.

CONTRIBUTORS

Ray Jones, Jean Folkerth

SAMPLE ENVIRONMENTS

Local park	Civic centers
Home	Community centers
Neighborhood	Universities
Local school	Museums
Shopping mall	Beaches/marinas
Amusement park	Local festivals
Bowling alley	Fitness centers

WHAT A SITE

SPACE REQUIREMENTS

Classroom or activity room

MATERIALS

Paper, pencils

GROUP SIZE

Small group

GOALS

1. To increase participants' awareness of leisure sites and facilities.
2. To increase participants' ability to recall vacations or leisure experiences.
3. To improve participants' ability to share past leisure experiences.

PREPARATION

Gather materials

ACTIVITY DESCRIPTION

Divide the group into 2 teams. Each team is to have 1 person as a recorder. Discuss vacations and other special leisure occasions. The purpose of the activity is to list as many vacation or special leisure sites as possible that persons on each team have visited. The team with the most sites listed within 5 minutes wins.

After completion of the lists, the winning team gets to tell about their favorite vacation spots, what happened there, who they went with, and why it was special. After the winning team members have finished the other team(s) can discuss the same questions.

DEBRIEFING QUESTIONS

1. Describe your favorite vacation spot.
2. What was special about the site or about the vacation?
3. What kinds of leisure activities did you take part in?
4. Who was with you on this special vacation?
5. Why are vacations different than everyday life?
6. What are ways to bring vacation "feelings" into everyday life?
7. How are others' vacation memories similar to or different from yours?
8. What makes vacations a good topic to discuss with people you may not know very well?

LEADERSHIP CONSIDERATION

1. Make sure the groups continue to generate ideas until the time limit. Some prompts may be needed—ask participants about vacations taken in childhood, family vacations, or weekend trips.

VARIATIONS

1. Ask players to vote on their top 5 vacation spots.
2. Discuss specific topics, such as low-cost, weekend, nearby, or family sites available for vacations.

CONTRIBUTORS

Cheryl Potter, Carol Holian, Peggy Bramlet, Kim Watson, Sharon Jester, Mary Miller, Jean Folkerth

AN EVENING OUT

SPACE REQUIREMENTS

Classroom or activity room

MATERIALS

Handout, telephone books, resource guides, pencils

GROUP SIZE

Small group

GOALS

1. To increase participants' awareness of leisure resources in the community.
2. To increase participants' ability to utilize reference guides for leisure participation.
3. To increase participants' knowledge of how and where to find different types of leisure resources.
4. To increase participants' ability to plan leisure experiences for themselves.

PREPARATION

Gather materials
Make one copy of the handout for each participant

ACTIVITY DESCRIPTION

Have the group form a circle and distribute the handout, telephone books, resource guides, and pencils. Explain the importance of planning leisure experiences. Discuss that people plan work and other events on a daily basis but may not think about planning for leisure. The purpose of the activity is to allow participants to plan a special evening out for themselves and one other person, with no limit on finances. They are to plan for:

- Transportation to a restaurant
- Dinner for two
- Transportation to a leisure activity after dinner
- After dinner leisure activity
- Transportation to overnight accommodations
- Overnight accommodations

They are not to discuss their ideas with other group members until each person has decided their

plans. Allow 10–15 minutes.

When plans are completed, ask each group member to share their evening out, including the information on the handout.

Discuss the feasibility of the plan, why each place or activity was chosen, and similarities or differences among group members.

DEBRIEFING QUESTIONS

1. Describe your evening out to the rest of the group.
2. What materials/resources did you use to make your plans?
3. How and why did you choose each of the places and activities?
4. How similar or different were the plans made by group members?
5. How did the lack of financial constraints affect your decisions?
6. Does your evening out resemble any that you've ever had?
7. How could you make a less costly evening just as special?
8. How important is the whole process of planning ahead for an evening out?
9. How well do you plan for your own leisure right now?
10. What did you learn about using leisure resources and planning for leisure?

LEADERSHIP CONSIDERATION

1. If resource guides and telephone books are limited, participants may share.

VARIATIONS

1. Limit the amount of money each person has to spend.
2. Have group members work together to come up with 1 evening that they could all agree on.
3. Give participants a season or theme to plan around.
4. Ask participants to make arrangements and follow through with their plans and report back to the group.

CONTRIBUTOR

Jean Folkerth

AN EVENING OUT

Transportation Options

Name of Company/Contact	Telephone Number	Other Information
_____	_____	_____
_____	_____	_____
_____	_____	_____
_____	_____	_____

Restaurant Options

Name of Restaurant	Telephone Number	Other Information
_____	_____	_____
_____	_____	_____
_____	_____	_____
_____	_____	_____
_____	_____	_____

After Dinner Activity Options

Name of Activity/Facility	Telephone Number	Other Information
_____	_____	_____
_____	_____	_____
_____	_____	_____
_____	_____	_____
_____	_____	_____

Overnight Accommodations Options

Name of Company/Contact	Telephone Number	Other Information
_____	_____	_____
_____	_____	_____
_____	_____	_____
_____	_____	_____

RESOURCE TIC-TAC-TOE

SPACE REQUIREMENTS

Classroom or activity room

MATERIALS

Masking tape, X and O cardboard markers, lists of sample leisure activities and leisure resources

GROUP SIZE

Small group

GOALS

1. To improve participants' knowledge of leisure resources within the community.

2. To improve participants' knowledge of activities that may occur in specific leisure environments.

3. To improve participants' knowledge of nontraditional leisure activities that may fit into their lifestyle.

PREPARATION

Gather materials
Draw a 3 x 3 grid on the floor with the masking tape

ACTIVITY DESCRIPTION

Have participants gather around a table or sit in a circle. Divide the group into 2 teams—Xs and Os—and hand out cardboard Xs and Os to the respective teams. Discuss the relationship of activities and where they take place.

Decide which team will go first. Call out an activity, and have the starting group decide if they have a leisure resource (X or O) where the activity can take place. If so, they may lay down their marker on any open square. If the opposing team challenges and the marker is judged unsuitable, the opposing team can lay one of their markers on any open square. Continue as a regular tic-tac-toe game—3 Xs or 3 Os in a row wins.

Summary discussion should focus on how creative participants were in determining which activities could occur in which environments, the variety of activities or experiences that can occur in each environment, and how the groups worked together.

DEBRIEFING QUESTIONS

1. How many different leisure environments were mentioned today?

2. On average, how many leisure activities were mentioned per environment?

3. Were the named activities active? passive? group activities? solitary activities?

4. How can we find out which activities are available in a specific environment? Where can we go for information?

5. If there are several activities that you may be interested in, how do you decide which to participate in?

6. What are the advantages of going to environments that can host several activities?

7. What is your favorite place that can offer several activities? What do you like to do there?

8. Describe what you learned about leisure activities and leisure environments today.

LEADERSHIP CONSIDERATIONS

1. Act as a judge to determine acceptable answers.

2. The group should come to a consensus before placing a marker on a square.

3. Participants should be familiar with how regular tic-tac-toe is played before the start of the game.

VARIATIONS

1. The difficulty and playing time can be increased by making a 4 x 4 square instead of a 3 x 3 square.

2. The leader may call out a leisure facility (e.g., a fitness center) and the X's and O's have the addresses and telephone numbers of the matching facilities.

CONTRIBUTOR

Jean Folkerth

SAMPLE LEISURE ACTIVITIES

Cooking
Walking
Eating
Sightseeing
Fishing
Dancing
Arts and crafts

SAMPLE LEISURE RESOURCES

Zoo
Community centers
Amusement parks
Beaches/marinas
Museums
Festivals

TOWEL VOLLEYBALL

SPACE REQUIREMENTS

Small gym or open area

MATERIALS

Volleyball net, volleyball, large towels

GROUP SIZE

Small group (even number of participants)

GOALS

1. To increase participants' awareness of the relationship between activities and the equipment used to participate in them.
2. To increase participants' listening and responding skills.
3. To improve participants' gross motor skills.
4. To provide participants with the opportunity to cooperate within their own team and compete with another team.

PREPARATION

Gather materials

ACTIVITY DESCRIPTION

Discuss the relationship between leisure activities and the equipment required to participate (e.g., tennis and a tennis racquet and balls). Divide group into 2 equal teams, and divide teams into pairs. Each pair receives one towel that they hold on the ends. The object of the game is to return the ball over the net using the towel while stating a piece of equipment in response to the activity called.

Begin play by throwing the ball over the net and calling out a leisure activity. One pair must name a piece of equipment that goes with the activity while they are returning the ball by using the towel. The team gets 2 points per each time a correct piece of equipment is named and the ball is returned over the net. First team to 10 points wins.

Summary discussion should focus on the types of activities that do and do not require equipment. Ask participants what types of equipment they have or where they could buy or rent leisure equipment.

DEBRIEFING QUESTIONS

1. How difficult or easy was it to name leisure equipment needed for the activity?
2. How familiar were you with the activities mentioned today?
3. How many of the activities have you participated in?
4. How many pieces of leisure equipment do you own?
5. Where are other places you can get leisure equipment if you don't own it?
6. Does every leisure activity require equipment?
7. What kinds of equipment can be used for more than one activity?
8. How well did you work with your partner?
9. What did you learn about leisure resources today?

LEADERSHIP CONSIDERATIONS

1. Depending on the physical skill level of the group, some practice volleys may be taken ahead of the start of the game.
2. Be prepared to call out activities quickly if volleys are returned so that the next pair has adequate time to respond.
3. Decide ahead of time certain rules of play (e.g., only one pair member can call out the piece of equipment).

VARIATIONS

1. Adapt scoring to the needs and skill levels of the participants.
2. Content may be changed to locations instead of equipment.

CONTRIBUTORS

Cheryl Potter, Carol Holian, Kim Watson, Sharon Jester, Mary Miller, Peggy Bramlet, Jean Folkerth

SAMPLE LEISURE ACTIVITIES
AND LEISURE EQUIPMENT

Water Sports
Skis, boat, snorkel, beach ball
Winter Sports
Skis, snowmobile, snowshoes, ice fishing rod
Outdoor Sports
Baseball, bat, soccer ball, tennis racquet, tennis balls
Cooking
Pots, pans, mixer, spoons, oven, cookbook
Reading
Books, newspaper, Internet
Hiking
Hiking boots, walking stick, map, water bottle
Dining Out
Menu, map, utensils, wine glass
Gardening
Hoe, rake, seeds, potting soil, plants, fertilizer

SCRAMBLED RESOURCES

SPACE REQUIREMENTS

Classroom or activity room

MATERIALS

Handout, pencils

GROUP SIZE

Small group

GOALS

1. To increase participants' awareness of leisure resources.
2. To increase participants' word recognition and problem-solving abilities.

ACTIVITY DESCRIPTION

Have the group form a circle and distribute the handouts and pencils. Discuss leisure resources and what is available in the community for leisure participation. Provide instructions for the word scramble activity and give a example. Have participants complete their forms. Participants may discuss their answers with one another. Allow 5 minutes.

When participants have finished, discuss leisure resources available for use. Topics might include what is available in their home communities or different types of leisure resources.

DEBRIEFING QUESTIONS

1. How many leisure resources were mentioned today?
2. How many of these are available for your use almost every day?
3. Which of these do you use almost every day?
4. Why is it important to know what leisure resources are available to you?
5. What is your favorite leisure resource?
6. Name 10 leisure resources available in your home community.
7. What did you learn about leisure resources today?

LEADERSHIP CONSIDERATIONS

1. Ensure that participants' cognitive skills are at a level needed to complete scrambled resources.

VARIATIONS

1. Modify the leisure resources to be unscrambled depending on the cognitive level of the participants.
2. Modify the leisure resources to be unscrambled depending on the topic of the leisure education discussion group.
3. Fill in the first letter of each word prior to distributing the handouts.

CONTRIBUTOR

D. Clawson

ANSWERS

1. Arcade
2. Art Museum
3. Book Store
4. Bowling Alley
5. Campgrounds
6. Community Centers
7. Dance Studio
8. Drawing Studio
9. Embroidery Shops
10. Exercise Programs
11. Fishing Tackle Store
12. Flight School
13. Golf Course
14. Garden Centers
15. Handball Courts
16. Health Clubs
17. Horse Stables
18. Hobby Shop
19. Ice Rink
20. Ice Cream Shop
21. Jogging Tracks
22. Jewelry Making
23. Karate Studios
24. Knitting Stores
25. Library
26. Leather Working
27. Museums
28. Music Stores
29. Night Clubs
30. Needlework Stores
31. Oil Painting
32. Orchestra Hall
33. Parachuting Lessons
34. Photography Lessons
35. Pet Store
36. Quilting Shops
37. Quarter Horse Riding
38. Racquetball Courts
39. Recreation Centers
40. Shopping Mall

SCRAMBLED RESOURCES

Directions: Unscramble each of the words below to uncover different leisure resources.

1. a r c a d e   rdeaca

2. _ _ _   _ _ _ _ _   atr smuemu

3. _ _ _ _   _ _ _ _ _   obok reost

4. _ _ _ _ _ _ _   _ _ _ _ _   ilngbwo layel

5. _ _ _ _ _ _ _ _ _   cgrdsnmuoap

6. _ _ _ _ _ _ _ _ _ _   _ _ _ _ _ _ _   moctyminu eesrcnt

7. _ _ _ _ _   _ _ _ _ _   cadne udstoi

8. _ _ _ _ _ _ _   _ _ _ _ _ _   widangr odtuis

9. _ _ _ _ _ _ _ _ _   _ _ _ _   yemrdebiro phsos

10. _ _ _ _ _ _ _ _   _ _ _ _ _ _ _ _   sieecerx msorprga

11. _ _ _ _ _ _ _   _ _ _ _ _ _   _ _ _ _ _   hisingf actlke ersot

12. _ _ _ _ _ _   _ _ _ _ _ _   gflthi locohs

13. _ _ _ _   _ _ _ _ _ _   oflg rcseou

14. _ _ _ _ _ _   _ _ _ _ _ _ _   dgnrae ncester

15. _ _ _ _ _ _ _ _   _ _ _ _ _ _   dblahanl uocsrt

16. _ _ _ _ _ _   _ _ _ _ _   htlhea ublsc

17. _ _ _ _ _   _ _ _ _ _ _ _   hsero bsltaes

18. _ _ _ _ _   _ _ _ _   bhbyo psoh

19. _ _ _   _ _ _ _   iec nkir

20. _ _ _   _ _ _ _ _   _ _ _ _ _   iec mcare pohs

21. _ _ _ _ _ _ _ _   _ _ _ _ _   gogjign ktrcsa

22. _ _ _ _ _ _ _ _   _ _ _ _ _   ljrwyee imgank

23. _ _ _ _ _ _   _ _ _ _ _ _ _   eaaktr dsstiou

24. _ _ _ _ _ _ _ _ _ _   _ _ _ _ _ _   ginktnti ssetor

25. _ _ _ _ _ _ _   yrlirab

26. _ _ _ _ _ _ _ _   _ _ _ _ _ _ _   terhlea kinrgow

27. _ _ _ _ _ _   mmsusue

28. _ _ _ _ _ _ _   _ _ _ _ _   smcui rotess

29. _ _ _ _ _   _ _ _ _ _   gnith sbclu

30. _ _ _ _ _ _ _ _ _ _ _   _ _ _ _ _ _   nleeedkwro erosts

31. _ _ _   _ _ _ _ _ _ _ _   loi ptininag

32. _ _ _ _ _ _ _ _ _   _ _ _ _   horsecatr lalh

33. _ _ _ _ _ _ _ _ _ _ _   _ _ _ _ _ _ _   tarauchgpni nsosles

34. _ _ _ _ _ _ _ _ _ _   _ _ _ _ _ _ _   phypohtoarg ssonels

35. _ _ _   _ _ _ _ _   tep erots

36. _ _ _ _ _ _ _ _   _ _ _ _ _   qlingitu ophss

37. _ _ _ _ _ _ _ _   _ _ _ _ _   _ _ _ _ _ _   uqatrre hsroe dingri

38. _ _ _ _ _ _ _ _ _ _   _ _ _ _ _ _   teqacruallb tsrcuo

39. _ _ _ _ _ _ _ _ _ _   _ _ _ _ _ _ _   treaiconter tseencr

40. _ _ _ _ _ _ _ _   _ _ _ _   pponigsh alml

UNIT SCAVENGER HUNT

SPACE REQUIREMENTS

Entire unit or facility

MATERIALS

Pieces of paper with various clues written on them

GROUP SIZE

Small group

GOALS

1. To improve participants' awareness of leisure resources within the unit and the function of each area.

2. To provide an opportunity for a supportive relationship to develop between new and current patients.

PREPARATION

Prepare clues
Note: Notify unit personnel in advance of the activity.

ACTIVITY DESCRIPTION

Have participants gather around a table or sit in a circle. Divide the group into at least 2 teams of 4–5. Groups should have an equal mix of new and current patients.

Explain that clues indicate the uses of each area of the unit, focusing on leisure (e.g., outdoor areas, cafeteria, TV room, game room). Each group is given their first clue and a time limit (approximately 20 minutes, but this may vary depending on the size of the facility). The clues are strategically placed so that each clue leads the groups to the location that the next clue can be found. All clues must be kept throughout the hunt. The first group back with all the pieces of paper wins. Close by using the following debriefing questions.

DEBRIEFING QUESTIONS

1. Describe (in order) where the clues led your group.

2. What leisure resources are located at each of these locations?

3. When might you use some of these resources?

4. Which of these resources can you use independent of staff?

5. Which of these areas have set rules you must follow? What are they?

6. How well did your team work together? What role did you play?

7. How can the information you learned in this activity help you while you're here?

LEADERSHIP CONSIDERATIONS

1. Color code the clues so that each group has a specific color that they are looking for.

2. Number the clues, so a group knows if they are at the right spot in the right sequence.

3. Designate someone in the group as a reader.

4. Inform other unit employees of the scavenger hunt ahead of time.

VARIATIONS

1. Require the group to do some activity (e.g., crawl, skip) between clues.

2. This game can be used to familiarize a group with a community center.

3. This activity can be used to acquaint a group to different resources in the area (by verbally answering the clues rather than requiring the group to physically go to the location).

CONTRIBUTOR

Cheryl Gordon

WHERE DO YOU GO?

SPACE REQUIREMENTS

Classroom or activity room

MATERIALS

Handout, pencils

GROUP SIZE

Small group

GOALS

1. To increase participants' understanding that moods affect leisure decisions.

2. To improve participants' understanding of how their individual moods establish patterns on which they base leisure choices.

ACTIVITY DESCRIPTION

Have the group form a circle and distribute the handouts and pencils. Discuss how moods affect leisure decisions. Give an example, such as when a person is in the mood for social company, he or she may go to a friend's house; when he or she wants to be alone, a drive into the country may be appropriate. Have participant give an example of how mood affected a leisure choice he or she made in the last week. Ask participants to answer the questions individually. Allow 3–5 minutes.

When participants are finished, ask them to share their responses with the group. Be prepared to discuss answers by asking questions concerning what types of places they chose, who they chose, how the mood affected the choice, and which choice was most prevalent.

DEBRIEFING QUESTIONS

1. Describe 3 of your answers for the group.

2. How do your moods affect your leisure decisions?

3. What types of places do you choose when you are happy?

4. What types of places do you choose when you want to be alone?

5. Do you most often choose places that let you stay in the mood or get you out of the mood?

6. Are there other choices that might be healthier?

7. Overall, describe the relationship of mood and leisure for you.

8. How is it alike or different from others in the group?

9. How often do you acknowledge that you can have a choice about your mood?

10. Summarize what you learned from this activity today.

LEADERSHIP CONSIDERATIONS

1. Participants do not have to share their answers.

2. Have good examples to start the discussion.

VARIATIONS

1. The questions on the handout may be modified to fit the theme or purpose of the leisure education session.

2. Have small groups of 3–4 discuss their answers before discussing in the larger group.

CONTRIBUTOR

Cheryl Gordon

WHERE DO YOU GO WHEN...

You're sad and you want to cheer up? _____

You're happy and you want to tell someone about it? _____

You want to be alone? _____

You want to just mess around? _____

You need help? _____

It's snowing? _____

It's really hot? _____

You want to celebrate? _____

You want to learn something? _____

It's dark outside? _____

You want to talk out a problem? _____

You want to avoid work? _____

You want to be entertained? _____

You want to enjoy nature? _____

You want to laugh? _____

You're running low on cash? _____

You're hungry? _____

You want to volunteer your time? _____

You want some companionship? _____

RESOURCE VALUES AND PRIORITIES

SPACE REQUIREMENTS

Classroom or activity room

MATERIALS

Handout, pencils

GROUP SIZE

Small group

GOALS

1. To increase participants' awareness of their values related to financial expenditures toward leisure.

2. To assist participants' in clarifying and making choices regarding expenditures for leisure experiences and opportunities.

3. To give participants a baseline from which to make future decisions regarding how finances are spent with regard to leisure.

ACTIVITY DESCRIPTION

Have the group form a circle and distribute the handouts and pencils. Discuss values and how they affect decisions made, often without our conscious awareness. This activity intends to help participants understand their values and how their money is spent on leisure-related activities.

Ask participants to consider their spending habits over the last year. Each participant is to rate the four areas from 1 to 4 (1 being highest) of how his or her money is spent. Allow 2–3 minutes. Next ask participants to indicate what types of items were bought or how the money was spent in each category. Allow 5–10 minutes.

Discuss the importance of values and how they affect the actions that each person takes. Ask participants if they were surprised at any categories or priorities they had made, what changes they would choose to make, and what actions follow these choices.

DEBRIEFING QUESTIONS

1. What values are most important to you?

2. How do these values affect your actions or behaviors?

3. How do these values relate to the money you spend on leisure?

4. What surprised you about what you spend money on?

5. How does your spending relate to your priorities?

6. What changes do you think you need to make?

7. What steps do you need to take to make these changes?

8. What do you need to do to spend according to your priorities?

9. What did you learn about your leisure values and priorities, and how you spend money?

LEADERSHIP CONSIDERATIONS

1. Group should be familiar with the concept of values before the start of the session.

2. Be aware that some individuals may not wish to share their answers.

3. Encourage acceptance of answers by group members.

VARIATIONS

1. Create another space on the form for delineating any changes the individual wants to make and actions that are required to make the changes.

2. The 4 categories may be changed, depending on the intent of the leisure education session and the characteristics of the group.

3. Add columns for how they currently spend their money, and how they wish they could spend their money.

RESOURCE VALUES AND PRIORITIES

Directions: Rate each of the following 4 values (1 being highest) reflecting how you have spent your money over the past year.

LEISURE VALUE	*HOW MONEY WAS SPENT*

SELF-IMPROVEMENT
Money spent on looking attractive,
developing abilities and interests,
being physically fit

SPECIAL INTERESTS
Money spent on musical instruments,
sports equipment, lessons, events related
to talents and interests

FAMILY LIFE
Money spent on family activities
and entertainment, making your home
comfortable and pleasant

KNOWLEDGE
Money spent on education, books,
seminars, tuition and fees, savings to
pay college costs

YOUR TOWN: FINDING THE WAY

SPACE REQUIREMENTS

Classroom or activity room

MATERIALS

Maps, paper, colored pencils.

GROUP SIZE

Small Group

GOALS

1. To increase participants' awareness of leisure resources within their community.
2. To increase participants' map-reading skills.
3. To provide stimulus skills for exploration of area leisure resources.

PREPARATION

Gather materials

ACTIVITY DESCRIPTION

Have participants gather around a table or sit in a circle. Encourage the group to brainstorm on what kinds of maps are available. Have participants look at various kinds of maps (e.g., city/county planners' map, nature trails/parks, biking, area transit authority, school maps). Identify the kinds of information found on the various maps.

Discuss what will be included in their map for recreation/leisure (e.g., recreation centers, libraries, major streets). Have group decide on symbols for the major buildings and sites of interest. Depending on the amount of information included on the map, can use special events, logos, puzzles, or quizzes as space fillers.

DEBRIEFING QUESTIONS

1. How can maps help you locate leisure resources?
2. With which kinds of maps are you most familiar?
3. What kinds of information can you find on most maps?
4. What kinds of leisure information was included on our map?
5. What additional information would you include on a map for your own personal use?
6. How often do we need to get new maps?
7. Where can you go to get the maps you need?
8. What did you learn from this activity today?

LEADERSHIP CONSIDERATION

1. Use "Where is...?" questions to help participants become familiar with map-reading.

VARIATIONS

1. Groups with limited map-designing ability can give verbal clues to the leader.
2. The group could highlight recreation or other familiar sites on a city/county planners' map.
3. Make a transparency of a map and have participants point out the route from point A to point B on the projected image.

CONTRIBUTORS

Carol Hoover, E. M. Williams

PLAY THE ARLINGTON WAY

ILLUSTRATED BY: LAURA BOYD

PREPARED BY:
THE OFFICE FOR TEENAGERS, ARLINGTON COUNTY,
DEPT. OF PARKS, RECREATION AND COMMUNITY RESOURCES;
YOUNG ADULT SERVICES, ARLINGTON COUNTY LIBRARIES
SUPPORTED BY:
FRIENDS OF THE ARLINGTON COUNTY LIBRARIES

NATURE AWARENESS: RECYCLING

SPACE REQUIREMENTS

Classroom or activity room, wooded area

MATERIALS

None needed

GROUP SIZE

Small group

GOALS

1. To improve participants' understanding of the importance of recycling.
2. To allow students to have fun while learning about the environment.

PREPARATION

None needed

ACTIVITY DESCRIPTION

This is a two-part program designed to heighten an individual's awareness of the need to recycle, and how he or she can contribute to the effort. Part One consists of an indoor session discussing the need to recycle, what can be recycled and how it is done. During this time, the group will participate in a series of activities stressing recycling and how they can do it. Activities include taking an inventory of things they use daily that are recyclables, and what nature can recycle naturally.

Part Two consists of a nature hike through a wooded area. During this walk, the leader should point out examples of natural recycling, and the impact of litter and garbage on the area, and have participants pick up any litter they find. At the end of the hike discuss the collected litter and how it can be recycled.

DEBRIEFING QUESTIONS

1. What things do you use every day that can be recycled?
2. Where do we take items to be recycled?
3. How does recycling benefit the earth?
4. Can recycling be considered a leisure activity?
5. What are the consequences of not recycling?
6. Is it more expensive to recycle or create and buy new items?
7. How can you encourage more recycling in your home, school, or town?
8. What will you do differently tomorrow after learning about recycling today?

LEADERSHIP CONSIDERATIONS

1. For younger groups, use more hands-on examples and limit the program to 1 hour.
2. Avoid areas where poison plants grow when picking up litter.

VARIATION

1. Bury certain items 3 weeks in advance (e.g., paper styrofoam cup, plastic jars, piece of wood, apple or banana). Dig up during nature hike and discuss the effect of how being exposed to nature's recycling process has affected the individual item.

CONTRIBUTORS

Tracy Smith, Patrick McCord

BOOKS BY VENTURE PUBLISHING

Leisure Education III: More Goal-Oriented Activities
by Norma J. Stumbo

Leisure Education IV: Activities for Individuals with Substance Addictions
by Norma J. Stumbo

Leisure Education Program Planning: A Systematic Approach, Second Edition
by John Dattilo

Leisure Education Specific Programs
by John Dattilo

Leisure in Your Life: An Exploration, Fifth Edition
by Geoffrey Godbey

Leisure Services in Canada: An Introduction, Second Edition
by Mark S. Searle and Russell E. Brayley

Leisure Studies: Prospects for the Twenty-First Century
edited by Edgar L. Jackson and Thomas L. Burton

The Lifestory Re-Play Circle: A Manual of Activities and Techniques
by Rosilyn Wilder

Models of Change in Municipal Parks and Recreation: A Book of Innovative Case Studies
edited by Mark E. Havitz

More Than a Game: A New Focus on Senior Activity Services
by Brenda Corbett

Nature and the Human Spirit: Toward an Expanded Land Management Ethic
edited by B. L. Driver, Daniel Dustin, Tony Baltic, Gary Elsner, and George Peterson

Outdoor Recreation Management: Theory and Application, Third Edition
by Alan Jubenville and Ben Twight

Planning Parks for People, Second Edition
by John Hultsman, Richard L. Cottrell, and Wendy Z. Hultsman

The Process of Recreation Programming Theory and Technique, Third Edition
by Patricia Farrell and Herberta M. Lundegren

Programming for Parks, Recreation, and Leisure Services: A Servant Leadership Approach
by Donald G. DeGraaf, Debra J. Jordan, and Kathy H. DeGraaf

Protocols for Recreation Therapy Programs
edited by Jill Kelland, along with the Recreation Therapy Staff at Alberta Hospital Edmonton

Quality Management: Applications for Therapeutic Recreation
edited by Bob Riley

A Recovery Workbook: The Road Back from Substance Abuse
by April K. Neal and Michael J. Taleff

Recreation and Leisure: Issues in an Era of Change, Third Edition
edited by Thomas Goodale and Peter A. Witt

Recreation Economic Decisions: Comparing Benefits and Costs, Second Edition
by John B. Loomis and Richard G. Walsh

Recreation for Older Adults: Individual and Group Activities
by Judith A. Elliott and Jerold E. Elliott

Recreation Programming and Activities for Older Adults
by Jerold E. Elliott and Judith A. Sorg-Elliott

Reference Manual for Writing Rehabilitation Therapy Treatment Plans
by Penny Hogberg and Mary Johnson

Research in Therapeutic Recreation: Concepts and Methods
edited by Marjorie J. Malkin and Christine Z. Howe

Simple Expressions: Creative and Therapeutic Arts for the Elderly in Long-Term Care Facilities
by Vicki Parsons

A Social History of Leisure Since 1600
by Gary Cross

A Social Psychology of Leisure
by Roger C. Mannell and Douglas A. Kleiber

Steps to Successful Programming: A Student Handbook to Accompany Programming for Parks, Recreation, and Leisure Services
by Donald G. DeGraaf, Debra J. Jordan, and Kathy H. DeGraaf

Stretch Your Mind and Body: Tai Chi as an Adaptive Activity
by Duane A. Crider and William R. Klinger

Therapeutic Activity Intervention with the Elderly: Foundations and Practices
by Barbara A. Hawkins, Marti E. May, and Nancy Brattain Rogers

Therapeutic Recreation: Cases and Exercises, Second Edition
by Barbara C. Wilhite and M. Jean Keller

Therapeutic Recreation in the Nursing Home
by Linda Buettner and Shelley L. Martin

Therapeutic Recreation Protocol for Treatment of Substance Addictions
by Rozanne W. Faulkner

Tourism and Society: A Guide to Problems and Issues
by Robert W. Wyllie

A Training Manual for Americans with Disabilities Act Compliance in Parks and Recreation Settings
by Carol Stensrud

Venture Publishing, Inc.
1999 Cato Avenue
State College, PA 16801
Phone: (814) 234-4561
Fax: (814) 234–1651

ISBN 978-1-892132-28-4

9 781892 132284

90000